Goodness and Rightness
in Thomas Aquinas's
Summa Theologiae

voluntaria, secundum hoc sunt duo mora- vi, non est actus domini, sed solum, in-
liter, & potest ex una parte inesse bonum, quantum procedit ex mandato domini,
& ex alia malum. unde sic non facit ipsum malum mala vo-
¶ Ad tertium dicendum, quod actus luntas servi.
servi, inquantum procedit ex voluntate ser-

---

tem esset mala, aliquid boni faceret, id, quod est con- quod fructus, idest actus unus, cum ab aliqua duarum
tra sanctum Evangelium. Per sententiam ergo illam arborum procedat, non potest simul esse bonus, & ma-
Mat. 7. Scriptura, tamquam scholastice loquens, dicit, lus. Secundo videt: quomodo, &c.

☞ IN corpore duo præstat. Primo statuit fundamenta- ad genus moris. Secundo infert conclusionem responsivam
lem hanc assertionem: Nihil probibet, aliquem a- 10 in genere moris negative, in genere naturæ affirmati-
ctum esse unum, secundum quod refertur ad genus na- ve, ibi: Si ergo accipiatur, &c.
turæ, qui tamen non est unus, secundum quod refertur

---

† al. De con-
sequentibus.
† De iis, quæ consequuntur actus humanos, ratione bonitatis, † & malitiæ, † al. vel.
in quatuor articulos divisa.

DEINDE considerandum est de his, quæ ¶ Secundo. Utrum habeat rationem lau-
consequuntur actus humanos ratione dabilis, vel culpabilis.
bonitatis, vel malitiæ. ¶ Tertio. Utrum habeat rationem meri-
ET CIRCA hoc quæruntur quatuor. ti, vel demeriti.
¶ Primo. Utrum actus humanus, inquan- ¶ Quarto. Utrum habeat rationem meri-
tum est bonus, vel malus, habeat ra- ti, vel demeriti apud Deum.
tionem rectitudinis, vel peccati.

ARTICULUS PRIMUS.

Utrum actus humanus, inquantum est bonus, vel malus, habeat rationem
rectitudinis, vel peccati.

Capt. 1. sent. dist. 5. quæst. 1. concl. 1. Medina quæst. 20 ne finis, & ejus prosecutione; ergo vide-
21. art. 1. tur, quod malitia actus non inducat ratio-
nem peccati.
AD PRIMUM sic proceditur. Vi- ¶ 3. Præterea. Si malitia actus induce-
detur, quod actus humanus, ret rationem peccati, sequeretur, quod,
inquantum est bonus, vel ma- ubicumque esset malum, ibi esset pecca-
lus, non habeat rationem re- tum. Hoc autem est falsum: nam pœna,
ctitudinis, vel peccati. Pecca- licet habeat rationem mali, non tamen ha-
ta enim sunt monstra in natura, ut dici- bet rationem peccati; non ergo ex hoc,
* tert. 9. tur in 2. Phys. * monstra autem non sunt quod aliquis actus est malus, habet ratio-
tom. 2. actus, sed sunt quædam res generatæ præ- nem peccati.
ter ordinem naturæ. Ea autem, quæ sunt 30 ¶ SED CONTRA. Bonitas actus humani,
secundum artem, & rationem, imitantur ut supra ostensum est *, principaliter de- * q. 19. a. 4.
ea, quæ sunt secundum naturam, ut ibi- pendet a lege æterna, & per consequens
dem dicitur; ergo actus ex hoc, quod est malitia ejus in hoc consistit, quod discor-
inordinatus, & malus, non habet rationem dat a lege æterna: sed hoc facit rationem
peccati. peccati. Dicit enim Aug. 22. contra Fau- * cap. 27. in
¶ 2. Præterea. Peccatum, ut dicitur in stum, quod peccatum est dictum, vel fa- princ. t. 6.
* tert.9. t. 2. 2. Phys. * accidit in natura, & arte, cum ctum, vel concupitum contra legem æter-
non pervenitur ad finem intentum a na- nam; ergo actus humanus ex hoc, quod
tura, vel arte: sed bonitas, vel malitia a- 40 est malus, habet rationem peccati.
ctus humani maxime consistit in intentio- ¶ RE-

Goodness and Rightness in Thomas Aquinas's *Summa Theologiae*

James F. Keenan, S.J.

GEORGETOWN UNIVERSITY PRESS / WASHINGTON, D.C.

COVER ILLUSTRATION: From the cover of the 3-volume commemorative published for the six hundredth anniversary of the canonization of Saint Thomas Aquinas (Rome, 1925, S. Szabó, ed.); courtesy of Lauinger Library, Georgetown University.

TITLE PAGE VERSO: Detail from the text page (reduced) of Question 21, Article 1 in the *Prima Secundae* of the *Summa Theologiae* (Rome, 1793, S. Capponi A Porrecta, ed.); courtesy of Woodstock Theological Library, at Georgetown University.

Library of Congress Cataloging-in-Publication Data

Keenan, James F.
    Goodness and Rightness in Thomas Aquinas's Summa Theologiae / James F. Keenan.
    p. cm.
    1. Thomas, Aquinas, Saint, 1225?–1274. Summa Theologiae. 2. Thomas, Aquinas, Saint, 1225?–1274—Ethics. 3. Christian ethics—History—Middle Ages, 600–1500. 4. Good and evil. 5. Right and wrong. I. Title. II. Title: Goodness and Rightness in Thomas Aquinas's Summa Theologiae.
BX1749.T6K44   1992
171'.2'092—dc20   92-3090
ISBN 0-87840-530-5 (pbk.)

Georgetown University Press, Washington, D.C.   20057-1079
© 1992 by Georgetown University Press. All rights reserved.
PRINTED IN THE UNITED STATES OF AMERICA
10 9 8 7 6 5 4 3 2 1   1992
THIS VOLUME IS PRINTED ON ACID-FREE ∞ OFFSET BOOK PAPER.

to Frank and Dolores

Contents

Introduction:
Initiating a Dialogue

I began this work seven years ago, believing the simple presupposition that goodness describes persons and rightness describes actions. When I read Thomas's *Summa theologiae*, however, I realized that Thomas rarely if ever spoke of actions, per se, and rarely if ever talked about goodness. Instead Thomas wrote about personal actions, intentions, ends, and virtues, but these concepts contributed less to the description of good persons than to right behavior.

As my work progressed I learned three new insights. First, rightness requires other objects of description than simple external acts. Second, the *Summa theologiae* cannot be parsed for goodness and rightness by simply presuming that intention or end is synonymous with goodness, and external act or object with rightness. Inasmuch as Thomas had other interests, I would have to find the primary concept that bears moral description. That concept would be key for finding the distinction between goodness and rightness. Third, virtue, which I had long considered as descriptive of personal goodness, began to appear as subject to rational observation and measurement. Virtue, in Thomas's writings, belongs not to goodness language, but to rightness language. Prompted by these insights, I began the investigation detailed in this book.

The book itself is divided into four parts. Part I introduces the work as a whole and treats the distinction of goodness and rightness. Goodness and badness describe whether or not we strive to the extent we are able to attain rightness in our lives and actions. Rightness and wrongness describe whether or not we attain the end that reason dictates is proper and necessary for our lives and actions. Chapter One investigates the origins of this distinction and its important applications to the topics of virtue and intention.

Part II establishes the legitimacy of this investigation by probing a significant shift in Thomas's writings. During his second regency in Paris, precisely while writing *De malo* 6 and question nine of the *Prima secundae*, Thomas develops a new position concerning the will's autonomy. The will's autonomy is a necessary condition for understanding moral goodness; without it, there can be no distinction. Chapter Two treats the writings prior to this shift, while Chapter Three discusses the shift and subsequent changes. Thus, the second chapter describes a moral psychology inadequate for bearing the distinction of goodness and rightness; the third chapter presents the psychology of the *Prima secundae* as an adequate one.

Part III also has two chapters. Chapters Four and Five examine the key areas of Thomas's work in morals: his treatises on the human act and the moral virtues. Thomas's only concern in these treatises is whether acts and persons are rightly ordered. The concept of moral goodness appears only in external acts commanded by charity and in the moral virtues perfected by charity.

Part IV of this work asks two questions. First, is there a concept of moral goodness distinct from moral rightness in Thomas's writings? Chapter Six argues that Thomas's concept of charity parallels our concept of moral goodness and that Thomas envisions an external act as subject to two measures: reason and charity. Whereas the measure of reason pertains to whether an act is right, the measure of charity is whether someone is good. The distinction between goodness and rightness finds a parallel in Thomas's distinction between charity and the acquired virtues.

Second, is there a concept of moral badness distinct from moral wrongness? Chapter Seven concerns sin and finds that the method Thomas uses to distinguish the goodness of charity from the rightness of the moral virtues is not employed in the treatise on sin. Rather, Thomas employs the same method in the treatise on sin as he does in the treatises on the human act and the moral virtues. In these treatises the starting point for consideration is always the object. In the treatise on charity, however, the starting point is the subject striving for union with God. Due to his singular concern with the disordered object, Thomas never attains a clear distinction between badness and wrongness in his treatise on sin.

Chapter Seven, which is also the last chapter, concludes by arguing that to some extent the distinction between goodness and rightness is in the *Summa theologiae*, but that Thomas never thematizes it. Thomas, distinguishes charity from reason and, therefore, implicitly goodness from rightness. But, he never actually entertains the distinction between badness and wrongness.

*   *   *

Three notes are needed here. First, this investigation will not establish what actually constitutes right living. The present debate between deontologists and proportionalists is a debate concerning the description of right action. Such debates have their own merits. My interest, however, respects the difference between rightness and goodness and asks only whether and how Thomas Aquinas similarly respects the difference. Second, I will conclude each chapter on Thomas by describing how the issues raised in his writings affect the contemporary insight into this distinction. Third, the focus of this work is specifically the *Summa theologiae*. In many ways the significance of the *Summa theologiae* speaks for itself as a logical choice for any investigation into Thomas's writings. But, as I will illustrate in Part II, it is only in the *Prima secundae* that Thomas achieved a synthesis on human freedom, founded on two distinct perspectives on human acting, which are evocative of, if not parallel to, the contemporary distinction. For this reason, I chose the *Summa theologiae* as the focus for this investigation.

Acknowledgments

I want to acknowledge the assistance I received in writing this book. First, I was fortunate to study with Josef Fuchs and Klaus Demmer at the Gregorian University. As priests, theologians, mentors and friends they enriched my life immeasurably. It was a privilege to be their student. At that time I met a fellow student, Tom Kopfensteiner, whose steadfast friendship has made these past years rewarding ones.

In addition to Fuchs and Demmer, I want to thank John Langan, Mark Henninger, John Boyle, John Breslin, and Joan Franks, for their extensive critical and helpful comments. Likewise, I was helped by the keen eyes of Craig Pilant, Robert O'Hare, and Martin Calkins. Finally, Georgetown University Press and, in particular, Patricia Rayner made the production of this book an easy and enriching operation. The shortcomings that the reader finds in these pages are significantly fewer due to the thoughtful assistance I received from these people.

I have always been blessed with many good friends. In writing this book, I wish to thank specifically four of them. Dick Dillon, Edie Mauriello, and Mark Massa made my years at Fordham not only productive, but more importantly, delightful. I have never laughed as much in my life as with these warm, clever, dedicated friends. Over the past fifteen years, John O'Malley's companionship has taught me the value of consolation. These friends, together with my colleagues, students and fellow Jesuits at Fordham and Weston, make my life a great one.

Finally, I have always been very close with my family, especially my brothers and sisters and their families. They are a very real part of my life. Even more, my Dad and Mom have been my best friends. From them I learned the importance of loving, of being just, and of being faithful. These two people formed me. After a number of very happy years and just as these pages went to press, my Dad died at an early age of heart failure. My Mom goes on, loving and teaching us more about justice and fidelity. To them I dedicate this book with esteem, gratitude, and love.

PART 1

Goodness and Rightness

CHAPTER 1

The Distinction
Between Goodness and Rightness

The contemporary distinction in moral theology and ethics between being good and living rightly is an incisive one. Goodness means that out of love we strive to live and act rightly. Rightness means that our ways of living and acting actually conform to rational expectations set by the ethical community. As this distinction permits the description of two different moral concerns, it represents a new foundation for moral investigation. But the distinction emerges from earlier questions in theology and philosophy.

This chapter examines the historical background that underlies this distinction and its presence in contemporary thought. It then considers the effect the distinction has on human freedom, virtue and intention, and concludes by examining its presence in the Hebrew and Christian Scriptures.

A BRIEF HISTORY OF MORAL DESCRIPTION

Formerly, philosophers held that to call a person "good," one had not only to do the good but also to want to do it because it was good: "Agathon oú to mè ádikein, álla to mēde éthelein."[1] Likewise, theologians maintained that a good person was one who did the good out of love or charity. In both sciences doing the good was a necessary but not a sufficient ground for describing a person as good.[2]

In the Middle Ages, theologians debated a question pertinent to the distinction.[3] They asked whether a person was bad if the person followed an erroneous conscience. According to Bernard, if one in conscience pursued an activity that one later learned was bad, that person who did the bad was bad. Breaking the law, knowingly or not, was sufficient grounds for calling a person bad. Abelard, on the other hand, believed that any person who acted conscientiously was always good. Thomas turned the debate right side up and asked whether a person who refused to follow the conscience was bad. He answered in the affirmative. He then asked, whether a person who followed an erroneous conscience was good. Thomas argued that a person who both could not have known the law and tried to do the good was "excused" from any moral blame for the bad action.[4]

Later, the manualists of the nineteenth century followed Thomas's insight and expanded it. Rather than simply excuse the agent, they offered a distinction between objectively good acts and subjectively good people. In their writings, "objectively good" described good or licit behavior. "Subjectively good" described people who acted conscientiously believing that their behavior was good. The description of such agents as good rather than excused represented a significant shift. To give pastoral guidance to confessors, the manualists discussed cases of people who performed objectively bad acts, e.g., an intrinsic evil, but who could still be called subjectively good. Nonetheless, their distinction functioned along the same lines as Thomas's had; that is, it excused agents from blame.

Until recently, therefore, moral theology has had only one source for moral description, the act. If a bad action was performed, mitigating circumstances were entertained to see if the agent was partially or completely exonerated of moral guilt. In fact, as recently as 1958, in John Ford's and Gerald Kelly's *Contemporary Moral Theology*, the question of subjective goodness was raised primarily and almost exclusively in the context of "imputability."[5]

Generally speaking, moral theologians did not examine cases on the other side of the distinction; i.e., they did not discuss people who do objectively good acts but on selfish grounds. Such an examination might have led them to the contemporary insight that executed acts are not necessary for the moral description of persons. Admittedly some manualists, Gury, Merkelbach, and Noldin among them, entertained certain questions related to beatitude, but their consistent point of departure was the human act. Consequently, they employed their distinction only to remedy the pastoral difficulties arising from cases in which persons performed bad actions but without blame. This is not to say that ignorance and drunkenness were not well discussed, but they were discussed as circumstances concerning the moral culpability of the action. The action remained always the point of departure.

Because the distinction between objectively good acts and subjectively good persons was only used in those pastoral situations in which an agent had committed a bad act in good faith or with excusing circumstances, the question of who the good person really was was not examined. Theologians in general presupposed that the one who did a good act was a good person, and the one who did bad acts was a bad person. Exceptions were noted, but grounds for these exceptions were not explored. If good people performed bad acts, and if bad people performed good acts, should there not be distinct moral descriptions for persons and acts? This question was not discussed, and the general presupposition remained: we are what we do.

Reinforcing this presupposition among theologians was the notion that the word "good" primarily described acts. Acts were described as bad or good and people who intended such acts were so described. Goodness was not used, as it is today, primarily and principally to describe persons.

In philosophy, on the other hand, goodness was descriptive of persons. Immanuel Kant argued that good was descriptive only of the will. Kant distinguished a person who acts out of duty from an act in accord with duty. An act in accord with duty, e.g., executing a prisoner, could not itself be called good. Rather, good acts were those done by persons acting out of duty, e.g., an execution by one who beheaded persons (solely) because it was his duty to do so.[6]

Kant, however, did not examine the distinction to see whether persons were good who acted out of duty but who performed acts not in accord with duty. Though Kant examined acts in accord with duty performed by people not acting out of duty, he did not explore the converse. A person acting out of duty to parent a child may err through too much leniency or rigidity. Is the parent good? Commentators may draw conclusions from Kant's work, but Kant himself did not raise the question. Rather, like Democritus, Kant presumed that a dutiful act was a necessary though not sufficient condition for naming an agent good.

According to Kant's description, not acts but willing persons are good. Yet his writings show that he did not share the same presupposition as the moral manualists. The philosopher's presupposition was not that we are what we do, but that we may not be as good as our actions appear to convey. That presupposition, however, was not complemented by another: we may not be as bad as our actions appear to convey.

Twentieth-century philosophers asked a new question. Instead of asking about goodness, they asked about rightness. Among these philosophers, G. E. Moore asked whether we could describe actions as right or wrong without considering the motives of the agent. Moore's answer to this question establishes the distinction between goodness and rightness.

In his *Ethics*, Moore sought to determine the objective notion of right. His definition is utilitarian: the act that "produces a maximum of pleasure" will always be called right and will never be able to be called wrong, for an act "can only be wrong if it produces less than a maximum."[7] To answer possible objections to his position, Moore drew the distinction between goodness and rightness. First, he distinguished the agent's motives from the act, by pointing out that the question whether an agent deserves praise or blame depends sometimes on the agent's motives; but the question of whether one's action is right or wrong never does.[8]

Second, he distinguished a person's perceptions of the right from what, in fact, is right. Even with the best of motivations, a person may not perceive the right. On the other hand, a person motivated by selfishness may nevertheless calculate what the right act is and do it. Thus, Moore concluded with a "paradox" concerning the act of a person with bad motivations: "A man may really deserve the strongest moral condemnation for choosing an action which actually is right."[9] Here emerges a new insight: that a person is bad does not affect the rightness of an action.[10]

Moore's "paradox" with its two distinct moral descriptions offered a way of overcoming the problem of the manualists: persons are "good"; actions are "right." Moore held that we can determine whether an action is right or wrong without having any information about the agent's motives. He did not, however, explore the converse: whether motives alone or only "sometimes" describe "goodness."[11] In fact, like Kant and Democritus, Moore did not call a person good who with good motives performed a wrong act. He also presumed that a right act was a necessary condition for calling an agent good. Still, he had come a considerable distance from the presumption that we are what we do: he had, in fact, made it clear that right actions can be done by good and bad people.

More recently, Bruno Schüller, a German moral theologian influenced by English philosophy, adopted and advanced Moore's distinction. With two distinctly different descriptions for persons and acts, he argued that persons are good who strive to realize the right, and actions are right when they satisfactorily meet the demands of protecting and promoting values.[12] Two other Germans, Josef Fuchs and Klaus Demmer, have also begun to establish this distinction as a foundational one in moral theology.[13] Together and in concert with others, they hold a new presupposition concerning moral description: good and bad people behave rightly and wrongly.[14]

The presupposition on which this distinction is based is radically different from all previous ones. With the (possible) exception of the manualists, philosophers and theologians have never really decided that a person who performs a wrong action can be called good for performing the action. And contemporary theologians, like Fuchs and Demmer, far outstrip the manualists by bringing this distinction into the center of their moral theory.

CONTEMPORARY DESCRIPTIONS OF GOODNESS

In order to appreciate the newness of the distinction between goodness and rightness, we must overcome old ways of thinking about the question of goodness. In the manualist tradition, the description that someone was subjectively good ordinarily followed the description of an action that was objectively good. In exceptional cases, someone was described as subjectively good who performed a bad act, but only if circumstances excused the agent from blame. General and exceptional judgments considered first the act, then the agent. In cases involving a bad act, the manualists asked whether any mitigating circumstances diminished or removed the blame that would ordinarily be attributed to agents who performed bad actions. Thus, an exceptional description of subjective goodness in a case of bad activity meant little more than "the agent did not mean it." This judgment was only a disclaimer; it negated any blame for bad action. Its function was negative: to deny blame where ordinarily it was presumed.

If goodness is consequent to questions of rightness or wrongness, then it is merely an appendage to moral reflection on right acting. In contemporary moral theology, goodness is not consequent to rightness, but antecedent to and distinct from rightness. Goodness does not ask whether someone meant to do the good act (manualist language); goodness asks whether one strives to realize right activity. In contemporary thought, we are good or bad before we are right or wrong in acting.

Goodness as antecedent to action no longer has an atomistic meaning. We no longer call people good if they do good actions. Rather, we call people good who strive to realize rightness in their lives and in the world. As goodness is antecedent to action, its contradictory is not bad or wrong action, but the failure to strive for rightness. People are bad, not when they perform "bad" actions (the manualists' term) or "wrong" actions (our term), but when they fail to strive to perform the right.

Badness, then, is not simply acting out of selfishness or malice.[15] Prior to any act, badness pertains to the failure to strive for rightness. Thus, a person described as bad may subsequently act out of hypocrisy, apathy, or malice, but this hypocrisy, apathy, or malice results from a prior failure to strive for right living.

Goodness, then, though distinct from rightness is not independent of it. When goodness is seen as independent of rightness, goodness becomes solipsistic. The claim that one is good at this particular moment is the claim that one is striving to realize right activity. The claim is not an empty one. Consider love. Loving parents seek to find right ways for their children to grow. Therefore, parents who simply dote on their children without seeking the right cannot claim to love their children. A claim may be made, but the claim remains empty.[16] Similarly, parents who strive to raise their children well but err through extreme severity or leniency truly love; that is, such parents are good, but their parenting is wrong.

Because goodness is an antecedent description, calling parents good means that they are striving for right parenting; it does not mean that they have attained right parenting. If good parents discover that their parenting activity is wrong, it will be unnecessary to tell them to discontinue the wrong activity. Being good, they will realize the need to change, and they will attempt to change. Only when we think of goodness as consequent to rightness do we make unnecessary admonitions.[17]

The contemporary description of goodness is antecedent to and distinct from the question of rightness. Goodness simply asks whether one strives out of love or duty to realize right activity. Rightness asks whether the activity itself protects and promotes values. Goodness is not a term of acquittal. If good people perform wrong actions, their primary concern will be to remedy the situation in which harm has been done. Being good they want to do the right.

HUMAN FREEDOM, VIRTUE, AND INTENTION

The contemporary understanding of moral goodness is fundamentally related to the concept of human freedom.[18] Each individual enjoys a distinct degree of personal freedom. Due to nature, nurture, economics, luck, and other causes, some people are more capable of realizing right activity than others. Some have a ready disposition to drink moderately. Some have greater ease in living chaste lives. Some never learned to be racist; others are by nature repulsed by sexual discrimination. Some are timid, while others are compulsive. And while some were taught to be discreet, others are born gossips. Personal strengths and weaknesses arise from a variety of formative sources.

Generally speaking, from their strengths people perform right activity, and from their weaknesses they perform wrong activity. Since each person has different weaknesses and strengths, each person is differently inclined to wrong or right acting. The reason that some people behave more rightly than others is not necessarily due to striving. Rather, people who behave rightly tend to be people who are rightly ordered. Disordered people are less likely to behave rightly.

The question of goodness, then, is simply whether one strives to become more rightly ordered so as to realize right activity for God and one's neighbor. To the degree that an individual enjoys personal freedom, to a similar and proportionate degree will one probably be able to make oneself more rightly ordered. Goodness does not ask whether a person *attains* a greater degree of freedom or order, but whether one *strives* to attain it. As the antecedent question, goodness asks whether one actually tries to make oneself more capable of realizing right activity. Rightness, on the other hand, always asks the question of attaining.

Rightness concerns, therefore, two dimensions of human living. First, rightness asks whether one is rightly ordered. If someone is inclined to excessive drinking, gossip, cowardliness, racism, sexism, promiscuity, dishonesty, that person has a disorder; the person is not rightly ordered in a particular dimension of life. Second, rightness asks whether one's action is rightly ordered. Not all people with drinking problems always drink excessively; nor do all racists always act with bias; nor do all cowards always walk away from urgent situations. Similarly, on occasion temperate people get drunk, just people discriminate, and the brave jump ship. No one, no matter how well-ordered one may be, is ever perfect. Nor is anyone, no matter how disordered one may be, ever an absolute failure. For these reasons, we distinguish between whether a person is actually living a rightly ordered life from whether a person's action is right. Neither description, however, depends on goodness.

Goodness asks whether one strives through right action to make oneself more rightly ordered. The good person consistently searches for opportunities to turn out a well-written first edition of oneself. The good person searches for those actions that will make one's weaknesses less debilitating and one's strengths more firmly anchored. The good person strives to become freer; the rightly ordered person is already free.

The description of persons as "virtuous" discloses particular difficulties in the use of the distinction between goodness and rightness. Generally speaking, we call a person virtuous who is both rightly ordered and presumably good.[19]

When we say that persons are just, temperate, or prudent, we mean something different from saying that they are virtuous. Attributing a specific virtue to someone predicts that in a particular area of living the person will enjoy acting rightly. A temperate person will generally enjoy a party without getting drunk. A chaste person will have loving and affectionate relationships that respect the sexual integrity of one's self and one's friends. A brave person will neither shun nor search for danger. A just person will take delight in the respect of persons. A prudent person will always weigh the pros and cons to achieve a balance. Each attribution of a virtue describes someone as rightly ordered in a particular area of human activity. Often, goodness is not even presumed.

Calling someone virtuous, however, signifies that in all dimensions of one's personality, the individual is generally inclined to right activity. The virtuous person is temperate, brave, just, and prudent. Moreover, this virtuous or rightly ordered person is presumably also good; that is, the person is striving to become more rightly ordered or virtuous. But is that presumption appropriate?

Consider prudence, the most important of the virtues. The selfish and the amoral are as capable as the saints of giving right advice. Similarly, temperance often has little bearing on moral goodness. We easily imagine the loving and the selfish as temperate. Likewise, we can imagine the wicked as brave.[20] Finally, if justice is giving one one's due, then it seems feasible that a person can sometimes act justly without necessarily being good.

Three additional points merit our attention. First, not all good people are virtuous or rightly ordered. If goodness describes striving out of love to become more rightly ordered, and rightness describes the attainment of integrated behavior, then many people may be good who have not yet attained the virtuous life. Not all good people are virtuous or rightly ordered. Some, perhaps many, good people are still disordered.

Second, when we judge someone to be virtuous, we may be asked to explain that judgment. We can answer with something like, "in light of my experience, this person has consistently acted rightly, has been comfortable with right actions, and has an uncanny way of striking a balance between excesses. I expect, therefore, that in future situations the person will behave similarly. It seems to be his [or her] second nature." Thus, we judge that someone is virtuous if our experience demonstrates that the person is rightly ordered. Were we also asked, "But is the person good; that is, does the person strive to become even better to serve humanity?" we would probably answer with a double negative: "I cannot imagine that the person is not good."

When asked these two questions we seem to appreciate that the judgment that one is rightly ordered is based on observation.[21] But the judgment that one is good is not subject to observation. We cannot actually know that one is good. Basically, to remark that a person is virtuous is to predict that the person will consistently perform rightly ordered behavior. The presumption that the person is also good is, at best, a presumption.

Third, and finally, what is the source of our presumption that a virtuous person is a good person? Do we presume that someone with the four virtues is good simply because we presume that he or she has a fifth, as yet unnamed, virtue? Is there a fifth virtue that actually accounts for the goodness of virtuous people? I think there is.

When we presume that a virtuous person is good, we are presuming that the person is also charitable or benevolent. In contemporary language a charitable person is one who performs charitable acts. We have, unfortunately, lost the original meaning of charity, which is the love that strives for greater union with God and neighbor through attempts to realize right living. Charity's original meaning provides a distinct description of a person's striving as opposed to one's other virtues that stress attainment.

Can we imagine a person with the four cardinal virtues but without charity? Again, I think we can. If someone has the virtues but lacks charity, then he or she is a rightly ordered person without goodness. Similarly, we can consider the person who has charity but lacks the four virtues. This person wants to be temperate, brave, just, and prudent but has not yet attained, and may never attain, such integration. Many people may have the virtue of charity, who are not temperate, brave, just, or prudent. Notwithstanding their failure to attain rightness, they often mean well, try hard, and certainly wish to be otherwise.

When moral description was keyed to the virtues, charity had a function that was similar to benevolence.[22] And, though some moralists would restrict benevolence to no more than well wishing, benevolence can, in fact, be the moral description for a person who literally strives to realize rightness.[23] The benevolent person's will is bent on right realization, but it may not attain the beneficial act.[24] The person is good; it is his or her behavior that continually misses the mark.

In many ways, benevolence can serve as a description for all good persons. Whereas charity is a theological virtue that presumes faith, benevolence describes good persons without the presumption of faith. In either case, this fifth virtue has a specific function different from any and all the other four.

The statement that a person is virtuous can be an unclear description. It describes a rightly ordered person, but it begs the question of whether the virtuous person is actually good. It acknowledges that knowing whether one is rightly ordered is different from knowing whether one is good. In making that admission it adds that though we can know through observation that one is prudent or just, we can only know that one is charitable, benevolent, or good by being the subject or the subject's intimate friend or confessor.[25] Finally, when we entertain the possibility that someone could have the four cardinal virtues and yet not have charity, we simply conclude that a virtuous person is a rightly ordered person.[26]

The distinction of goodness and rightness describes the four cardinal virtues as right making virtues, because they make the agent and the agent's actions right. Since rightness describes two dimensions of human living, persons and actions, each of the four virtues describe the rightness of the agent and the action. On the other hand, goodness, charity, or benevolence describes the agent solely, i.e., the one striving through action to become a more rightly ordered person.

This insight that virtue language needs a specific concept of goodness is hardly new. Both Aristotle and Augustine recognized it. Aristotle considered cleverness (*deinotes*) as the capability of "carrying out the actions conducive to our proposed aim and of achieving that aim." Since cleverness belonged to both good and bad people, cleverness is called prudence only in the good person: "One cannot be prudent without being good." The good person who is clever is prudent.[27]

Augustine, having the concept of charity as goodness, raised the problem of observation.[28] He argued that whereas the contrary vice of prudence was imprudence, there existed a vice that was a "deceptive resemblance" to prudence: craftiness. Craftiness is the cleverness of a bad person. Prudence is the cleverness of a good person.[29]

Augustine argued that the moral virtues have both contrary vices and "deceptive resemblances." Thrift has prodigality as its contrary vice and niggardliness as its "deceptive resemblance." Niggardliness is the thrift of a selfish person. In contemporary terms, thrift is right behavior, prodigality is wrong behavior, but niggardliness is a bad person's thriftiness. Similarly, Augustine distinguished between justice's contrary vice, injustice, and its "deceptive resemblance," vengeance. Vengeance belongs to the selfish and justice to the charitable.[30]

Augustine's use of "deceptive resemblances" is insightful. Injustice, imprudence, and prodigality are observable and, therefore, not deceptive. Vengeance, niggardliness, and craftiness are deceptive. Though they share the same material qualities as justice, thrift, and prudence, their formal quality, selfishness, is no more observable than charity itself. Charity, as the moral motivation for being just, prudent, courageous, and temperate, also provides the "moral" significance to the moral virtues.

Why, then, did Augustine need to posit these distinctions? Perhaps he realized that of themselves the "moral" virtues are not descriptions of morally good persons. The observation of "thrifty" acts or "prudent" dispositions can be deceptive. They can actually be bad acts or dispositions, notwithstanding that the behavior is right. Just as a "right act" can be either good or bad, so, too, can a "prudent" act or a "just" or "temperate" disposition be exercised by either good or bad people.[31]

In summary, rightly ordered persons are persons with virtues. Their will, reason, and passions are ordered. As "habits of living or conduct," virtues belong to those who live rightly.[32] In turn, virtues enable persons to act rightly. The virtues are acquired not by repeatedly performing the same types of actions but by intending and executing the same types of actions. The virtues are acquired willfully, not accidentally.

A virtue is defined as a "constant disposition" that "produces promptness and facility of action" as well as "joy in acting."[33] Though the virtues are interior dispositions, they do not pertain to goodness. As rightly ordered interior dispositions, they enable us to intend and execute other rightly ordered acts. Whether they are acquired out of goodness or badness pertains to whether the agent has charity or not. The egotistical politician can easily desire to be just for the sake of political gain. The sexually frigid individual may find sanctuary in chastity. The aging alcoholic may find temperance a valid way of life. The young rookie may find that the virtue of courage is an indelible aspect of her career. And even though we call it niggardliness, the miser cultivates thrift.

These desires for a specific virtue are simply the formal notions of that virtue. They tell us only that one wants a rightly ordered disposition; they do not tell us why. We need some other form, charity or benevolence, to explain that the person who intends to acquire virtue is intending rightness out of goodness.

Do intentions, therefore, pertain to goodness or rightness? Generally, we associate intentions with a person's goodness, but in the case of virtuous people, intentions are specifically rightly ordered. To remedy the dilemma Klaus Demmer and Josef Fuchs, among others, suggest that we distinguish between motivation and intention. Goodness pertains to the former, rightness to the latter.

Though the distinction may seem contrived, it proves itself in ordinary affairs. In the Irangate episode, for instance, when we asked why arms were sold, we were given two different answers. We heard President Reagan say that this was the best way to free the hostages. Freedom for the hostages was his intention. But did he adequately consider the ramifications of such an intention? Did he consider what this act would signal to terrorists or allies? Did he really think that this form of diplomacy would remain secret? These questions ask whether the president's thinking was right. Intention here is measured as right or wrong thinking. On the other hand, had we asked the president about his motivation, he may have said that he acted solely out of love for the hostages and their families. This response concerns goodness. It does not imply that President Reagan's reasoning was right, but that his motivation was good.

Motivation is a relatively new concept in philosophy, though it has long been used in ordinary language.[34] Thus, when we say, "she did this out of love," we are not describing the moral rightness of one's behavior but one's moral goodness. The phrase "out of" (aus, ex, and their equivalents) has always been used to make moral judgments specifically of goodness. In fact, Kant himself distinguished goodness and rightness precisely by distinguishing "an action done out of duty" (Handeln aus Pflicht) from an action "in accordance with duty" (pflicht-mässiges Handeln).[35] Out of love, hate, jealousy, disregard, contempt, loyalty, people move themselves to action. The boundary between goodness and rightness is marked by the distinction between motivation and intention: moral goodness depends solely on the motivation of the person.[36]

Rightness pertains not only to intention but also to choice: one can actually have the right intention but, lacking prudence, make the wrong choice; or one can make the right choice even if one's intention is not completely ordered. Rightness has two realms: the executed act (choice) and the agent's reason for acting (intention).

Occasionally, authors consider intention within the sphere of moral goodness.[37] These authors err because, wanting to discuss the elements of rightness pertaining to an action itself, they identify rightness with choice alone. Whereas exclusion of intention from judgments concerning choice is acceptable, the inclusion of intention in judgments concerning moral goodness is mistaken. Intention pertains to rightness.

Similarly, psychological motivation is distinct from moral motivation.[38] When used *psychologically*, motivation concerns questions of rightness or wrongness. When used *morally*, it concerns whether one moves oneself out of charity or benevolence to realize oneself or one's action rightly.

Moral motivation explains the agent's fundamental disposition. Why is one interested in chastity, truth-telling, or parental duty?[39] Is one motivated out of self-aggrandizement or egoism? If so, one is immoral. Is one motivated out of love for God or one's neighbor or both? If so, one is a moral person. Only one question, the question of moral motivation, concerns the fundamental, formal self-movement of the agent.[40] This moral motivation gives moral significance to all right dispositions or actions, and it alone is the singular description of moral goodness.[41]

We distinguish the moral from the psychological uses of motivations. A greedy person, for instance, is psychologically motivated to act greedily. In this way, neither the person nor the person's actions are rightly ordered. But being greedy is not necessarily an indication of badness. Whether the person is bad depends on whether the person has failed to strive to be free from greed in order to serve God and neighbor. The person's striving to be free makes the moral (or formal) motivation good, though the psychological (or material) motivation is wrong to the extent that it remains greedy. The person's goodness is solely dependent on whether that person has been trying to overcome the greed; the person's rightness is dependent on whether that person has overcome the greed. In this distinction, too, goodness remains antecedent and formal.

*   *   *

Goodness, then, is descriptive of the first and most formal movement in a person. Unlike earlier approaches, goodness is not a judgment consequent to action, but a judgment antecedent to action. Rightness, on the other hand, concerns whether one's life and actions attain what is necessary for the protection and promotion of values. As attaining pertains to rightness, striving pertains to goodness.

As a judgment antecedent to rightness, goodness asks whether one is willing to move oneself into and toward right acting. Goodness concerns the most formal motivation for human acting and the most formal virtue for the virtuous life. Goodness moves one to strive for rightness. Badness is failing to move oneself.

Though goodness describes striving and is antecedent to rightness or attainment, it is not the starting point of questions concerning rightness. Moralists familiar with scholastic terminology may be tempted to think that goodness is the *terminus a quo* of human action, rightness the *terminus ad quem*. But there is no such direct sequence. The *terminus a quo*, or point of departure, for rightness is not goodness, but reason itself.

In examining a wrong act, for instance, we may ask why it is wrong. Here we search for errors in one's thinking. Sometimes an error is simply a mistaken choice. Sometimes a mistaken choice has its source in an erroneous intention. Sometimes the error in intention or choice is merely the result of disordered psychological motivations. But always the explanation for right or wrong activity will be found in one's reasoning.

Therefore, when persons want to correct wrong action they need advice, not exhortation. The exhortation to good people to try harder is not advice for correcting wrong actions. Being good, they have been trying. They need right reason, not a good will; they need prudence, not charity. Similarly, if a wrong action is performed by a person who simply fails to strive, exhortation will not make the action right. Exhortation is certainly needed, but for the sake of goodness, not rightness. The bad person, being converted to goodness, will need advice to learn to act rightly. The exhortation to bad people to strive harder for the interests of others may be an invitation to goodness, but it is not advice for rightness.

MORAL GOODNESS AND THE SCRIPTURES

In the Bible, the heart is designated as the locus of morality. The heart as moral motivation appears in the synoptic gospels in passages that emphasize the moral motivation of the pharisees: the pharisees "seek to destroy Jesus" (Luke 19:47), and they ask questions so that "they might accuse" Jesus (Matt 12:10) or "provoke" him (Luke 11:53-54). But Jesus knows the motivations of the pharisees (Luke 6:8; 9:47; 18:17). These motivations are considered descriptive of the pharisees' moral worth. Thus, despite their right action, the Lord criticizes them directly: "you justify yourselves before men, but God knows your hearts" (Luke 16:15). John's gospel makes the accusation even clearer: "I know that you have not the love of God in your hearts" (John 5:42).

In fact, the famous "woes" are precisely an attack on the distinction between one's conduct and one's motivation (Luke 11:37-54; Matt 23:1-36). The pharisees are righteous; one could even say "right-doers." Against them stand the sinners, clearly "wrong-doers." Jesus opts for the latter: he did not come to invite the righteous, but sinners (Luke 6:32; 15:7; cf. Matt 8:11-12). Jesus associates with these sinners (Luke 7:33-34; Matt 11:18). Notwithstanding their "wrongfulness," he sees in them the possibility for being good. In the righteous, he does not.

The issue of motivation is not restricted solely to the pharisees. Throughout the New Testament we can find any number of distinctions between goodness and rightness, from the judgment on Judas's remark at Bethany: "This he said, not because he cared for the poor but because he was a thief" (John 12:5-6), to Jesus' post-resurrection encounter with Peter (John 21:15-19), "Do you love me?"

Two particular passages underline the New Testament's use of this distinction. The first appears in the story of the widow's mite

(Mark 12:41-44; Luke 21:1-4) in which Jesus deliberately contrasts the extent of the widow's gift to the generosity of her heart. He praises the impoverished one who strives to answer the needs of another. Here is the heart of the distinction. What matters is not what we do or who we become but whether, despite our material, intellectual, or emotional poverty, we strive to do what we can.

The most striking indication of the New Testament's awareness of the distinction between goodness and rightness appears in the pauline hymn of love:

> If I speak in the tongues of men and of angels, but have not love, I am a noisy gong or a clanging symbol. And if I have prophetic powers, and understand all mysteries and all knowledge, and if I have all faith, so as to remove mountains, but have not love, I am nothing. If I give away all I have, and if I deliver my body to be burned, but have not love, I gain nothing (1 Cor 13:1-4).

To claim that such acts as speaking in tongues, prophecy, understanding, and faith are as nothing compared to love is a powerful claim. But that an apostle to the early Christians would distinguish even martyrdom from charity indeed highlights the radical nature of the distinction. Not even the right act of self-sacrifice can confirm the martyr's goodness. Goodness comes from the heart alone.

NOTES to Chapter One

1. Democritus, *Fragmenta Moralia*, n. 109. Cited in Stephen Toulmin, *An Examination of the Place of Reason in Ethics* (Cambridge: Cambridge University Press, 1958), 170.

2. For a partial list of authors and references on this point, see Bruno Schüller, *Die Begründung sittlicher Urteile* (Düsseldorf: Patmos, 1980), 140.

3. Josef Fuchs, *Christian Morality: The Word Becomes Flesh* (Washington, D.C.: Georgetown University Press, 1987), 105–117.

4. *Summa theologiae*, I.II.19.5c and 6c (hereafter, S.T.).

5. John Ford and Gerald Kelly, *Contemporary Moral Theology* (Westminster, Maryland: Newman Press, 1958).

6. Immanuel Kant, *Foundation of the Metaphysics of Morals* (Indianapolis: Bobbs-Merrill, 1969), Part 1.

7. G. E. Moore, *Ethics*, (London: Thornton Butterworth, 1912), 80.

8. Ibid., 187–189. Later, R. M. Hare refined this distinction by identifying good acting with good motives (*The Language of Morals* [Oxford: Oxford University Press, 1952], 185).

9. G. E. Moore, *Ethics*, 193–195.

10. For Hare's thoroughgoing elaboration of the linguistic differences between the words "good" and "right," see *The Language of Morals*, 151–152, 186; *Freedom and Reason* (Oxford: Oxford University Press, 1962), 152–156; and "Right and Wrong," *Dictionary of Christian Ethics*, ed. John Macquarrie (London: SCM Press, 1967), 299.

11. For why Moore failed to make the identification, see H. J. Paton, "The Alleged Independence of Goodness," in *The Philosophy of G. E. Moore*, ed. Paul Schilpp (New York: Tudor Publishing Co., 1952), 113–134.

12. Bruno Schüller, "Gewissen und Schuld" in *Das Gewissen*, ed. Josef Fuchs (Düsseldorf: Patmos, 1979), 34–55; "Neuere Beiträge zum Thema 'Begründung sittlicher Normen,'" *Theologische Berichte* 4, ed. Franz Furger (Zurich: Benziger, 1974), 109–181; "Various Types of Grounding Ethical Norms" in *Readings in Moral Theology* 1, ed. Charles Curran and Richard McCormick (New York: Paulist Press, 1979), 184–198.

13. Josef Fuchs, *Personal Responsibility and Christian Morality* (Washington, D.C.: Georgetown University Press, 1983), 84–111; *Essere del signore* (Rome: Gregorian University Press, 1981); *Christian Ethics in a Secular Arena* (Washington, D.C.: Georgetown University Press, 1984), 100–113; *Christian Morality: The Word Becomes Flesh*, 48–67, 105–117, 131–153.

Klaus Demmer, "Sittlich handeln aus Erfarung," *Gregorianum* 59 (1978): 661–691; "Sittlich handeln aus Zeugnis geben," *Gregorianum* 64 (1983): 453–485; *Deuten und Handeln* (Freiburg, Switzerland: Universitätsverlag, 1985).

14. See also Bernard Hoose, *Proportionalism: The American Debate and its European Roots* (Washington, D.C.: Georgetown University Press, 1987); Louis Janssens, "Ontic Good and Evil," *Louvain Studies* 12 (1987): 62–82; Richard McCormick, *Notes on Moral Theology, 1981 through 1984* (Lanham, Maryland: University Press of America, 1984); "Bishops as Teachers and Jesuits as Listeners," *Studies in the Spirituality of Jesuits* 28 (1986).

15. See John Langan, "Sins of Malice in the Moral Theology of Thomas Aquinas," *The Annual of the Society of Christian Ethics* 12 (1987): 179–198.

16. The nature of moral claims is a constant theme in Josef Fuchs. See notes 3 and 13 above.

17. See Bruno Schüller, "The Debate on the Specific Character of Christian Ethics," *Readings in Moral Theology* 2, ed. Charles Curran and Richard McCormick (New York: Paulist Press, 1980), 207–233.

18. See Bruno Schüller on "ought implies can": "L'importanza dell'esperienza per la giustificazione delle norme di comportamento morale," in *Fede Cristiana e Agire Morale*, ed. Klaus Demmer and Bruno Schüller (Assisi: Cittadella Editrice, 1980), 338–339; see also note 12 above.

Philip Keane also raises the question of one's "maturity" as expressive of one's freedom and hence the question of rightness in "The Objective Moral Order: Reflections on Recent Research," *Theological Studies* 43 (1982): 274–278.

19. On the conflation of the virtues in the virtuous person, see Alasdair MacIntyre, *After Virtue* (Notre Dame: University of Notre Dame Press, 1981), 210–226.

20. See, e.g., Alasdair MacIntyre, *After Virtue*, 166–167; Karl Rahner, "The Theological Concept of Concupiscentia," *Theological Investigations* 1 (Baltimore: Helicon Press, 1961), 365–366.

21. See Stuart Hampshire, *Thought and Action* (Notre Dame: University of Notre Dame Press, 1982).

22. Karl Rahner, "The Commandment of Love in Relation to the Other Commandments," *Theological Investigations* 5 (Baltimore: Helicon Press, 1966), 439–459; "Reflections on the Unity of the Love of Neighbor and the Love of God," *Theological Investigations* 6 (Baltimore: Helicon Press, 1969), 231–252.

23. William Frankena, *Ethics* (Englewood Cliffs, New Jersey: Prentice Hall, 1973).

24. See especially Bruno Schüller, *Die Begründung sittlicher Urteile*, 68ff.; "Various Types of Grounding Ethical Norms," 188ff.

25. On the difference between the knowledge of observers versus the self-understanding of the agent, see Stuart Hampshire, *Thought and Action*, 113, 125, 152.

26. For a different position, see William Frankena, *Ethics*, 70 and "McCormick and the Traditional Distinction," *Doing Evil to Achieve Good*, ed. Richard McCormick and Paul Ramsey (Chicago: Loyola University Press, 1978), 146ff.; Vernon J. Bourke, "Aquinas and Recent Theories of the Right," *American Catholic Philosophical Association* 48 (1975): 187–197.

27. *Nicomachean Ethics* 6.12.1144a22–35.

28. John Langan, "Augustine on the Unity and the Interconnection of the Virtues," *Harvard Theological Review* 72 (1979): 92.

29. Augustine, *Letters*, Fathers of the Church Series, 30 (New York: Fathers of the Church, 1955), letter 167.

30. Ibid., 167.6.

31. See Klaus Demmer, "Erwägungen zum 'intrinsece malum,'" *Gregorianum* 68 (1987): 613–637.

32. Austin Fagothey, *Right and Reason* (St. Louis: C. V. Mosby Company, 1959), 227.

33. Servais Pinckaers, "A Virtue Is Not a Habit," *Cross Currents* 12 (1962): 75.

34. "Not until the 20th century did motivation seem to enter the vocabulary of philosophy and psychology. The concept was not in the *Dictionary of Philosophy and Psychology*, publication of which was completed in 1911; the word 'motive' was listed, but in the sense of awareness of desire or purpose, rather than as a moving force" (Encyclopedia Britannica's *Macropaedia* [Chicago: Benton, 1974], 12:557).

35. Bruno Schüller, "Various Types of Grounding Ethical Norms," 191. Schüller uses *aus* with some regularity, e.g., when describing goodness as that which comes "aus der sittlicher Ureinsicht" in *Die Begründung sittlicher Urteile*, 136, 304.

36. See William Frankena, *Thinking about Morality* (Ann Arbor: University of Michigan Press, 1980), 48; R. M. Hare, *The Language of Morals*, 185. See also note 13 above.

37. William Frankena, "Conversations with Carney and Hauerwas," *Journal of Religious Ethics* 3 (1975): 50; Garth Hallett, *Christian Moral Reasoning* (Notre Dame: University of Notre Dame Press, 1983), 19–28. For a more sophisticated approach to rightness, see Stuart Hampshire, *Thought and Action*.

38. Peter Knauer makes an analogous distinction in "The Hermeneutic Function of the Principle of Double Effect," *Readings in Moral Theology* 1, 4f.

39. Stephen Toulmin, *An Examination of the Place of Reason in Ethics*, 155–160; 201–211.

40. Similarly Bruno Schüller continually returns to this fundamental level of the person in which the moral self-determination of the person logically precedes all other acting, by using such terms as "sittliche Uralternative," and "sittliche Ureinsicht," and "Grundhaltung" in *Die Begründung sittlicher Urteile*, 137–138, 300; and "Urgewissen" in "Gewissen und Schuld," 40.

41. See Bruno Schüller, "The Debate on the Specific Character of Christian Ethics," especially 214.

PART 2

Choosing the *Summa Theologiae*

CHAPTER 2

Difficulties Before the *Prima Secundae*

The contemporary distinction between goodness and rightness marks the difference between whether we strive to know the right and whether we know the right. Striving to know pertains to goodness and requires an autonomous will. When we strive both to understand what right activity is and to execute that activity, we are good. But, in order to strive or will to know the right, we must have a concept of the will as that which moves the reason to understand.

In the literature of the thirteenth century—and most important— in Thomas's own writings, we find this question: do we will only what we know or do we will to know? If we can will to know, then the will is autonomous. If we can will only what we know, then the will is not autonomous. Without an autonomous will, we could not ask whether a person strives to find the right.

Nevertheless, Thomas does not clearly establish the will's autonomy until he writes the *Prima secundae* of the *Summa theologiae*. In earlier writings, Thomas maintains that the will is a moved mover, first moved by reason. He describes this movement by reason as exerting a causality similar to final causality. This description, in effect, precludes any autonomous movement of the will, because any movement is ultimately derived not from what is moved, but from the mover. Insofar as Thomas describes reason and not the will itself as the will's mover, any achievement or any fault in the will must, therefore, originate in reason. If, therefore, every moral fault is ultimately a fault in reason, then all moral faults are due to error. If this is true then any moral fault will simply be moral wrongness and any question regarding moral goodness or badness will be precluded.

As late as the *Pars prima* of the *Summa theologiae*, Thomas does not yet have a synthesis to explain the relation between reason and the will. Thus he asks whether the will, like the intellect, ought to be divided into a passive will and an active will. Thomas answers: "The intellect is compared to the will as moving the will. And therefore there is no need to distinguish in the will an active and a passive will."[1] In the *Pars prima* Thomas does not admit an autonomous will.

In the *Prima secundae*, Thomas reverses his earlier position and writes in the ninth question: "It is evident that the intellect through its knowledge of the principle, reduces itself from potentiality to act, as to its knowledge of the conclusions; and thus it moves itself. And, in like manner, the will, through its volition of the end, moves itself to will the means."[2] In order to make this reversal, Thomas will have to employ several distinctions not made in earlier writings.

In this chapter I present what I believe are two competing views in Thomas's pre-*Prima secundae* writings. On the one hand, Thomas recognizes the importance of the will's autonomy in dealing with moral praise and blame. Thus, Thomas affirms the will's autonomy. On the other hand, Thomas explains the will's movement by attributing the cause of that movement to reason. Thus, he asserts that as reason is the source of both freedom and sin, the will is a passive power.

THE WILL'S AUTONOMY

Thomas's *Commentary on the Sentences* (1252–1256) clearly maintains that the will moves all the other powers. The assertion is made to explain that only voluntary acts are meritorious; the role of charity as mover; and how habits incline one to action.[3] Thomas writes that the will moves the intellect, in fact, all powers, and is, in short, the first mover.[4]

In *De veritate* (1256–1259) Thomas argues that in movement the will precedes the intellect, that merit is derived from this movement, and that the first mover is the will. Furthermore, the will as efficient cause wills both itself to will and the intellect to understand. Therefore, under the aspect of moving, the will is more noble than reason.[5]

While at Orvieto (1261–1265) Thomas argues in the *Summa contra gentiles* that the will has in its power to will or not will, to make the intellect think or not think, and to make it ponder this or that.[6] In the same work he argues that for a substance to move itself is the property of the will.[7] Underlying this property of movement is the efficiency of the will, through which reason moves. Insofar as the will moves efficiently, the will thus moves as agent.[8]

In Rome (1265–1268) Thomas writes to the Dominican master general that in acting the intellect is not distinguished from the will, because the intellect in acting does not move unless mediated by the will.[9] The same point is often made in *De potentia*: the will, as mover and mediator, moves the intellect to understand.[10]

Finally, even in the *Pars prima*, Thomas argues that the will moves the intellect, that to be moved voluntarily is to be moved from itself (*ex se*), and that this movement from self is the necessary condition for merit or demerit.[11]

From the first cited text to the last, Thomas holds that the will's function as mover is the ground for attributing any merit or demerit to the will: to move something is nothing other than to be the cause of something.[12] Clearly, this argument for the will's autonomy in movement is consistent with the distinction between goodness and rightness. We cannot speak of merit or demerit unless we can assert that the will is primarily autonomous in its movements. Whether we are right or wrong in thought or action is one thing; whether we will or strive to find and execute the right, is another. The latter, Thomas realizes, pertains to merit or demerit.

Thomas is even firmer on this point when he considers the role of ignorance in sin. In his *Commentary on the Sentences*, Thomas argues that ignorance is culpable when it is in the power of the agent to know otherwise: under such conditions ignorance does not cause the act to be involuntary, but voluntary, and thus the sin is in the will as cause.[13] Further, ignorance can be attributed to the will as cause, if the will does not restrain the passions that absorb reason's estimative capability, but behaves irresponsibly and chooses whatever it pleases.[14] If ignorance is ever blameworthy, it is blameworthy when the will has failed to act as it could.

A few years later in *Quodlibetales* 8 (1256-1259), Thomas again argues that ignorance neither excuses nor diminishes sin if one is capable of knowing the right.[15] Later, in his commentary on Dionysius (Rome, 1265), Thomas argues that the will is culpable for ignorance, if the will does not want to be directed by reason.[16] And, finally, in *De malo*, Thomas writes: "An act of the will can precede an act of the intellect, just as when someone wishes to understand; and by the same notion ignorance can fall under the will and be voluntary."[17] Thomas recognizes here the importance of the will's autonomy in order to understand the will's accountability for sin. If our understanding of sin is founded on the responsibility of the will, then we must not only say that ignorance can be attributed to the will, but also that the will can will ignorance. Thus, Thomas concludes, not only can the will move the will to understand, it can also directly will ignorance. The autonomy of the will is the cornerstone of any discussion of a person's moral state.

The themes are constant: the will moves itself, and it precedes reason both by moving reason to think and by mediating reason's own movement. Failure to try to understand and failure to be governed by reason are both moral failures. In short, Thomas develops the efficiency of the will's movements in arguments concerning moral responsibility; and rightly so, since Thomas consistently attributes efficient causality to the will.

Given this data, it appears that Thomas in his early writings upholds the will's autonomy. But there are other texts, and the data are conflicting.

REASON AS THE CAUSE OF THE WILL'S MOVEMENT

As early as his *Commentary on the Sentences*, Thomas argues that the intellect moves the will. And the movement of the will follows the movement of cognition, because reason moves the appetite.[18]

In subsequent writings he develops the argument consistently and substantially. Citing Aristotle's *De anima* III, 10, Thomas argues in *De veritate* that the apprehended good moves the appetite and that the will, therefore, is a passive power. Thus, only knowledge of an end moves the will and an end, therefore, is an object, presented by the reason, moving the will. Thomas concludes that the reason moves in the manner of an end. If then the end is the cause of the efficient cause, then the will only moves at the command of reason.[19] In *De veritate* Thomas argues with greater frequency than in the *Commentary on the Sentences* that reason moves the will.

In the *Summa contra gentiles* Thomas argues from the outset and consistently that the intellect is not an efficient or moving cause, but because it moves the will by proposing the object, reason moves the will as final cause.[20] Just as reason moves the will by presenting the object, so reason moves the will as an end.[21]

Earlier, in *De veritate*, Thomas argued against any precedence of reason over the will. Instead, he argued, reason's presentation of the object is at once the will's movement: the movement is instantaneous.[22] Now, in the *Summa contra gentiles*, Thomas reverses this position: the will must first be moved by reason; no movement of the will precedes reason.[23] In the new argument against any priority of the will over reason, Thomas specifically excludes motivation as prior to reason's presentation of the object.[24] Thus, he concludes that lacking this priority the will cannot move reason as reason moves the will; reason moves the will *primo et per se*, but the will moves reason *quasi per accidens*.[25]

Thus, it should not surprise us that Thomas also contradicts his earlier assertions concerning the will as first mover: if reason moves as end, then reason must be the superior mover, the first mover.[26] Thomas's answer to the question, whether the will is moved by itself or by reason is clear: reason moves the will.

In the *Pars prima*, Thomas argues that the end moves the efficient cause; that the end in the intellect moves the will; and that the intellect precedes the will as the motive power precedes the thing moveable and as the active precedes the passive.[27] On the same grounds, he argues that the object is to the passive power as moving cause and that every movement of the will must be preceded by an apprehension of the intellect. Clearly, the apprehended good moves the will.[28]

When Thomas considers whether the will ought to have some active power in itself that moves it to action, he argues against such a claim: "The intellect is compared to the will as moving the will. And therefore there is no need to distinguish in the will an active and a passive will."[29] Thus, despite Thomas's assertions, we are hard pressed to find clear evidence for the will's autonomy from reason in any of his works before the *Prima secundae*.

It is clear that Thomas finds the metaphysical explanation of the will's movement in reason's presentation of the object to the will. This finding, however, compromises Thomas's earlier assertions. Insofar as reason moves the will, the will is a passive power that cannot move reason to consider anything other than reason's own objects. This passivity of the will becomes more evident in Thomas's description of the final cause.

In his *Commentary on the Sentences*, Thomas declares that it is in the end, as the cause of the causes, that the meaning of good is to be found.[30] This affirmation that the end is "the cause of the causes" continues throughout his writings. Similarly, he holds the end as the "first of all the causes."[31] These titles are used fundamentally to affirm causal primacy: without the end, the agent does not act.[32]

Because the end moves the agent, all other causes derive their causality from the end, and all other causes receive from the final cause their status as causes.[33] Moreover, the end is not simply the cause of the causes, nor the first cause of the causes in general, but of each cause specifically. From the *Sentences* (1252-1256) to the *Commentaries* on Aristotle (1269-1272), Thomas consistently maintains the primacy of the final cause.[34]

EXPLAINING REASON'S CAUSALITY ANALOGICALLY

Before the ninth question of the *Prima secundae*, Thomas explicitly designates the causal relation between the will and reason in reason's presentation of the object to the will as analogous to final causality. This designation occurs in *De veritate*, in the *Summa contra gentiles*, and in the *Pars prima*. Consistently, Thomas argues that reason moves the will in the way that an end moves something.[35]

> Primarily and directly the intellect moves the will; indeed, the will, as such, is moved by its object which is the known good. . . . The intellect moves the will in the way an end moves something since the good that is understood is the end for the will.[36]

The importance of reason's movement is here underlined:

> That the will is higher than the intellect in the sense of moving it is again clearly false. For primarily and directly the intellect moves the will. . . . Hence, it is evident that the intellect is, without qualification, higher than the will.[37]

Thomas's affirmation that reason moves the will in the way an end moves something is always stated in careful analogical language. Thomas does not state that reason is the final cause but that reason moves the will as an end or as a final cause moves something. By the same token, however, Thomas refers to no other causality. Final causality alone is Thomas's best description of reason's presentation of the object to the will. By this presentation, the will is moved to act. Without this presentation of the (known) good, the will remains a passive power. "The intellect precedes the will, as the motive power precedes the thing movable, and as the active precedes the passive; for good which is understood moves the will."[38]

Despite these passages, I believe that Thomas is reluctant to conclude his own reflections on the matter. This reluctance arises from the fact that if we describe the causal effect of reason's presentation of the object as final, we ultimately preclude the will's accountability. Thus, along with assertions that the will moves itself, I find other statements in these works that are incompatible with this description of reason as final cause. These statements concern the will's freedom to accept or reject reason's object and the will's movement by God.

First, consider the will's freedom. The first cause or the cause of the causes is also that which causes movement. But, the end is not a cause unless the will is moved by it.[39] Insofar as the will has the end, the end is the cause of the causes: the principle of causality rests in the will. If an end exerts final causality only when the will accepts it, then the end is subject to being accepted or rejected by the will.

In addition, Thomas explicitly rejects the necessary movement of the will by reason.[40] In his early writings, however, Thomas offers no explanation for this position. Only on the very eve of writing the *Prima secundae* does Thomas explain that because the object presented is always a particular good, reason does not of necessity move the will, whose object is the universal good.[41]

Second, in Thomas's earlier writings, he argues that the will is moved by God, who is inevitably the first mover.[42] In the *Pars prima* he argues that only the last end moves the will such that the will cannot not will the last end.[43] No other end exerts such influence over the will. It would seem, then, that only this end and no other end presented as an object could necessarily move the will.

Thomas argues that the very ability of the will to move itself is derived from God. These two movements of the will by God and by reason are not adequately distinguished in Thomas's earlier writings. That the will can will at all is derived from God. And that the will wills something requires that an object be presented to it by reason. But is that "presentation" final causality? Does not such an object become an end only insofar as the will inclines itself toward it? If this is so, then reason's presentation of the object must signify some other causality than the final one.

These arguments notwithstanding, Thomas does not assert another causal explanation until *Prima secundae* 9. Until that shift occurs his position on the will's autonomy remains unclear and— what is worse—inadequate. Thus, when Thomas argues that reason's presentation of the object exerts final causality, he draws some disturbing conclusions. We turn now to the difficulties in Thomas's position.

THE DIFFICULTIES IN THIS POSITION

Inasmuch as Thomas attributes final causality to reason and not the will, all motion is eventually attributed to reason and the will is left without autonomy.[44] The results for moral theology are startling: if reason is the final cause, sin comes from error, the will is a passive power, and reason alone explains freedom.

Earlier, in his *Commentary on the Sentences*, Thomas distinguished the root of sin from its specification. This distinction lends itself to the distinction between goodness and rightness, because that we sin is distinct from the specific "sinful" act.[45]

Thomas changes this position in *De veritate*, the first work in which he argues that reason acts as final cause in any act of the will. This argument logically leads to the position that any "bad" end of the will necessarily requires a preceding "wrong" or "erroneous" object in reason. Thomas develops this thought when he distinguishes the will as either natural or subordinate to reason.

The will as nature inclines necessarily to the good. Since this is a necessary movement it can never be classified as meritorious or blameworthy. Rather praise and blame pertain to the will either as subordinate to reason or as it is specified.[46] Sin, therefore, pertains not to the fact that we desire happiness (which we do necessarily), but that we desire this particular happiness. In desiring a particular happiness that we should not desire, we sin. But the sin is the fact that the happiness we desire is the wrong happiness. Thus, "if anyone were by erroneous reasoning to be brought to desire as his happiness some particular good, for example, bodily pleasures, in which his happiness does not in fact consist, he incurs demerit by so desiring."[47] As opposed to his earlier position, Thomas now argues that demerit is derived from the specific act.

Thomas presumes that since reason presents the object, which, in turn, acts as final cause, bad action can only result from erroneous thinking: "where there is no failure in apprehending and comparing, there can be no willing of evil even when there is a question of means."[48] A necessary condition for sinning is specific error: there can be no "sin in the motion of the will so that it tends to evil unless there previously exists some deficiency in the apprehensive power."[49] Badness is explained in terms of wrongness.[50]

Thomas refines this position considerably in the *Summa contra gentiles*. Thomas argues that an external act would have "nothing to do with moral evil if the external act were defective by virtue of a defect having no reference to the will."[51] The defect cannot pertain to the natural will, because being unchanging its defect would cause every act of the will to be morally evil.[52] Thus, though Thomas turns to the will as subordinate to reason, he places the defect in the will, not in reason. If good action results from a proper end and proper subordination to reason, then sin in the action of the will results from a defect in the will's subordination to reason and to a proper end. Thomas contends that these defects can occur by the will's breaking forth into action in pursuit of a sensible apprehension rather than a reasonable one, or by reason's presentation of a good that is not consonant with the final good.[53]

Because reason, however, and not the will is the final cause in an act of the will, the problem remains: if the final cause is derived from reason, what grounds has the will to deny the object that reason presents? We are hard pressed to explain sin in any terms other than those of *De veritate*.

Thomas's premise that the will is a passive power is a second effect that results from the identification of the presented object with final causality.[54] It occurs, for example, in *De veritate*. Thomas writes that whatever belongs to reason stands as active in relation to the end, while whatever is directed or referred to the end by reason stands as a passive power. Inasmuch as intention is an act of the will in subordination to reason, the will is passively directed by the active direction of reason.[55]

Thomas also asserts the will's passivity in the *Summa contra gentiles*. First, he argues that the object willed is to the one willing as moving is to moved. Then he draws the same analogy, this time using reason presenting the object.

> The active should be proportionate to the passive, the moving to the movable. But in things having cognition the apprehending power is related to the appetitive power as mover to movable, for that which is apprehended by sense or imagination or intellect moves the intellectual or animal appetite.[56]

On one occasion, however, Thomas argues that for a substance to move itself is the property of the will.[57] But this does not presuppose that the will moves itself. Instead, Thomas argues that, for a substance possessing an intellect, to move itself is the property of the will. Thus, the necessary condition for movement is the intellect. Movement comes from the will, but the antecedent question is whether the will is first moved by itself or by reason.

The problem, therefore, is this: if the final cause is the cause of the causes, and if all movement is derived from this cause, then, inasmuch as the final cause is attributed to reason, the source of all movement is derived from reason. Thomas maintains precisely this position in the *Pars prima* when he rejects the need for positing an active and a passive will.[58] If, however, self-movement belongs to the will, then self-movement is only possible if final causality is derived from some source other than reason. If not, then there is no self-movement, and the will becomes a passive power. The result is not freedom but an intellectual determinism in which we only sin if we first err.

In *De veritate*, when asking whether humanity is endowed with free choice, Thomas argues that freedom comes from reason. His argument is clear: we act because we are moved, we are moved by a judgment, the judgment comes from reason. Thus, as freedom is derived from movement, so freedom comes from reason.[59]

By identifying freedom with the power of self-reflection, Thomas decisively identifies reason and not the will as the source of freedom.

To judge about one's judgment belongs only to reason, which reflects upon its own act and knows the relationship of things about which it judges and of those by which it judges. Hence the whole root of freedom is located in reason. Consequently, a being is related to free choice in the same way as it is related to reason.[60]

Thomas adds to this a puzzling remark: "Though judgment is a function of reason, the freedom of judging belongs immediately to the will."[61] It may seem that Thomas is in fact correcting his text.[62] But Thomas expressly points out that the will has no autonomy: "Free choice does not refer to the will absolutely but in subordination to reason."[63] Furthermore, Thomas establishes freedom in the will solely through the power of reason. Reason alone is the ultimate ground of freedom.

When Thomas treats freedom of action in the *Summa contra gentiles*, he similarly argues that the will is the mover moved by the intellect and that freedom in acting is derived from judgment. As judges, we are able to move ourselves by the power of reflexive judgment, which is the source for free choice as well as freedom in acting.[64] Any specific role for the will as explanatory of freedom is overcome by Thomas's intellectualism. Here, as in *De veritate*, Thomas recognizes that freedom comes from the will, yet when he explains freedom, he derives none of his argument from the will. Instead, Thomas attributes freedom exclusively to reason.[65]

A change occurs, however, after the *Summa contra gentiles*. In *De potentia* 3, Thomas asks whether God works in the world and includes in his reflections the objection that God could only work in agents who were not free in acting. In the body of the text, Thomas argues that God is the cause of our action in that God gives us the power of acting. In response to the objection, however, he distinguishes God as the cause of our ability to act from reason as the cause of our freedom in action.[66] This development sets the stage for the later distinction in the *Prima secundae* between the free exercise of the will in general and its freedom for specific action, that depends on reason. In terms of the later distinction, this one is its seed.

In the following year, Thomas returns to the question of freedom in the *Pars prima*. As in earlier writings, he insists that free choice belongs to humans precisely as rational creatures. He then asks, however, whether the voluntary quality of actions is lost if God first moves the will. Thomas answers negatively, again stating that God works in each thing according to its nature.[67] Once more, Thomas has discussed freedom of the will without any reference to reason.

These texts from Rome on the eve of the *Prima secundae* are not far from Thomas's earlier theme about God as final cause. They raise the same question, i.e., whether God can move the will, and they prepare the ground for the decisive shift to come in the *Prima secundae*.

EVALUATING THE POSITION

We have seen the tension in Thomas's early writings. On the one hand, the autonomy of the will is asserted; on the other, final causality is attributed to reason. The second of these assertions is the undoing of the first one. It leads to the conclusion that sin consists in error, that the will is a passive power, and that reason is the root of freedom. This fundamental position precludes any discussion of the distinction between goodness and rightness.

Thomas's moral criterion at this point is solely whether we understand the right, not whether we strive to realize the right. Insofar as the will is at least implicitly passive, and insofar as Thomas denies that the will has any original active agency, reason is the entire measure of morality. For this reason, I argue that no one should attempt to investigate the distinction between goodness and rightness in the writings of Thomas before question nine of the *Prima secundae*. Until then, the contemporary notion of moral goodness is simply precluded by Thomas's insistence that reason, not the will, ultimately causes and explains the will's movements.

But, prior to the *Prima secundae*, what, if anything, do we make of Thomas's fundamental position? Reason's presentation of an object to the will is nothing more than what we in modern language call "getting an idea." Thus, Thomas is asking, "whence the idea?" But Thomas's response, that the idea finds its cause in reason, is perplexing developmentally, morally, and epistemologically. It is perplexing developmentally because growth would become impossible unless one's reason could of its own accord present new ideas, new visions, new activities. Only reason that made new presentations would help an individual to grow, but whether reason did or did not make new presentations would not be subject to the agent's will or desire. Ideas would be presented not because the agent wanted new ideas, but simply because reason, of its own final accord, was beneficent. Thus, to make any effort toward self-examination or to search for legitimate goals would be meaningless. Only a very intelligent person with a naturally creative reason could grow.

Morally speaking, Thomas's position suggests that only an intelligent person can be a possible candidate for the moral life. Without an autonomous will, only persons whose reason could and would present right objects would be described as potentially moral. But, as there would also be no antecedent benevolence, we have to ask, why would even intelligent reasons be beneficent? Since we cannot say that it is because the agent wants or is striving to become beneficent, we are left with intellects that simply present objects on their own. Thus, the position terminates in a moral elitism that is also solipsistic.

Finally, this position is obviously epistemologically troublesome. It so destroys the will that not only are we at the mercy of reason to present its objects, but worse, we are at reason's mercy to replace a wrong object with another one. If reason acts as the ultimate cause of all presentations, not only would we be unable to refuse an object; we would also be unable to look for another.

It is clear, however, that Thomas was not satisfied with this position and, even while holding it, raised other questions, particularly about God's movement of the will. In crystallizing an answer to this question, Thomas arrived at a shift in his explanation of the relationship between reason and the will that not only affords us a port of entry into his writings; it also enables us to explore the possible existence in the *Summa theologiae* of the distinction between goodness and rightness. To that shift we turn.

NOTES to Chapter Two

1. S.T. I.83.4.ob3. and ad3: ". . . intellectus comparatur ad voluntatem ut movens. Et ideo non oportet in voluntate distinguere agens et possibile." On reason and intellect being the same power, see I. 79.8. Since reason refers there to movement, I usually refer to reason rather that the intellect.

2. I.II.9.3c: "Manifestum est autem quod intellectus per hoc quod cognoscit principium, reducit seipsum de potentia in actum, quantum ad cognitionem conclusionum: et hoc modo movet seipsum. Et similiter voluntas per hoc quod vult finem, movet seipsam ad volendum ea quae sunt ad finem."

3. III Sent.d.27.q.2a.4sol.3c., and IV Sent.d.49q.3a.5sol.3ad2.

4. III Sent.d.23q.1.a.2ad3: ". . . voluntas quodammodo movet intellectum, dum intelligo, quia volo." See also d.23q.3a.1a. for the will as the "primi motoris," and II Sent.d.38q.1a.2ad5. on the will as moving all the powers.

5. See *De veritate* 14.5.ad5; 22.12.c and ad5 (hereater, DV).

6. *Summa contra gentiles*, III.10.nr.1950 (hereafter, SCG).

7. SCG II.47.nr.1238. In his commentary on *De div nom*, Thomas also states that the appetite moves itself (4.9.nr.402) but then later states that "voluntas nostra non est causa rerum, sed a rebus movetur" (4.10.nr.439).

8. SCG III.26.nr.2092. See also SCG II.23nr.992.

9. *Responsio ad fr. Joannem Vercellensem de articulus 108*, nr. 22.

10. *De potentia* 3.15c; 6.3ad2 and ad7; 10.4.ad17. See also the later *De unitate intellectus*, 3.

11. S.T. I.82.4.ad1. and I.105.4.ad2 and ad3. See also the *Commentary on De anima* (1269) in which he makes the same affirmation, cf. 3.15.nr.7.

12. S.T. I.2.3c; 75.1.ad1.

13. In II Sent.d.22q.2a.2 and ad.3.

14. In II Sent.d.39q.1a.1ad4, and d.43q.1a.1ad3.

15. *Quodlibetales* 8q.6a.15: ". . . ut cum procedit ex ignorantia eius quod quis scire tenetur et potest."

16. In *De div nom.* c.13 l.4nr.1004: "si qui enim voluntarie ignorant, dirigi nolunt."

17. *De malo* 3.8c: ". . . voluntatis actus potest praecedere actum intellectus, sicut cum aliquis vult se intelligere; et eadem ratione ignorantia sub voluntate cadit, et fit voluntaria." (hereafter, DM).

18. II   Sent.d.26q.1a.2ad2.   III   Sent.d.26q.1a.1ad5;   IV Sent.d.14q.1a.2sol.2c.

19. DV 14.5ad5; 22.3c; 12.ob3 and ad3; 6.2.ad3; 25.4c.

20. SCG I.72.nr.623; II.48nr.1243 and 1246; II.60.nr.1373; II.76.1579; III.73.2479; III.88.2638; III.107.2827.

21. SCG I.72.nr.623; III.26.nr.2092.

22. DV 29.8c. and ad3.

23. SCG III.26.nr.2092: "Nam primo et per se intellectus movet voluntatem: voluntas enim, inquantum huiusmodi, movetur a suo obiecto, quod est bonum apprehensum. . . . Et in hoc ipso intellectus voluntatem praecedit."

24. Ibid.: "Quod autem quinta ratio (2076) proponit, voluntatem esse altiorem intellectu, quasi eius motivam, falsum esse manifestum est."

25. SCG III.26.2092.

26. SCG III.25.2064: "superior motor"; II.60.1373.

27. S.T. I.18.3c; 48.1.ad4; 82.3.ad2, 4c., and 4.ad2; 105.5c.

28. I.77.3c; 82.4ad3 and 111.2c.

29. I.83.4.ad3.

30. I Sent.d.38q.1a.1ad4. Cf. I Sent.d.45q.1a.3c.

31. S.T. I.II.1.2c.: "Prima autem inter omnes causas est causa finalis." See also I Sent.d.8q.1a.3c; *De div nom.* 1.3; S.T. I.5.4c; I.39.8ob4 and 8c; I.44.4.ob4; I.82.3.ob1.

32. S.T. I.5.2ad1.: ". . . agens non agit nisi propter finem."

33. II Sent.d.37q.3a.2c.: ". . . finis movet agentem ad operandum." DV 28.7c.: ". . . sicut finis, qui dicitur causa causarum, quia a causa finali omnes aliae causae recipiunt quod sint causae."

34. See I Sent.38.1.1.ad4; DV 21.3.ad3; S.T. I.5.2.ad1; *In Sent. libri Ethicorum* I.1.5.nr.58; In Meta.II.1.4.nr.318.: "Remota autem causa finali, removetur natura et ratio boni: eadem enim ratio boni et finis est."

35. See Odon Lottin, "La preuve de la liberté humaine chez Thomas d'Aquin," *Recherches de Théologie ancienne et médiévale* 23 (1956): 323–330. Klaus Riesenhuber, "The Basis and Meaning of Freedom," *American Catholic Philosophical Association* 48 (1974): 99–111.

36. SCG III.26.nr.2092: "Nam primo et per se intellectus movet voluntatem: voluntas enim, inquantum huiusmodi, movetur a suo obiecto, quod est
bonum apprehensum . . . intellectus autem voluntatem per modum quo finis
movet, nam bonum intellectum est finis voluntatis."

37. Ibid.: ". . . voluntatem esse altiorem intellectu, quasi eius motivam,
falsum esse manifestum est. Nam primo et per se intellectus movet
voluntatem. . . . Unde apparet intellectum simpliciter esse altiorem voluntate."

38. S.T. I.82.3.ad2: "Intellectus est prior voluntate, sicut motivum mobili, et activum passivo: bonum enim intellectum movet voluntatem."

39. II Sent.d.1q.2a.2ad3.: "Finis non est causa rei, nisi secundum quod
est in voluntate agentis."

40. DV 22.15c: "Non enim voluntas de necessitate sequitur rationem."
Cf. SCG III 10.nr.1950: "Nam in potestate ipsius voluntatis est velle et non
velle."

41. S.T. I.82.2.ad2. See also ad3.

42. II Sent.d.15q.1a.3c; DV 22.8, 9; SCG I.13.nr.91; SCG III.88,89,91,92;
DM 3.3; S.T. I.105.4; I.106.2.

43. S.T. I.18.3c.: "non potest non velle."

44. DV 22.12c; SCG I.72.nr.623; SCG III.26.nr.2092; S.T. I.82.4c; Cf. DV
6.2.ad3; 22.12.ad3; 22.13c; ST I.82.3.ad2.

45. II Sent.d.42q.2a.1c: "Actus autem peccati non proprie nomen radicis
habet, quin potius ipse ex radice est."

46. DV 22.7c.: "Patet igitur quod volendo id quod quis naturaliter vult,
secundum se non est meritorium nec demeritorium; sed secundum quod
specificatur ad hoc vel illud, potest esse meritorium vel demeritorium."

47. Ibid.: "Si vero aliquis per rationem erroneam deducatur ut appetat
aliquid speciale ut suam beatitudinem, puta corporales delectationes, in
quibus tamen secundum rei veritatem sua beatitudo non consistit; sic appet-
endo beatitudinem, demeretur."

48. DV 22.6c.: "Nam ubi non est defectus in apprehendendo et confer-
endo, non potest esse voluntas mali in his quae sunt ad finem. . . ."

49. Ibid., 24.8c: "Unde non potest esse peccatum in motu voluntatis,
scilicet quod malum appetat, nisi in apprehensiva virtute defectus praeexistat,
per quem sibi malum ut bonum proponatur."

50. Interestingly, Thomas is much more nuanced when speaking of
merit. Here, Thomas distinguishes the specification from the motivation,
charity, and attributes merit to the latter. DV 24.1 ad2: ". . . opus meritorium
a non meritorio non distat in quid agere, sed in qualiter agere: nihil enim est
quod unus homo meritorie agat et ex caritate, quod alius non possit absque
merito agere vel velle." Whereas charity provides Thomas with a description
for goodness or merit, no contrary exists for badness or demerit. We shall
return to this in the final chapter.

51. SCG III.10nr.1946: "Nihil autem ad malitiam moralem pertineret si
actus exterior deficiens esset defectu ad voluntatem non pertinente."

52. SCG III.10.nr.1947.

53. SCG III.10.nr.1949 and 1950.

54. Odon Lottin, *Psychologie et morale aux XIIe et XIIIe siècles* (Gembloux: Duculot, 1942), I:384ff.; III:594.

55. DV 22.13.ad4 and ad10.

56. SCG II.47.nr.1240: "Activum oportet esse proportionatum passivo, et motivum mobili. Sed in habentibus cognitionem vis apprehensiva se habet ad appetitivam sicut motivum ad mobile: nam apprehensum per sensum vel imaginationem vel intellectum, movet appetitum intellectualem vel animalem." See also SCG I.76.652.

57. SCG II.47.1238.

58. S.T. I.83.4.ad3.

59. DV 24.1c.

60. Ibid., 24.2c: "Iudicare autem de iudicio suo est solius rationis, quae super actum suum reflectitur, et cognoscit habitudines rerum de quibus iudicat, et per quas iudicat: unde totius libertatis radix est in ratione constituta. Unde secundum quod aliquid se habet ad rationem, sic se habet ad liberum arbitrium."

61. DV 24.6.ad3: "Quamvis iudicium sit rationis, tamen libertas iudicandi est voluntatis immediate."

62. "Intellektualistischer Ansatz und voluntarische Korrekturstehen hier noch unversöhnt nebeneinander" (Klaus Riesenhuber, *Die Transzendez der Freiheit zum Guten* [Munich: Berchmanskolleg Verlag, 1971], 181).

63. DV 24.6.ad1: "Quia liberum arbitrium non nominat voluntatem absolute, sed in ordine ad rationem. . . ."

64. SCG II.48.nr.1243.

65. See SCG III.112.nr.2857. Riesenhuber suggests that perhaps two theories of freedom are operative before the ninth question in *Die Transzendenz der Freiheit zum Guten*, 183–187.

66. *De potentia* 3.7c; ob14 and ad14.

67. S.T. I.83.1c and ad3.

CHAPTER 3

A Shift and a Distinction

In the ninth question of the *Prima secundae*, Thomas shifts his description of the causal relation between reason and the will. Here, for the first time, he attributes formal, not final, causality to reason's presentation of the object to the will.[1] The will, he now argues, insofar as it is first moved, is only moved by God, who created the will and gave it the inclination to the universal good. Now God alone is the final cause or ultimate mover of the will.

The conceptual shift, from reason as final to reason as formal cause, is made possible by distinguishing two dimensions of movement: that in which the will moves itself, the intellect, and all other powers in the continuous exercise of its power as efficient mover, *quantum ad exercitium*, and that of the actual act, which is derived from the object alone, *quantum ad specificationem*.[2]

This differentiation between the two dimensions of movement offers a metaphysical ground for the distinction between goodness and rightness. Goodness concerns the will's movement insofar as it strives, that is, *quantum ad exercitium*. Rightness concerns the will's movement insofar as it is specified.[3] Thus the distinction is not between willing and reasoning, but *within* the will's movement itself. Every movement of the will can be right or wrong and good or bad. What marks the distinction between goodness and rightness is whether the act stems from the will's movement as *exercitium* or as specification.

Before examining this shift in Thomas's development, however, we must answer two important historical questions. First, what inspired Thomas to make the shift; second, how has the shift been noted by Thomas's researchers?

HISTORICAL CONSIDERATIONS

Until very recently, commentators presupposed that Thomas wrote the *Summa theologiae* in Rome (1265–1267), Viterbo (1267–1268), Paris (1269–1272), and Naples (1272–1273).[4] Now, however, they reject the suggestion that Thomas lived a year in Viterbo. They argue instead that Thomas stayed three years in Rome (1265–1268), during which he wrote the entire *Pars prima* and after which, for the most part, he wrote the *Pars secunda* and the *Pars tertia*, in Paris and Naples, respectively.[5]

Leonard Boyle, in his *The Setting of the Summa Theologiae of Saint Thomas*, holds that understanding Thomas's reasons for writing the *Summa theologiae* requires an understanding of the early apostolate of the Dominicans.[6] In 1221, four years after the approval of the Order of Preachers, the new order received a second mission: hearing confessions. To meet the demands of this new mission, a plethora of manuals was produced, among which was Raymond of Peñafort's *Summa de casibus*. These manuals helped the Dominicans understand the specific wrongness of sinful actions. They made up the substance of the lectures that all "fratres communes," even the prior, had to attend. These lectures were predominantly practical in nature rather than speculative like the work prescribed for the select few at any of the five studia throughout Europe. Until 1265, therefore, Dominican formation consisted either of lectures at the priory or of studies for the elite at the studium.

In 1265, Thomas was assigned to open a studium at Rome that had none of the distinction of the other five. His assignment appears to stem from his own suggestion, at the provincial chapter at Anagni in 1265, that the study of theology must include more than the practical matters then being taught at the priories. Since its existence coincided with Thomas's tenure there, Boyle argues that the "studium" at Rome was a "studium personale" designed for and by the master, in an attempt to break away from the simple practical approach to the teaching of theology.

Thus, Thomas literally wrote for "beginners" in an order of preachers and confessors, in a province in which the more treasured works were confessional manuals. The *Summa theologiae* is not speculative but pedagogical. Through it, Thomas taught the student to make determinations or judgments. Coming out of a tradition in which acts were "specified" for confessional purposes, Thomas offered a new approach to future confessors. He did not neglect their interest in "specificity," but he provided a theological context from which "specific" acts could be understood. Thus, the practical interest of Thomas's students was to understand why certain ways of living were described as right or wrong.[7] Not surprisingly then almost all of Thomas's moral discussions concern specification rather than *exercitium*.

Most contemporary commentators, like Weisheipl and Boyle, hold that Thomas completed the *Pars prima* and had just begun the *Prima secundae* when he was called to Paris in 1269. Thus, in the middle of a major work, Thomas returned to Paris for a rare second appointment to the Dominican chair, after first closing the Roman studium. On his arrival in January 1269, Thomas learned that John of Vercelli, the Dominican master general, had suspended the entire Dominican masters' program.

Thomas was recalled to the university for two major reasons: (1) to respond to the renewed anti-mendicant fervor at the university, which was led by Gérard d'Abbeville, and (2) to respond to the growing dominance of the Latin Averroists, led by Siger of Brabant. Our concern is with this latter group who were the subject of a condemnation by Bishop Stephen Tempier. On December 10, 1270, the Bishop issued a list of thirteen treatises of the Latin Averroists that were forbidden to be taught at the university.[8]

Two of the condemned theses concern the will: (1) that the will is a passive power and not an active one, and (2) that the will necessarily wishes what it chooses. These theses are explicitly critiqued in Thomas's *De malo* 6. The title of *De malo* 6 echoes one thesis and an objection echoes another.[9]

The irony is that Thomas had explicitly written one of these theses and implicitly endorsed the other. Now, having been called to confront the agenda of the Averroists, he finds his position on the will both condemned by the Church and supported by the Averroists. The situation is even more ironic when we note that Thomas's new solution is along the same lines as Gérard d'Abbeville's. Yet Thomas's new solution does not simply appear in one article; the subject of *De malo* 6 also has clear parallels with the ninth question of the *Prima secundae*, and two central premises of the Averroist position, cosmic determinism and the impossibility of self-movement, are critiqued in both works.[10] Contemporary scholars hold therefore that both articles were written on the occasion of the condemnation. *De malo* 6 is the first draft in response to the controversy; the ninth question of the *Prima secundae*, its later refinement.[11]

There seems, however, a logistical problem in supposing that the two works were written after the condemnation of December 1270. First, Thomas arrives in Paris in or about January 1269, after having spent two years beginning a very ambitious work. Arguing that the *Prima secundae* was not begun until after December 1270, one wonders why Thomas would have waited almost two years before resuming his work. Second, since we know that Thomas completed the entire *Pars secundae* in the spring of 1272, to posit the writing of the ninth question as subsequent to the condemnation's publication would mean that Thomas wrote the entire *Pars secundae* in about 15 months. In light of the extraordinary amount of work produced during his tenure at Paris, restricting the writing of the *Prima secundae* to the last 15 months seems an improbable suggestion.

Furthermore, inasmuch as *De malo* 6 and the ninth question do unquestionably reflect the two theses on the will, then it would seem that the dating of Thomas's works must coincide, not necessarily with the promulgation of the condemnation, but with its writing. Since we know that the proposed list was in circulation for some time before the actual promulgation, it is possible that both of Thomas's works were written before the promulgation, perhaps at the beginning of 1270, if not earlier.[12]

The arguments in the *Prima secundae* constitute a reversal of Thomas's earlier position on the will. Odon Lottin and his contemporaries, however, were the first commentators who recognized the need to admit a "development" in Thomas's writings and, therefore, the need to construct a chronology. Thus, it is not until Lottin that this significant shift was discovered.[13] In fact, its initial discovery went unnoticed, though a few writers attempted to deny it.[14] Now, however, it enjoys considerable acceptance and has prompted further investigations.[15]

Commentators are at a loss to explain whence Thomas derived the distinction *quantum ad exercitium* and *quantum ad specificationem*. Lottin argues that though Thomas recognizes the existence of this double liberty in earlier writings, the formula is "a creation" of *De malo* 6.[16] Otto Pesch agrees with Lottin.[17] Nevertheless, a passage of striking similarity to the distinction does appear in the *Commentary on the Sentences*, a much earlier writing.

De Malo 6c:	*In IV Sent.* d.49.q.3 a.5 sol.3 ad2:
. . .potentia aliqua dupliciter movetur: uno modo ex parte subiecti; alio modo ex parte obiecti. . . . Prima quidem immutatio pertinet ad ipsum exercitium actus, ut scilicet agatur vel non agatur aut melius vel debilius agatur: secunda vero immutatio pertinet ad specificationem actus, nam actus specificatur per obiectum.	. . . habitus inclinat ad actum dupliciter. Uno modo ad hoc ut actus exerceatur; et sic inclinare ad actum non est nisi habitus in parte appetitiva existentis: quia appetitus qui habet bonum et finem pro obiecto, movet seipsum et vim cognitivam in actum: ex desiderio enim actus vel finis provenit quod aliquis aliquem actum exerceat, dummodo non sit ex necessitate naturae. Alio modo quantum ad modum agendi, ut scilicet illud quod agitur, recte agatur; et sic quilibet habitus inclinat ad actum.

In both writings, Thomas distinguishes the exercise of an act from the specification of an act. The difference between them is that the formula in *De malo* 6 addresses the freedom of the will vis-á-vis reason. In the earlier writing, however, Thomas simply addresses two modes of examining an act and treats neither reason nor the will's freedom. Still the distinction is there and can be construed as having significant relevance for our investigation.

Later, in the *Commentary on the Sentences*, the distinction appears again. This time, Thomas distinguishes charity as exercise from wisdom as directive. The distinction between the *exercitium* of the act (charity) and the specification of the act (wisdom as directive) obviously parallels our own distinction.[18] Unfortunately, however, we find no other reference to this distinction in his earlier writings, and certainly no attempt to use it as explanatory of the will's freedom vis-á-vis reason. Why?

It seems that Thomas did not use this distinction to ascertain the will's autonomy precisely because in the *Commentary on the Sentences*, as in all the other writings prior to *De malo* 6, reason, in presenting the object to the will, presents the end. In the *Commentary on the Sentences*, Thomas identifies the object, that is, the *materia circa quam*, with the end. In the *Prima secundae*, however, he identifies the object with the form of the determination.

In III Sent. d.36q.1a.5ad4.	*Summa theologiae* I.II.18.2.ad2.
Ad quartum dicendum, quod est duplex materia: ex qua, vel in qua, et materia circa quam; et primo modo materia dicta non indicit in idem cum fine, sed secundo modo est idem cum fine, quia obiectum finis actus est.	Ad secundum dicendum quod obiectum non est materia ex qua, sed materia circa quam: et habet quodammodo rationem formae, inquantum dat speciem.

Because in the earlier writings, Thomas argues that the object presented to the will is the end, he sees no need to posit any other metaphysical argument to explain the will's self-movement: reason's presentation of the object expresses sufficiently and finally the will's movement. Only later, when Thomas detaches the object from the last end, will he need the distinction. The distinction between *exercitium* and specification, therefore, only takes on significance in Thomas's writings when Thomas makes the shift from final to formal causality in his explanation of reason's influence on the will.

From this brief history two points emerge. First, Thomas's shift is more directly concerned with freedom of the will than with morality. The title of *De malo* 6, for instance, raises the question of necessity and freedom in the will's movement, and the title of question nine of the *Prima secundae* simply addresses *de motivo voluntatis*, "of that which moves the will." The shift and the distinction have moral significance for us, but that significance is derived from the purpose they serve in establishing the will's autonomy. Their significance for Thomas's moral arguments is debatable.

Second, though the distinction occurs as a prelude to morals (as is evident by the place it holds in the *Prima secundae*), Thomas's moral argument uses the will's movement *quantum ad specificationem* or *ad determinationem* but not the will's movement *quantum ad exercitium*.[19] Rather, as Maritain notes, when it comes to morality, Thomas seems to value only the order of specification, not the order of exercise.[20]

MAKING THE SHIFT

In the *Prima secundae* Thomas makes the distinction between the movement of the will as an autonomous movement and the movement of the will as a specific movement informed by some object. In order to make this distinction, Thomas must change or shift his earlier position to remove the obstacle that had impeded it: the confusion concerning final causality.

Thomas must first respond to a fundamental objection: what is moved is in potentiality, what moves is in act; therefore, the same thing cannot be in potentiality and in act. This objection appears in an article that treats a question new to Thomas: "whether the will moves itself."[21] Thomas responds to the objection interestingly enough by using a parallel to the active and passive intellect and arguing that similarly the will in wanting the end reduces itself from potency to act with respect to the means.[22] Nonetheless, Thomas fails to meet the objection in this article. His analogy offers no real structure to explain how the will can be both passive and active, in potentiality and in act.

In the next article, "whether the will is moved by some exterior principle," Thomas returns to the problem. Here, he affirms that the will is moved by an object, but only insofar as the will seeks specification. Yet, insofar as the will first exercises itself, the will is not moved by an object, though it is first moved by some exterior principle. If the will is the efficient cause of all human acts, where does the will first get the ability to move itself and other powers? Since there is some point at which the will is not in movement, the will requires a first mover.[23]

What moves the will finally? More exactly, what is the mover that enables the will to move itself? In *De malo* 6 Thomas answers this question rather straightforwardly: not any apprehended good, but the last end, God, moves the will efficiently. Thomas makes this point repeatedly.[24]

In the ninth question of the *Prima secundae*, Thomas provides a much more elegant structure. In the first article he eliminates reason as the mover of the will's efficiency. In the second, he eliminates the sensitive appetite as the mover. In the third, he affirms that the will moves itself. In the fourth, he raises the question: must not the will be moved, if at some point the will never willed? He says that as self-mover, the will is the proximate agent of itself, a contradiction of his earlier assertion in the *Summa contra gentiles* that the good understood is the proximate agent of the will.[25] The position here is that in moving itself, the will is its own immediate cause. Yet, Thomas has made it clear in this fourth article that we must have some prior mover, a first mover, which moves the will interiorly. In the fifth article, he raises the Averroists' position on cosmic determinism only to disprove it. Finally, he concludes the question with the article, "whether God alone moves the will." Through a process of elimination, Thomas leads us to God as the final cause of the will's efficiency. Only God is the cause of the will's first movement, *quantum ad exercitium*.[26]

Thomas argues here that the only exterior principle which can move the will to will is the cause of the will itself. The cause is God, for (1) God has created it and (2) the will's finality is the "universal good" which is God. Here, then, Thomas understands the final cause of the will as the creator of the will. He concludes the question: as the universal mover, God moves the human will to the universal object, the good. Without this movement the human cannot will anything. But once one wills, one wills through reason specifically.[27]

This question ultimately resolves the problem of the final causality of the will. God is the final cause of the will. Only the last end, the universal good, moves the will. By God's creative act, this inclination is already in the will, and thus the final cause is already in the will prior to any presentation of an object by reason.[28] Any object accepted by the will can become the end for an intended, specific action, but that end can never be the last end, and only the last end can be the final cause of the will's willing. It alone can ultimately explain the will's movements. On the other hand, the object now simply provides the form for the specifically willed act. By designating reason's presentation of the object as the formal cause of the specific act of the will, Thomas has an argument to support his assertions that the will is autonomous.[29]

In summary, the distinction between *exercitium* and specification arises because Thomas distinguishes between whether the will can will and what the will can will. He makes this distinction by differentiating the final causality provided by God from the formal causality provided by reason. That the will can will, *quantum ad exercitium*, is not caused by reason, but by God. What the will can will specifically, *quantum ad specificationem*, is occasioned by reason's presentation of the object, which when accepted, becomes the form of the act.

AND THE DISTINCTION

The central issue in the *Prima secundae's* ninth question is the will's freedom: "Whether the will can move itself?"[30] This question is new. To answer it, Thomas repeats a fundamental assertion: "The will is mistress of its own act, and to it belongs to will and not to will."[31] But he also adds something new to the assertion: an adequate explanation of it. "But this would not be so, had it not the power to move itself to will. Therefore, it moves itself."[32] To be autonomous the will must be free to move itself.

Thomas must now distinguish between how the will moves, *quantum ad exercitium*, in a way other than by reason's presentation of the object, *quantum ad determinationem*. He must also prove that the will is the mover of all powers, including itself and the intellect, and that its self-movement takes precedence over all other movements.[33]

Having attributed final cause to God's creative act, Thomas will consistently argue that the will moves all the other powers in subsequent articles in the *Summa theologiae*. Still Thomas needs a device to explain this assertion. Granted that the will has the power to move through its created, innate inclination to the universal good, how is it able to exercise that power?

Thomas asserts with significant regularity the fact that the will moves itself, *voluntas movet seipsam*. He uses, in fact, even more significant forms of expression to highlight the independence of the will's efficiency: his forms are reflexive. Riesenhuber, calling these "decisive expressions . . . which characterize freedom as reflexive self-disposal," cites two forms: *se movere* and *se reducere de potentia in actum*.[34] To Riesenhuber's two I add that the will can will itself to will, *potest velle se velle*.[35]

Thomas had already used the phrase *se movere* in reference to the will in *De potentia* 6.6c. In the same sentence, however, he had argued (pre-1270) that the will is moved by the appetible object understood. *Se movere*, of itself, does not guarantee the will's autonomy. The autonomy of the will is only established when the will can reduce itself from potency to act. Thus, the importance of these reflexive forms is precisely the expression *se reducere*, which is the metaphysical possibility for *se movere*. The newness of the contribution rests in the fact that prescinding from whether or not *se movere* existed in earlier writings, the possibility of understanding the expression as indicative of the will's autonomy is only found insofar as the will is able *se reducere de potentia in actum*. Thomas did not attribute this power to the will in earlier writings.

Taking this discovery further, Riesenhuber suggests that the structure for understanding the will as self-mover is exactly parallel to the active and passive intellect.[36] The validity of Riesenhuber's suggestion can be found in Thomas's own writings. In the earlier *De spiritualibus creaturis*, Thomas had raised the objection *nihil reducit se de potentia in actum*, and answered by distinguishing the active and passive intellect.[37] Now, in attributing *se reducere* to the will, Thomas draws a clear parallel from the active and passive intellect.[38] Though he does not actually establish an active and passive will, Thomas's only explanation for a power reducing itself from potency to act is from the intellect.

In any case, we need to imagine how the will reduces itself from potentiality to act. Thomas proposes that the will in wanting the good in general, not in particular, moves itself to willing the means. He argues that the will moves itself *quantum ad exercitium* into the willingness to be determined; that is, the will through its own volition of the end moves itself to willing the means.[39] Wanting the good in general, the will (*quantum ad exercitium*) encounters reason or any other faculty presenting objects to it. It is free to accept or reject any object provided that object is not the universal good.[40] Since reason cannot present the universal good, the will is completely free vis-á-vis reason. Once the will wants an object as end, the will moves reason to counsel it for appropriate means. The will moves itself toward willingness to be counseled by reason, thus entering the realm of particulars.[41]

Thomas explicitly compared the will and the intellect in this action. The comparison yields one dissimilarity: "They are dissimilar indeed *quantum ad exercitium actus*, for the intellect is moved by the will to what is to be done, but the will is not moved by any other power but by itself."[42] The will moves the intellect but the intellect cannot move the will into movement. In subsequent writings, Thomas will consistently maintain that the will moves the intellect.

The possibility of movement is explained by God's first movement as final cause. This movement and the efficient movement of the will account for the will's movement into acts of determination. These two movements, that of the last end and the will's efficient self-movement, explain the will's willingness to be presented with any object.[43] Therefore, Thomas can now restore the primacy of the will in movement and name it the first mover with considerable frequency, in clear contradiction to earlier assertions, in the *Summa contra gentiles*, for example, that had presented reason as the first mover.[44] As first mover, the will's movement is independent of and prior to reason's presentation of the object, and thus movement becomes the key for understanding the will. The will is the "principle of movement" for "to move pertains absolutely to the will."[45]

The only object that can move the will necessarily *quantum ad determinationem* is the universal good. For this reason, we long for beatitude. But if the human is a free subject, how could the will be free to reject the universal good if it is already determined to this object? Indeed, Thomas is free of intellectual determinism, because reason cannot present the universal good; i.e., the universal good can never be an object presented by reason. But can Thomas avoid divine determinism, which would as surely compromise human freedom? What if God were to present the universal good to the will?[46] Thomas explains that we are free from all necessary movement of the will *quantum ad exercitium* because the will has the ability to avoid thinking of beatitude: "No object moves the will necessarily, for no matter what the object be, it is in man's power not to think about it and consequently not to will it actually."[47]

This point, which Thomas also makes twice in *De malo* 6, highlights the scope of the will's freedom. But we should note that Thomas also argues that we cannot will the opposite of the universal good. Were we presented the object that is universally good, the will would tend to it of necessity, "if it wills anything at all."[48] In the present life the will is passive but only to God. Yet this passivity to God is not a necessary one, because though we cannot not will the universal good, we can will *quantum ad exercitium* not to think about it.[49] Though the will cannot not will the universal good were it to be presented, the will can, nonetheless, avoid the universal good, simply by the power that the will exerts as mover. We can, in effect, avoid goodness in one way: by not attending to it.

EFFECTS OF THE SHIFT

Two particular effects arise in the shift from reason's domination to the will's freedom. Thomas distinguishes the "end" and the "object" and introduces the concept *conveniens*. Logically, a third effect could result: the use of the concept *exercitium* to describe moral goodness. We consider now all three points.

Prior to the *Prima secundae*, Thomas does not clearly differentiate the object presented to the will and accepted as an end for action from the last end that moves the will. But this difference is at the root of the distinction between specification and *exercitium*. As Riesenhuber rightly comments, the solution is based on the separation of specification, which has an a posteriori influence on the will, from *exercitium* which, by having the last end already in the will, has an a priori possibility for self-opening.[50]

In light of the distinction, the only "end" to which the will is passive is the last end, "the universal good."[51] The only a priori is the will's inclination to the universal good, and the will in having this inclination already has the last end.[52] By having the last end, we can will. The last end, the end that has no other antecedent end, constitutes, therefore, the foundation of motivation.[53] The last end is the only end that exists a priori in the will. All other ends are merely the means, originally presented as objects by reason, exerting only an a posteriori influence on the will. All other ends are properly and originally objects. These ends only specify, precisely because they are objects. They do not move the will into action because an object cannot be the last end. Riesenhuber remarks that "the finite good known by the intellect is no longer in the strict sense the goal of the will; in the new terminology it is reduced to an object and is only a means to the ultimate and proper goal."[54]

An object is an object precisely because its influence is a posteriori. In order to will anything, we need an object. Inasmuch as the object is that by which we will anything, the object cannot be the last end; it is, instead, always in relation to something antecedent, that is, as a means.[55] That object, when accepted by the will, becomes the end for a specific act or series of acts of the will. As we shall see, the "object" is the genus for all questions concerning specificity.

Thus, on the two occasions when "object" and "end" are juxtaposed, the former is the more specific means, the latter is the less specific end.[56] But the "end" is first presented as an object and then accepted by the will as the goal of an action. Then, to achieve that specific end, a second object or the means is considered and accepted by the will. The end still remains the first object willed. Thus, a specific end is the first object presented to the will, whereas the means to that end is a second object. Again, the possibility that any end, but the last end, can be a means, is derived precisely from the fact that any such end is originally an object. For this reason, Thomas tells us that both the formal notion of object and the proximate end give species.

Though Thomas develops the concepts of object and end, he leaves us with a certain problem concerning the last end. He writes:

"The first act of the will is not out of the direction of reason but out of the instinct of nature, or of a higher cause."[57] Later, when he discusses charity, he argues that charity is the response to the instigation of a "higher" cause. Inasmuch as charity is a theological virtue, however, we have to ask what response in the natural order can instigate the will to move itself to understand and execute the right? When can we say that our response to that movement is properly called good other than by invoking charity? Thomas gives no answer and leaves his twentieth-century reader with a significant lacuna.[58]

A second effect of the new distinction is the developing use of the concept *conveniens*. Thomas determines that no object except the universal good moves the will by necessity to determination.[59] But Thomas asks whether the will is inclined to some objects more than others. The issue arises when the object that moves the will to determination is that which is apprehended as "good" and "fitting." Thomas writes in *De malo* 6: "If something good is proposed that is apprehended under the meaning of good, and it is not also under the meaning of fitting, it will not move the will."[60] The concept of "fitting" (*conveniens*) serves as a new condition for explaining why the will is prone to accept one object over another.

Thomas develops the concept in the *Prima secundae*. Because objects are accepted by the will according to the objects' suitability to the will, objects serve as the indication of the will's dispositions. Our dispositions will incline us more to one object over another.[61]

The object, however, pertains only to the will *quantum ad specificationem*. Inasmuch as this applies to rightness, the will's attraction to any given object tells us not whether the will is good but whether the will is "rightly ordered." When the will is inclined to a right object, we know that the will is well-ordered, when inclined to a wrong object, we know that the will is disordered.

In certain ways, however, different objects are always fitting to the will. For instance in the order of specification, the universal good is always fitting to the will: once considered, the universal good naturally attracts the will absolutely. The general notions of being and truth are always fitting to us. We could not hate them. We could, however, consider a particular being or truth unfitting. If we did so consider a particular truth, it would indicate that we had a wrongly ordered disposition in us: we would be unable to recognize as fitting what in fact is fitting.[62]

The good, however, whether particular or general, is always fitting and, therefore, it can never be hated. The fitting is good. Thomas clarifies this by adding that something may be apprehended as good, though it truly is not; it is apprehended as good precisely because it is apprehended as fitting.[63] "Fitting" continuously links the will with the object and distinguishes a particular truth from a particular good. We can hate a particular truth; we cannot hate a particular good. An object, then, is apprehended as good, because it is fitting.[64]

We can, moreover, be inclined to an actual evil, to something that would *truly* not perfect us. But we can be inclined to a particular evil only inasmuch as our disposition is disordered, for we tend to anything as it appears fitting to us. Being fitting to our disordered will, a particular evil will appear good and be willed as such. We cannot will an actual or apparent evil as evil.

The concept of fitting, then, serves two functions. First, it stipulates that an object presented by reason can only be accepted by the will to the degree that the will is disposed to it. Second, the concept of fitting distinguishes the good from the true. Usually, fitting is used to describe the relation between an object and an agent. It has, therefore, the meaning of the good and the good, unlike the true, always bears a relation to the agent.[65] Whether the good is truly or rightly so, that is, whether it, in fact, perfects us, is a subsequent judgment.

The good is the object of our love because the good is fitting for our wills. Thus, the term "good" is not a primary concept but its meaning is defined by fittingness. Its moral significance arises in the question that concerns which goods are truly or rightly fitting for us. The good, like the fitting, are objects and thus pertain to the will's movement *quantum ad specificationem*.

Finally, a "command," Thomas states, is *essentially* an act of reason, which presupposes an act of the will.[66] That act of the will is the first movement of the will *quantum ad exercitium*, coming as we have seen from a natural instinct or from a superior cause.[67] This *exercitium* is always antecedent to specification. The will must first be willing to consider any object offered by reason for its acceptance. That the will must first be willing means that the will must first move itself and reason. Without that antecedent willingness, reason does not influence the will with its objects. By establishing this antecedent self-exercise of the will, Thomas distinguishes between God as final cause of the will, *quantum ad exercitium*, and reason as formal cause of the will's movement, *quantum ad specificationem*. This antecedent *exercitium* provides the foundation for Thomas's assertion that the will is free to move itself and reason.

Later, in describing how we develop habits, Thomas uses the word *exercitium* in a different way. Through the exercise of "good deeds," we acquire the habits of the moral virtues. If we exercise ourselves only in certain matters and not in all, we acquire a habit, but not a virtue, because we are not exercised in all matters.[68]

Thomas had adopted from Avicenna the position that virtue is acquired through *studium et exercitium*.[69] Thomas writes that moral virtues are acquired through the exercise of virtuous acts or the exercise of right principles.[70] He distinguishes the acquired virtues from the infused virtues by arguing that the former are acquired through *exercitium*, the latter through grace.[71]

Occasionally, Thomas becomes more specific and argues in agreement with Aristotle that we already have a natural aptitude for virtue, but that the perfection or realization of that aptitude occurs either through grace or *exercitium*.[72] Thus, in speaking of prudence, Thomas writes: "Aptitude for prudence is in our nature, while its perfection comes through practice (*exercitio*) or grace."[73] Bringing a disposition to completion requires exercise or grace.[74] Moreover, just as the acquired virtues are perfected through exercise, so are the infused virtues.[75] Similarly, merit increases by the exercise of divine charity, and the greater the exercise, the greater the merit.[76]

These instances demonstrate that, in acquisition and in increase, *exercitium* is not a first movement but multiple later ones; *exercitia* refers not to motivation, but to the regular performance or execution of particular acts. After questions nine through seventeen of the *Prima secundae*, *exercitium* is found primarily in writings concerning the acquisition of virtues and the development of acquired and infused virtues. In each case the underlying premise is that through exercise we move toward the perfection of virtue. And, in other works contemporaneous to the *Summa theologiae*, exercise has much the same role; it serves as a description for the way virtues are acquired and developed. Even wisdom itself is not gained except through studious exercise.[77]

In later questions, the concept of *exercitium* appears with uncanny regularity.[78] Indeed, Thomas develops the notion of attaining perfection through exercise most fully in his writings in the *Summa theologiae* on the religious life. Thomas asserts in the first question on religious life that our perfection consists in adhering wholly to God. This perfection is lived in the religious life, which has as its end the perfection of charity, which is the perfection of us all. Thus, as Thomas defines religious life: "the religious state is a school or exercise for the attainment of perfection, which some strive to reach by various practices."[79]

This complete giving of ourselves to God is not a simultaneous giving, but a successive giving. Thus, we need a training school or an *exercitium* in which we can exercise the giving, which in itself is our growth toward perfection. Thomas names this lifelong series of exer-

cises, commonly called the religious life, "an exercise of perfection."[80]
Exercise is a key for understanding Thomas's idea of religious life.

To a lesser extent, Thomas applies *exercitium* to the perfection
of Christian life. He notes that the effects of Baptism do not take away
all the penalties of the present life. Yet, these penalties provide the
opportunity for "our spiritual exercises, namely by fighting against
concupiscence and other defects to which he is subject, man may
receive the crown of victory."[81] Similarly, both the process of penance
and the process of redemption as a return to God require, among other
things, the exercise of virtues or good works.[82] As in his theology, so
also in his philosophy, Thomas argues that the unhappy person will
need to struggle through a long period of exercise to return to happiness.[83]

Speaking generally, the word *exercitium* has an athletic or military
nature. Effectively, we become strong through exercise: the greater
the exercise, the stronger the habit.[84] Commenting on Paul's Letters,
Thomas writes that we win the prize by fighting temptations and
exercising ourselves in good works.[85] In fact, Thomas appears to
appreciate the word precisely for its pauline roots: Commenting on I
Timothy 4.7, Thomas writes that Paul chooses the verb to train (*exerce*),
rather than to perform (*fac*), because exercise demands promptness
and what has been exercised becomes lighter, more enjoyable, and
stable.[86]

In each context after question 17 of the *Prima secundae*, Thomas
uses *exercitium* solely to describe the way we can acquire or develop
the virtues. But this use differs significantly from the use of *exercitium*
found in the beginning of the *Prima secundae*.

THE APPLICATION OF THOMAS'S DISTINCTION TO CONTEMPORARY THOUGHT

We have examined in this chapter Thomas's reflections on the will's
freedom. Earlier, we saw the difficulties advanced by the argument
that reason moves the will as final cause. This earlier position maintained that the will is moved by reason; that the will is passive to
reason; that the cause of sin is reason; that the root of freedom is
reason; that the first mover in human activity is reason. But through
a distinction of *quantum ad exercitium* from *quantum ad specificationem*,
Thomas shifts to formal causality to explain reason's involvement in
the will's act. This distinction allows Thomas to maintain that the will
is an active power; that it moves itself and all other powers; that the
will is the source of freedom; that the final end is in the will; that

the first mover is the will; and, that the will is free of all necessary movement.[87]

This distinction marks the questions between whether the will wills and what the will wills. Subsequently, the distinction causes a shift in the use of the word "object." Thomas now holds that "object" exerts only an a posteriori influence on the will: the object becomes an end only if the will accepts it. Furthermore, Thomas has modified this influence by introducing and developing the concept of fitting. This notion provides the foundation for a more dynamic understanding of how we grow "rightly ordered." We will only choose rightly ordered acts to the degree that they appear *conveniens* to us. A more "rightly ordered" will can recognize "rightly ordered" objects as more fitting than a will less "rightly ordered." Similarly, to better ourselves, to make ourselves more rightly ordered, we will have to exercise ourselves in right actions.

These changes are the source of Thomas's greatness: he introduces distinctions and shifts and develops concepts. Oddly, however, he literally abandons use of the formal concept, the last end, the only end that moves the will. This last end is, in fact, God who moves the will as having created it and having ordained it to the universal good. This last end grants us the power to move ourselves to understanding. It is the fundamental assertion concerning human freedom: we can will to understand.

Strangely enough, Thomas does not develop these writings into a moral description of the will as consenting and exercising itself in terms of this last end. In the *Prima secundae*, having established the distinction between *exercitium* and specification Thomas develops his moral theory solely within the context of specification, or rightness. Thus, Thomas provides no moral description of the agent who seeks to understand and to act rightly. There is no moral description of one seeking to exercise oneself precisely according to the natural instinct. There is no moral description of an agent acting out of benevolence, but judging wrongly. But this is not surprising. Having overcome the challenges of the condemnation of Paris, Thomas continues his interest in specification; that is, he continues to lead his Dominican students toward an adequate notion of growing in perfection. He has now determined the exact parameters of specification and develops his moral theology solely within that context.

Yet, we may ask: in light of this distinction, what if Thomas had applied these ideas to his moral theory? I suggest that three important applications of Thomas's material would accord well with the contemporary distinction of goodness and rightness.

First, from Thomas's argument on freedom versus intellectual and divine determinism, we have the material for a refined notion of moral badness. Let us recall that, according to Thomas, no one can will anything unless he or she is first moved by the universal mover who ordains each will to the universal good.[88] It would be impossible, therefore, to will contrary to the universal good. But we are free not to will the universal good; that is, we have in our power *quantum ad exercitium* the ability not to consider. The power to reject the universal good, which is the power to be bad, rests in the power we enjoy not to consider the good. It does not rest in the power to will the contrary.

Thomas's insight corresponds with our concept of moral goodness. Moral goodness always requires that we strive to realize the right. Failure to strive to realize the right is moral failure. This striving is not simply wishing; it is, rather, the actual self-motivation willing to consider all the factors necessary for moral living, to deliberate about them, and to execute the decision. In many ways the contrary of moral goodness is not the willingness to be bad, but the failure to be good. As we suggested earlier, even the sin of malice is nothing other than an effect of the original failure to strive. Maliciousness finds its roots in moral apathy.

Thomas establishes the scope of human freedom precisely on the grounds that contemporary moral theologians presuppose. For us, the real measure of moral goodness is found in whether we are willing to understand. For Thomas, the foundation of human freedom is based on the fact that the human person is free from any necessity to consider value. Thomas does not, however, draw the moral conclusion inherent in his position on human freedom, which is that the will becomes or is morally bad precisely in its failure to consider. That conclusion, though not drawn by Thomas, derives from his proposed explanation for human freedom.

Second, Thomas, as we noted earlier does not give a moral description for the will's response to the natural instinct for the good. But, as Klubertanz, Leclerq, and Lottin noted, without a moral description of this response to the first movement, that leaves only charity to describe a person's cooperation with this instinct. Not surprisingly, then, Karl Rahner will ask "whether all interhuman love, provided only that it has its own moral radicality, is also *caritas*."[89] From Thomas's writings, Rahner rightly concludes that charity, whether explicit or implicit, is the only moral description of our response to the first movement that inclines us naturally to the universal good. As other writers have recognized, however, Thomas could have developed some nontheological expression of charity, e.g., benevolence. But he did not.

In any event, we recognize that moral goodness is found in the *exercitium* and that, despite claims to the contrary, after making the distinction, Thomas does not develop this notion of the last end present in the will.[90] In fact, he omits completely any discussion of the moral issues involved in responding to this natural instinct. Yet, precisely here is the contemporary issue of moral motivation or moral goodness: by exercising ourselves according to this instinct we are good. Though not drawn by Thomas, this conclusion also derives from his proposed explanation for human freedom.

Finally, the distinctive uses of *exercitium* could have been developed significantly into a virtue ethics that specifically entertains questions of goodness and rightness. As Thomas notes, we only grow in virtue, if we exercise acts. Those acts, however, must be right ones: if we do not exercise right or virtuous acts, we do not become rightly ordered or virtuous. Unlike Thomas's use of *exercitium* in questions nine through seventeen of the *Prima secundae*, wherein *exercitium* precedes and is independent of reason, Thomas generally uses *exercitium* to describe that dimension of the act *consequent* to the judgment, that is, its actual execution. For this reason he says that *exercitium* needs both encouragement to execute the act and wisdom to know which act to execute.[91] In these cases, then, *exercitium* follows reason.

Thomas could have used the concept of the primary *exercitium* to develop a concept of goodness. Using benevolence as an example of goodness, Thomas could have asked a simple question to determine whether we are good in a particular action: do we exercise ourselves out of benevolence? For instance, out of benevolence a parent may judge it right to overlook the wrongdoing of a child. The parent is good, because the parent is seeking what is right for the child. But perhaps the child actually needs in this particular instance to be corrected, punished, or even spanked. If so, then the act of "overlooking" is wrong in this case. Furthermore, by exercising this wrong judgment, the parent fails to grow in parental prudence.

Thus, there are two exercises: the primary exercise out of which the parent moved, i.e., benevolence, and the second exercise, the execution of the imprudent judgment to overlook. The first exercise has no connection to rightness. It does not necessitate a right judgment, though it requires the willingness to exercise oneself toward what one believes is right judgment. This primary notion of *exercitium* describes goodness. The second exercise requires right judgment if the act is to be right and if we are to grow in prudence. This latter exercise alone is what Thomas continuously has in mind when discussing exercises in the virtuous life, the religious life, or the Christian life.

Had Thomas considered the exercise of benevolence or charity, then Thomas would have had a *distinct* concept of goodness. In fact, as we shall see in Chapter Six, there are clear signs of this in his treatment of the supernatural virtues, but within the concept of the moral virtues, *exercitium* is only used for the actual realization of right ways of living.[92] Had Thomas used both the primary and the secondary *exercitium*, he may have discovered the notion of goodness as distinct from rightness. I state this because by explaining reason's presentation of the object as formal and not final causality, Thomas establishes a unique concept: a primary *exercitium*. Had he used his own concept of the primary *exercitium* (rather than Aristotle's or Avicenna's secondary *exercitium*, an *exercitium* of right judgment), he may have arrived at moral goodness. For that conclusion, though not drawn by Thomas, also derives from his proposed explanation for human freedom.

NOTES to Chapter Three

1. "Il faut toutefois ajouter que nulle part avant le De malo, cette raison, cause formelle de la nature humaine, n'est présentée comme cause formelle de l'activité humaine." Odon Lottin, "La preuve de la liberté humaine chez Thomas d'Aquin," *Recherches de théologie ancienne et médiévale* 23 (1956): 325.

2. S.T. I.II.9.1.ad3: "Voluntas movet intellectum quantum ad exercitium actus: quia et ipsum verum, quod est perfectio intellectus, continetur sub universali bono ut quoddam bonum particulare. Sed quantum ad determinationem actus, quae est ex parte obiecti, intellectus movet voluntatem: quia et ipsum bonum apprehenditur secundum quandam specialem rationem comprehensam sub universali ratione veri. Et sic patet quod non est idem movens et motum secundum idem."

3. George Klubertanz, e.g., writes: "Cognition is on the side of form or specification" (*Habits and Virtues* [New York: Meredith Publishing Co., 1965], 106).

4. See James Weisheipl, *Friar Thomas d'Aquino* (Garden City: Doubleday and Company, 1974), 355–405.

5. René Gauthier, "Quelques questions à propos du commentaire de S. Thomas sur *De Anima*," *Angelicum* 51 (1974): 438–443; Leonard Boyle, *The Setting of the Summa Theologiae of Saint Thomas* (Toronto: Pontifical Institute of Medieval Studies, 1982), 8; James Weisheipl does not fully accept Gauthier's position, though he no longer accepts Madonnet's (cf. *Friar Thomas D'Aquino*, 2nd ed. [Washington, D.C.: Catholic University Press, 1983], 470–474).

6. Leonard Boyle, *The Setting of the Summa Theologiae of Saint Thomas*, 1–4.

7. It is not surprising, therefore, that the most popular section of this Dominican work was the *Secunda secundae*, which has twice as many extant manuscripts as any other section. The *Secunda secundae* often had its texts abridged or simply "lifted", it sold for a higher price, and it was more often cited (see Leonard Boyle, *The Setting of the Summa Theologiae of Saint Thomas*, 23ff.).

8. James Weisheipl, *Friar Thomas d'Aquino*, 2nd ed., 236–242 and 276. See also Thomas's *De unitate intellectus contra Averroistas*.

9. DM 6: "Utrum homo habeat liberam electionem suorum actuum, aut ex necessitate eligat." Thesis 3: "Quod voluntas hominis ex necessitate vult vel eligit."

DM 6.ob7: "Ergo voluntas est potentia passiva, et velle est pati. . . . Ergo videtur quod voluntas de necessitate moveatur ab appetibili." Thesis 9: "Quod liberum arbitrium est potentia passiva, non activa; et quod necessitate movetur ab appetibili."

10. On cosmic determinism: DM 6.ob21 and S.T. I.II.9.5; on self-movement: DM 6.ob20 and S.T. I.II.9.3, particularly ob1.

11. Otto Pesch in his article "Philosophie und Theologie der Freiheit bei Thomas von Aquin in quaest. disp. 6 *De malo*" (*Münchener Theologische Zeitschrift* 13 (1962): 1–25), argues against Odon Lottin's claim that *De malo* is the first work (*Psychologie et morale aux XIIe et XIIIe siècles* [Gembloux: Duculot, 1942–1954], 1:260. Klaus Riesenhuber sides with Lottin and argues that *De malo* "seems to show the still fresh traces of a controversy," whereas I.II.9 appears in its wording "more settled and academic" ("The Basis and Meaning of Freedom in Thomas Aquinas," *American Catholic Philosophical Association* 48 [1974]: 109).

12. See Vernon Bourke, *Aquinas' Search for Wisdom* (Milwaukee: Bruce Publishing Co., 1965), 171–172. James Weisheipl argues that *De malo* 6 was disputed in 1270 and that the *Prima secundae* was, in fact, *completed* in December 1270 (*Friar Thomas d'Aquino*, 2nd ed., 361, 366).

13. Though Lottin first presented his findings in *La theorie du libre arbitre depuis S. Anselme jusqu'à S. Thomas d'Aquin* (Louvain: St. Maximin, 1929), it was systematically presented in his acclaimed *Psychologie et morale*, 1:221–262, 345–346, 374–375, 382–387; 3:590–591.

14. In his "The Root of Freedom in St. Thomas's Later Works" (*Gregorianum* 42 [1961]: 701), George Klubertanz noted, "Among the expositors of St. Thomas's thought, I have been able to find only one who made use of St. Thomas's text according to this historical view as presented in the 1929 version, Bernard Lonergan, S. J." Klubertanz lists more than thirty-five works that omitted any reference to a change in Thomas's thought.

On the attempt to deny this development, see Rosemary Lauer, "St. Thomas's Theory of Intellectual Causality in Election," *The New Scholasticism* 28 (1954): 317–19; Tibor Horváth, *Caritas est in ratione* (Münster: Aschendoffsche Verlagsbuchhandlung, 1966), 56–57.

15. Giuseppe Abbà, *Lex et Virtus* (Romas: LAS, 1983), 165–173 and 215–217; Mario Gigante, *Genesi e struttura dell'atto libero in S. Tommaso* (Naples:

Giannini, 1980), 72–119; Karl-Wilhelm Merks, *Theologische Grundlegung der sittlichen Autonomie* (Düsseldorf: Patmos Verlag, 1978); Dorothée Welp, *Willensfreiheit bei Thomas von Aquin* (Freibourg: Universitätsverlag, 1979). See also Pesch and Riesenhuber, note 11 above.

16. Lottin refers the reader to II Sent.d.7,q.1ad1 and ad2 and DV 22.6c. ("La preuve de la liberté humaine chez Thomas d'Aquin," 328).

17. Otto Pesch, "Philosophie und Theologie der Freiheit bei Thomas von Aquin in quaest. disp. 6 *De malo*," 10.

18. In IV Sent.d.49q.5a.5sol.1ad1.: ". . . nec tamen hoc verum est, quod docere sit actus prudentiae; immo potius est actus caritatis vel misericordiae, secundum quod ex tali habitu inclinamur ad huiusmodi exercitium, vel etiam sapientiae ut dirigentis."

19. One minor exception is a reference to charity in S.T. II.II.83.1.ad2.

20. Jacques Maritain, *Neuf Leçons sur les notions premières de la philosophie morale* (Paris: Téqui, 1950), 31–33, 84, 85; and *Moral Philosophy*, trans. M. Suther (New York: Charles Scribner's Sons, 1964), 24. See also John McDermott, "Moral Systems: Maritain and Schüller Compared," *Divus Thomas* (1985): 6.

21. S.T. I.II.9.3. The only parallel question is in *De malo* 6.

22. S.T. I.II.9.3c.,ob1., and ad1.

23. S.T. I.II.9.4c.

24. DM 6.ob11. and ad11.; 6c., ad1, 3, 4, 17 and 21.

25. See S.T. I.II.9.4.ad3: "Voluntas quantum ad aliquid sufficienter se movet, et in suo ordine, scilicet sicut agens proximum." For the earlier, contradictory assertion, see SCG III.88.nr.2638.

26. I.II.9.6c.: "Voluntatis autem causa nihil aliud esse potest quam Deus."

27. I.II.9.6.ad3.

28. See Klaus Riesenhuber, *Die Transzendenz der Freiheit zum Guten* (Munich: Berchmanskolleg Verlag, 1971), 116.

29. Riesenhuber calls this argument: "diese Befreiung des Vollzugs des Wollens aus der Herrschaft der Erkenntnis" (*Die Transzendenz der Freiheit zum Guten*, 118).

30. I.II.9.3c.

31. I.II.9.3sc: "Sed contra est quia voluntas domina est sui actus, et in ipsa est velle et non velle." See also I.83.1.

32. "Quod non esset, si non haberet in potestate movere seipsam ad volendum. Ergo ipsa movet seipsam."

33. See Cornelio Fabro, "Orizzontalità e verticalità della liberta," *Angelicum* 48 (1971): 326–327. That precedence had been attributed explicitly to the reason; see esp. I.82.3.ad2; I.82.4c.; SCG III.26.nr.2092; DV22.12c.

34. Klaus Riesenhuber, "The Basis and Meaning of Freedom in Thomas Aquinas," 108, note 33.

35. II.II.25.2c.

36. Klaus Riesenhuber, *Die Transzendenz der Freiheit zum Guten*, 178–179.

37. *De spiritualibus creaturis* 10.ob4 and ad4.

38. I.II.9.3c.; DM 6.ad20. The inference is especially clear in DM 6c.

39. I.II.9.3c. and ad1; DM 6c.ad17 and ad20; II.II.82.1.ad1.

40. I.II.10.2c.

41. DM 6c.: "Sed cum voluntas non semper voluerit consiliari, necesse est quod ab aliquo moveatur ad hoc quod velit consiliari; et si quidem a seipsa, necesse est iterum quod motum voluntatis praecedat consilium, et consilium praecedat actus voluntatis."

42. DM 6.ad10: "Dissimile quidem quantum ad exercitium actus, nam intellectus movetur a voluntate ad agendum, voluntas autem non ab alia potentia, sed a seipsa."

43. See DM 6.ad17.

44. On the will as first mover, see I.II.16.1c.; 17.1c and 81.1; II.II.88.1ad2; III.18.3sc.

45. II.II.47.9.ad1; II.II.47.8.ad3: ". . . movere absolute pertinet ad voluntatem." Cf. III.63.5.ad2.

46. Thomas argues that the universal good is God in I.105.4c.; I.II.2.8c.

47. I.II.10.2c.: "Primo ergo modo, voluntas a nullo obiecto ex necessitate movetur: potest enim aliquis de quocumque obiecto non cogitare, et per consequens neque actu velle illud."

48. I.II.10.2c.: "Unde si proponatur aliquod obiectum voluntati quod sit universaliter bonum et secundum omnem considerationem, ex necessitate voluntas in illud tendet, si aliquid velit; non enim poterit velle oppositum."

49. I.II.10.2c.: ". . . illud solum bonum quod est perfectum et cui nihil deficit, est tale bonum quod voluntas non potest non velle: quod est beatitudo." Cf. Lottin, *Psychologie et morale*, 1:256, 260.

50. Klaus Riesenhuber, *Die Transzendenz der Freiheit zum Guten*, 186.

51. I.II.10.2c.; cf. I.II.9.6.ad3. DM 6.ad7.

52. I.II.10.1c.; 17.9.ad2. Cf. I.60.2c.

53. I.II.1.4c. See also Klaus Riesenhuber, *Die Transzendenz der Freiheit zum Guten*, 168–169.

54. Klaus Riesenhuber, "The Basis and Meaning of Freedom in Thomas Aquinas," 101.

55. I.II.11.4.ad2.

56. I.II.18.6c. and 7c. See also Klaus Riesenhuber, *Die Transzendenz der Freiheit zum Guten*, 112.

57. I.II.17.5.ad3.: "Primus autem voluntatis actus ex rationis ordinatione non est, sed ex instinctu naturae, aut superioris causae" (author's translation). Cf. I.II.9.4c.

58. George Klubertanz states his own, as well as Lottin's and Leclerq's difficulties, with this lacuna in "The Empiricism of Thomistic Ethics," *Proceedings of the American Catholic Philosophical Association* (1957): 22.

59. I.II.10.2c.: "Voluntas a nullo obiecto ex necessitate movetur."

60. DM 6c.: "Si aliquod bonum proponatur quod apprehendatur in ratione boni, non autem in ratione convenientis, non movebit voluntatem."

61. I.II.10.3c. and ad2.

62. I.II.29.1c.,ad1 and 5c.

63. I.II.29.1.ad2.

64. George Klubertanz argues that goodness as such is not an object but the aspect under which the will wills (*Habits and Virtues*, 67).

65. I.II.29.1c.: "Sicut autem omne conveniens, inquantum huiusmodi, habet rationem boni; ita omne repugnans, inquantum huiusmodi, habet rationem mali."

"Goodness is always a relative term expressing a relation between an object and an appetite" (George Klubertanz, *Habits and Virtues*, 68).

66. Cf. II.II.47.8.ad3.

67. I.II.17.1c. Cf. I.II.17.6c.

68. I.II.65.1.ad1.

69. III Sent.d.33.q.1a.2sol.2.

70. S.T. I.II.65.3.ad2. and II.II.47.16.ad2.

71. II.II.47.14.ad3. See also III Sent.d.25q.2a.2sol.1ad1.

72. II Sent.d.39.q.2.a.1c.; DV 11.1c.; S.T. I.II.63.1c.; *In Sent. libri Ethicorum* 10.14.2143.

73. S.T. II.II.49.1.ad2.: "Prudentia aptitudinem quidem habet ex natura, sed eius complementum est ex exercitio vel gratia."

74. II.II.51.3.ad1.

75. DV 11.1c. Cf. S.T. II.II.47.14.ad3.

76. II.II.182.2.ad2.

77. In Pol.1.1.nr.32. *De virt card* 5.2.ad3; 5.3.ad13; In Mat. 25.2.2045.; In 2 Cor 5.2.; 12.3; Serm. 12.3.

78. See especially S.T. II.II.186. and 188.

79. II.II.186.2c.: "Status autem religionis est quaedam disciplina vel exercitium ad perfectionem perveniendi. Ad quam quidem aliqui pervenire nituntur exercitiis diversis."

80. II.II.186.7c.: "exercitium perfectionis."

81. III.69.3c. ". . . hoc est conveniens propter spirituale exercitium: ut videlicet contra concupiscentiam et alias passibilitates pugnans homo victoriae coronam acciperet."

82. In Tit I.4.46.; Ps. 37.2; 51.1. See also S.T. III.86.5.ad3.

83. *In Sent. libri Ethicorum* I.16.199.

84. *De virt card* 3.ad13. See also S.T. II.II.182.2.ad2; III.86.5.ad3.

85. In 2 Cor 5.2.nr.168: "Sequitur de praeparatione ad praemium, quae fit per pugnam contra tentationes et per exercitium bonorum operum. . . ."

86. In 1 Tim 4.2.nr.154. "Et dicit 'exerce,' non 'fac,' quia exercitium dicit promptitudinem; et hoc ideo, quia exercitatus facit levius, delectabilius, et stabilius."

87. S.T. I.II.17.1.ad2.: "Radix libertatis est voluntas sicut subiectum: sed sicut causa, est ratio."

88. I.II.9.6.ad3.

89. Karl Rahner, "Reflections on the Unity of the Love of Neighbor and Love of God," *Theological Investigations* 6 (Baltimore: Helicon Press, 1969), 238.

90. Klaus Riesenhuber, *Die Transzendenz der Freiheit zum Guten*, 325 n. 221.

91. In 1 Tim 4.3.171. "Ad exercitium autem necessaria est exhortatio nostra quantum ad agenda, doctrina quantum ad cognoscenda."

92. Odon Lottin, who discovered the shift in Thomas's writings, refers to this second *exercitium* as the act of the will following judgment (*Psychologie et morale*, 3:664ff).

PART 3

Living Rightly

CHAPTER 4

Specification and the Object

In this chapter, I demonstrate that Thomas's entire discussion of such concepts as intention, choice, and internal or external acts are rooted in his concept of the object. Object is the primary notion for Thomas's moral writings.[1] Grasping the significance of this concept, we also grasp the insight that these moral writings remain within the concept of specification, that is, solely within the sphere of rightness.

The object is subject to inquiry; it reveals to us what exactly we intend, what meaning we give to our actions, and whether our intentions and chosen actions are right or wrong. It provides the context of intelligibility for any species of action. Without an object, we cannot understand what an action is. An intention without an object reads: "I intend . . ." With an object, we can understand what we intend, e.g., "I intend to pay back a debt." An object gives species and intelligibility to our intentions and actions.

Being the source of the intelligibility of an action, the object also provides the context for measuring or evaluating whether an internal or external action is suitable for rational judgment.[2] Intending to pay a debt, for example, is measured by rational judgment as suitable; knifing someone in the back is measured as generally unsuitable. Through rational judgments, we can measure whether the objects of internal or external actions are suitable or not.

> The difference in good and evil considered in reference to the object is an essential difference in relation to reason, that is to say, according as the object is suitable or unsuitable to reason. Consequently it is evident that good and evil diversify the species in human actions; since essential differences cause a difference of species.[3]

Thomas has, then, a central presupposition: "Now in human actions, good and evil are predicated in reference to the reason."[4] In effect, an act is "good" (Thomas's term) because reason judges it appropriate or fitting. In terms of our distinction, however, we call an act that reason judges either fitting, "right," or not fitting, "wrong."

This chapter is divided into six sections. In the first, I argue that for Thomas the context of specification is completely dependent on the object; in the second, that the object gives species; and, in the third, that Thomas identifies the end with the object. In the fourth section, I examine the object as form and as *materia circa quam* in order to demonstrate (in the fifth) the relationship the object has with the following concepts: intention, circumstances, internal and external acts, form and matter. I conclude in the sixth that the descriptions of moral acts, both interior and exterior, are measured according to reason. Those measurements that yield what Thomas calls "goodness," we call "rightness." What we, on the other hand, call "goodness" corresponds to a primary *exercitium* and is not found in Thomas's treatment of the ends and objects of human acts.

TO WILL IS TO WILL SOMETHING

In the ninth question of the *Prima secundae*, Thomas achieves a new system by distinguishing *exercitium* or "that the will can will" from specification or "that the will can will this or that".[5] By the former, the will alone enjoys the freedom to move itself, reason, or any other power. In *exercitium*, the freedom of the will to will or to think is not limited. But this freedom is not the same as the freedom to intend or choose this or that. This latter movement, *quantum ad specificationem*, the willing of this or that, depends on the object that reason presents to the will. If something is not presented, the will cannot will it. Thus, in the *exercitium* the will requires no object; in the *specification*, it does. Freedom in specification is limited.

The freedom to think this or that depends on whether reason can present this or that object. For example, the famed Tasaday Indians cannot contemplate a war because, to date, they have no such concept in their language. For the same reason, Thomas could not contemplate the effects of nuclear deterrence, and infants cannot contemplate matrimony. The scope of human freedom is limited by the horizon of reason. The form of our willed actions is shaped by the objects that reason presents to the will. Thomas achieves this insight in the ninth question.

If we are to will, then we must will something, some object. Unfortunately, the word object is often used (in neo-Scholastic language) as equivalent to an act of choice or an external act. For Thomas, however, the object is that which the will first needs in order to will anything. The first object the will needs is not what it chooses, but what it intends. The first object becomes the internal act, not the external one.

"An intention," Thomas writes, "means to tend to something."[6] But the will needs something toward which to tend: "The will has no inclination for anything except insofar as it is apprehended by the intellect."[7] Thus, the will can desire no "good" (Thomas's term) unless it has first been apprehended by reason, because the good is not the object of the will except as apprehended.[8] The good understood is the object of the will, because the will tends to its object as presented by reason.[9] The will as inclination has no meaning without an object apprehended.

The end as end is derived from the will. But that end is a purely formal notion. It derives its substance only when the object presented by reason is accepted by the will.[10] The will needs the object precisely because the end is purely formal, i.e., it is simply movement without any direction or purpose. The end without the object is not inclined toward anything.[11] For this reason, an intention requires an antecedent act of apprehension, that presents the object to the will.[12]

The will needs the object not only to will something, but also to will something good or bad (Thomas's terms). The goodness or badness of an act of willing is, according to Thomas, derived from the object. In question nineteen of the *Prima secundae*, Thomas asks about the goodness of the interior act of the will. Throughout the question he never asks whether the goodness of the will is derived from the end. Instead, he begins by stating that good and evil are acts differing in species whose specific differences are determined by objects.[13] He then points out that the good is presented by reason to the will as its object, a point he repeats with particular regularity in the question.[14] The object, then, is that which becomes the end when the will accepts it. The entire discussion of the goodness of intentions revolves around the object, not the end.[15] The will's goodness depends *solely* on the object's goodness.

Twice Thomas asks whether the will's goodness can be independent of the object. He first asks whether the will is good before having an object. He responds that the good that the will desires must first be apprehended by reason before the will can want it.[16] He then asks whether right apprehension depends on right appetite and responds that the desire of the due end presupposes a "right apprehension of the end" (*rectam apprehensionem de fine*).[17] Thomas reminds us that we are solely within the context of specification, not *exercitium*, and allows no exceptions: if we are to will, we are to will something and that something makes our actions good or bad. Thomas's good end in practical matters is derived from the rightness of the object presented to the will (Thomas's terms). The important assertion that a "right appetite is a good will" means that the will is "good" when reason's object is right.[18]

In Thomas's writings on specification, the end is a purely formal concept. For this reason, the will must assume some object in order to give meaning and order to the will's movement.[19] Nonetheless, the end determines whether actions are moral, for human acts are acts done for an end and such acts are moral ones.[20] Though species are always derived from objects, moral species are derived from an end. Thus, an object alone does not determine the morality of an action, but whether the object is willed. The object willed is the end.

The importance of the end is derived from Thomas's concept of voluntariness.[21] Moral acts are voluntary and being voluntary they have an end.[22] The voluntary is broader and more inclusive than the end is, for the voluntary applies not only to acts as intended, but also to those omissions wherein we have the power and the duty to perform certain obligations, but fail to act. An omitted act is, therefore, a voluntary omission. The end in such cases of omission is the aversion to the due but omitted end.[23] Thus, even acts of omissions have ends, which may be derived from a consideration of the object that should have been willed.

In summary, if an act is moral, it must somehow be attributed to an end. Its morality, however, must have content. The act must have intelligibility, some meaningful directionality or inclination. Its intelligible content is derived from an object apprehended by reason and accepted as an end or as informing the end. By informing the end, the object gives the species to the moral act.

THE OBJECT AS SPECIFYING

Thomas regularly maintains that the object gives species to our actions, but he especially does so in question eighteen "Of the Good and Evil of Human Acts in General." There, Thomas argues eight times that the object gives species to both internal and external acts.[24]

Though question eighteen concerns the good and evil in human acts, its individual articles address the issue of specification because the difference in species is the difference between good and evil. "The good and evil will are acts differing in species. Now the specific difference in acts is according to objects. Therefore, good and evil in the acts of the will are derived properly from objects."[25] The classification of the will's acts as good or bad will depend on that one thing, the specific object.

The interior act of the will begins with the acceptance of the presented object, through which the act is specified.[26] The specification of the interior act, which is a specification of the end or the will's proper object, is derived properly from this first presented object.[27] This first object, if it is in accord with reason, "causes moral goodness in the will."[28]

This causal goodness is singular. The goodness of the interior act is caused by one thing alone (*ex solo uno illo*): the object.[29] Since the goodness of the will depends properly on the object, and since the object is presented by reason, "the goodness of the will depends on reason, in the same way as it depends on the object."[30] Likewise, since the end is the object received by the will, the goodness derived from the object does not differ from that derived from the end.[31]

After Thomas distinguishes the two movements of the will, *quantum ad exerticitium* and *quantum ad specificationem*, he chooses to enter solely into the movement of specification, carefully and with regularity, excluding the last end. The object no longer moves the will as end but instead provides the formal principle for an action. That object provides the intelligibility and measurability for both external and internal actions of the will.

The interior act of the will is not, therefore, an action whose meaning is derived from *exercitium* or the last end. The meaning of the interior act is taken from specification. When Thomas speaks of the end as giving species, he clearly distinguishes the last end from any other end and from the end that gives species. Thus, though human acts are specified by their ends, this specification is derived from "but one proximate end."[32] Later, he excludes the possibility of the last end's being willed as an act of the will and declares it impossible that an act be specified by the last end.[33] Still later, he writes, "Moral matters do not receive their species from the last end, but from their proximate ends."[34] We find, then, two concepts pertaining to the giving of species: an object and a proximate end, and both are identified precisely as something other than the last end. Thus, restricting the interior willed act to specification and excluding the last end, Thomas has provided a way of measuring the specific end. This end, the object in the intention, is measured by reason.

In contemporary moral discussion, such a measure is the measure of rightness or wrongness. The concept of end, insofar as it refers to the proximate end, pertains to rightness alone. The measure of the end in specified acts, both internal and external, is derived not from the last end, which moves the will according to *exercitium*, but from the object alone, which moves the will as form in giving specification.

THE END AS SPECIFYING

I have argued that the object gives moral species to an act when the will accepts it and tends toward it as the intended end. But my thesis also stands on a recurring pattern of argument: in every article dedicated to the relationship between the object and specification, Thomas refers in one of his objections to the end and responds to the objection by identifying the object with the end that gives species, that is, the proximate end.

The context and structure of the argument is the same, whether the subject is power, act, goodness, virtue, or sin. In each case, Thomas introduces the question of specification as derived from an object. He does not begin with an end, because an end cannot have species unless it is first informed by an object.[35] But he introduces an objection: doesn't the end give species? Here, he implicitly asks whether the assertion that the object gives species is contradicted by the assertion that the end gives species. He answers that the assertions complement rather than contradict one another. Moreover, by using the notion of end, he offers a corrective concerning the object: not any object, but the object in the will, the formal object (as opposed to the object in the external act, the material object) gives species in moral acts.

In the first use of this pattern Thomas asks what distinguishes powers, and answers that powers are distinguished by objects.[36] To the objection that objects are extrinsic and subsequent to powers, Thomas responds that objects are principles or ends of action.[37] By asserting that the object is principle or end, he underlines the object as an intrinsic starting point in giving species.

The next instance of this pattern appears in question eighteen of the *Prima secundae*. Thomas dedicates this entire question to the issue of specification and integrates four concepts: object, species, goodness, and reason. To answer whether good or evil is derived from its object, Thomas affirms that good and evil are derived from the object because it is through the object that every action derives its species.[38]

Having established the identity between the object and the specification of acts, Thomas asks whether ends give species. Here Thomas introduces two actions: internal and external actions, each of which has an object. He identifies the end with one of these objects: "The end is properly the object of the interior act of the will."[39] He raises, however, the objection that since the object gives species to action, how then can the end give species? The end gives species because it has the "meaning of the object."[40]

In question nineteen, Thomas asserts that the goodness of the will comes from the object alone. He then raises the objection: is not the end also a source of goodness? He responds that the goodness derived from the object does not differ from that derived from the end.[41] Thus, the species of "goodness and badness" (Thomas's terms) or "rightness and wrongness" (our terms) is the same whether derived from the end or the meaning of the object.

The pattern appears again at the very beginning of the treatise on the virtues. Thomas argues that habits are specified by objects. The objection, that habits are specified by their end, is raised by way of an example: giving money to someone can be done either for God's sake, in which case it is an act of charity, or it can be done to repay a debt, in which case it is an act of justice.[42] Before he answers this objection, Thomas distinguishes the "meaning of the object" from the object considered "materially." He argues that habits and potencies are specified by the former.[43] This distinction serves to answer the above objection: ends are objects of internal acts.[44] Thus, the object formally taken, e.g., paying a debt, is the end and specifies the act and the habit.

The pattern reappears in the question of whether there is only one moral virtue. Having already explained that the moral virtues are habits of the appetitive faculty, and that habits differ specifically according to their objects, Thomas distinguishes the virtues from one another precisely according to their objects.[45]

Thomas elaborates: "in moral matters the reason holds the place of commander and mover, while the appetitive power is commanded and moved."[46] This movement is not a movement of *exercitium* but of specification, wherein reason does not move the will "univocally" (*univoce*) but by presenting objects. Nonetheless, the objects that give species are antecedent and not subsequent to willing. The object specifies a virtue as temperate or just, not as it is materially realized, but as it is accepted by the will, that is, in the intention.

To this position that the virtues are specified by the object, Thomas raises the common objection: things pertaining to morals are specified by their end. But the end of virtue is happiness. Therefore, there is only one moral virtue.[47] He responds: "Moral matters do not receive their species from the last end, but from their proximate ends."[48] The end that gives species to things in morals is always the object that gives species to things in morals. Thomas concludes the question by writing that the difference of objects always causes a specific difference of virtues.

The function of the object as antecedent to any act of the will is to establish the specific virtues. Prudence, justice, temperance, and fortitude are each distinguished by their formal object's relation to reason; thus, a matter pertaining to rights among individuals will differ from a matter dealing with sexual passions. In a similar vein, the specification of these objects as right or wrong, temperate or intemperate, just or unjust will equally be established by the relation to reason. For just as a virtue is determined by the formal object's relation to reason, that is, by its intelligibility, so, too, the same formal object is determined as either "good or bad" (Thomas's terms), virtue or vice, or right or wrong (our terms) by its fittingness to reason.[49]

The last instance of the pattern appears in the section on sin. Thomas writes that sins differ in species according to their object. Then, with thorough consistency, he raises the objection: are not sins specified by the ends rather than by objects?[50] He responds:

> The aspect of good is found chiefly in the end: and therefore the end stands in the relation of object to the act of the will which is at the root of every sin. Consequently it amounts to the same whether sins differ by their objects or by their ends.[51]

The end that gives species is the object that gives species. There is no difference between the two because the proximate end is the will's inclination informed by a conceived, presented, and accepted object. The original source of the object is not the will, but reason, and the object as intelligible is measured by reason. Its measurability gives species to the various dimensions of moral matters.

In six different contexts, Thomas affirms the statement he made in the ninth question: the object gives species. And on each occasion he introduces an objection: the end gives species. By incorporating the end in each of these contexts, Thomas draws certain conclusions. First, the end that gives species is the object that gives species. Second, the object giving species is the object formally understood.[52] Third, the end is the proximate end, not the last end which does not give species. Fourth, the end gives species only by the will intending the object as it is conceived, not as it is realized. Fifth, the species establishes the essential difference between good and evil. Sixth, the difference between good and evil is determined by the object's fittingness (we can now say, correctness) to reason.

THE OBJECT AS FORM AND *MATERIA CIRCA QUAM*

There are two types of operations: immanent and transient.[53] Immanent operations remain in the agent and are acts and perfections of the agent; transient operations pass into external matter and are acts and perfections of the patient. Immanent operations perfect the internal matter, the agent. Insofar as they are perfections of the agent, all "moral" acts are immanent acts.[54]

As the operations differ, so do the objects. In transient operations the object is external to the agent; in immanent operations the object is within the agent, and thus bears the same relationship to actions as the form does in other agents.[55] Through these operations, furthermore, form is made actual and is able to perfect its matter, the subject, and itself. Thus, in all immanent operations, the object acts as form and perfects its matter, the subject and itself.[56]

As Thomas begins the *Prima secundae* he argues (particularly in questions nine and eighteen) that the object acts as form or formal cause. Despite the impression of the last chapter, this shift is not entirely new: already in the *Pars prima* Thomas had established the object as the form in immanent operations.[57] He had, however, also taught that the object moves the will as final cause. Now, in question nine of the *Prima secundae*, Thomas concretely decides on the form over the final end, so that in the remaining sections of the *Summa*, he must explain not only how the object acts as form but also how it acts within the moral agent. Yet an object by definition is something exterior to the subject. If it is exterior, how can it act as form for an agent's acting? How can "the object" be within the subject?

In question eighteen of the *Prima secundae*, particularly in the article that asks whether good and evil are derived from the object, Thomas presents the problems through "objections." First, he asks in objection two: if the object is the matter of an action, how can goodness be derived from matter when goodness is derived from form? Thomas responds that the object of the act is not natural matter, *materia ex qua*, but a *materia circa quam*. This matter somehow has the meaning of form in that it gives species.[58] The "matter" about the object does not preclude the object from being a form.

The next objection asks, if an object is the effect of an active power, how can it be the cause of goodness? Thomas explains that the object as *materia circa quam* acts as form and is not always an effect. An object, Thomas writes, only has the nature of an effect in an active power after it has been "transformed." He uses a highly illustrative example: "Thus food when transformed is the effect of the nutritive power; whereas food before being transformed stands in relation to the nutritive power as the matter about which (*materia circa quam*) it exercises its operation."[59]

An object is an effect only insofar as it is first the matter about which (*materia circa quam*) the will is concerned.[60] When the object is realized it stands in relation to the will as effect. But before the will can produce an effect, it needs some "subject matter" about which it can intend. The object is the subject matter which the will's acceptance transforms into an end being sought. What the will intends is precisely what reason or any other power presents to the will first: the object. This object is not the object realized, but the object as it is in the intention, which gives form to the act.[61]

There are two notions of object: (1) that which is offered to the will, which stands as the *materia circa quam* of the intention and therefore provides the form and species of the act, and (2) that which is realized by the will. The former notion, the *ratio obiecti*, is that which gives species, a point Thomas makes with thorough frequency.[62] Because the object acts as form, and since form gives species to operations, the object gives species.[63] Thus, both form and object are identified as giving the grounds of intelligibility. The formal object is the object not as it is realized in some external act, but as it is conceived and accepted as the principle of acting.[64]

A simple example may serve to clarify how the form gives intelligibility and therefore in operations, species. Formally, a telephone is an instrument by which two or more people separated by distance can communicate through speech. As matter, a telephone is a unit that has a dial or push buttons, an ear and mouthpiece, and a square, oblong, or round unit containing many wires. The matter has meaning to the extent that it has form. If someone pointed to this object on my desk and asked what it is, I would not say that it is a unit with a dial, an ear and mouthpiece, and many wires. Rather, I would give its form. Similarly, were I engaged in a phone conversation and someone asked what I was doing, I would not say that I was holding a unit with many parts. I would refer to form and say that I was speaking to someone at another location. The action or operation finds its meaning in form, not matter.

On a number of occasions, Thomas relies on form to designate the proper notion of the object that gives species to actions.[65] For instance, Thomas derives the particularlity of prudence as a virtue, not from the material consideration of the object (*materialem considerationem*), but from the formal meaning of the object (*rationem formalem*), which is the end.[66] The end is the formal aspect of the object and gives species.

In the *Secunda secundae*, when Thomas asks whether one is unjust by doing an unjust thing, he raises the objection that habits are specified by the objects; therefore, the one who does an unjust act is unjust. He responds that the object as it is formally accepted, not as it is materially realized, specifies habits.[67] Though the act or external object is unjust, the "operation" is not called an injustice, because the operation takes its name and species from the object per se, not the object per accidens. The object per se is that which is intended; the object per accidens is outside the intention (*praeter intentionem*).[68] The formal aspect of the object is the object in the intention, that is, that which has been accepted by the will as that toward which to tend.[69] The end is the intention's object.[70]

For Thomas, the end is first in intention and last in execution. But the former gives moral species.[71] Likewise, the object as formal is first in intention and as material, last in execution. The formal object is the end.

Not only does Thomas join end and object, he also joins form and *materia circa quam*. The object gives species because it has intelligibility, and because it has intelligibility, it is the *materia circa quam*, the matter about which actions, both interior and exterior, are concerned. "Moral" species, then, are derived from the matter about which the internal act is concerned.[72]

The *materia circa quam* is always related to Thomas's use of object. In both the *Commentary on the Sentences* and the *Prima secundae*, Thomas describes the object as *materia circa quam*.[73] Before the shift, the object or *materia circa quam* is the end; after the shift, it is the form, giving species to an act.

The identity between object and *materia circa quam* is simply a way of describing what an object is and its use is similar to its use in English: subject matter. The object of the internal act and the object of the external act are their respective subject matters.

When *materia circa quam* first appears in the *Prima secundae*, it both underlines the intelligibility of the object and upholds its status as form of the act: it is the matter about which the will is intending, not the matter which is effected.[74] It is clearly not the external act, but the formal object.

Inasmuch, however, as the object becomes matter realized and not simply matter conceived, the *materia circa quam* also becomes the matter of the external act.[75] This assertion does not deny the *materia circa quam* of the intending will. Rather, the matters of the will and the external act differ from one another exactly as formal and material objects differ from one another.

Just as Thomas ascertains the nature of the object in giving species, so does the concept *materia circa quam* become the device to express the object as form and as matter, as cause and effect, and as conceived and as realized. In question eighteen, Thomas clarifies the point he had made earlier: an "object" is that "matter" presented by reason; it is whatever is discussable, because it is whatever is offered for consideration. If the will accepts this object or matter or "apprehended form," it becomes the matter about which the will or the end is concerned. As accepted, it becomes the form of the act to be realized.[76] When the will realizes the external act, the second object becomes the matter about which the exterior act is concerned.

The importance of the concept of the *materia circa quam* is that it permits Thomas to overcome important objections that could incline us to think of the object as external matter, as a *materia ex qua*. That is, through the concept of the *materia circa quam* Thomas overcomes objections that might have relegated the object to being an effect of realized matter. Instead, it is the stuff which gives form to the species.

OTHER CONCEPTS RELATED TO MORAL ACTION

The interrelationship among the four concepts of end, object, form and *materia circa quam* sets the context for understanding other concepts related to human or moral actions: intention, circumstances, internal and external acts, form and matter.

Since that which gives moral species is the proximate end or the formal object, we cannot speak of the end as specifying without some *materia circa quam*, some matter about which, the intended end can be measured by reason. Inasmuch as Thomas writes that the formal aspect of the object gives species, or that the proximate end gives species, Thomas also argues that that which is intended gives species. Let us consider some examples.

In the *Secunda secundae*, discussing whether it is lawful to kill in self-defense, Thomas remarks that "moral acts take their species according to what is intended."[77] He uses the same term to determine whether we are called unjust for performing an unjust act, in questions about scandal and lying, and in questions pertaining to the religious life.[78]

The instance of lying underlines Thomas's understanding of intending an end. In the question whether lying is always opposed to truth, he provides a threefold division of the act of lying: falsehood materially, formally, and effectively. First, Thomas argues that if we intend to be truthful but tell a falsehood, our act does not belong to the species of lying because the falsehood was not the "proper object." Though a material falsehood is stated, the formal object is lacking and we have not lied. Second, if we intend to tell a falsehood, then the act formally contains falsehood and belongs to the species of lying. Even though a material falsehood may not be stated, still the formal object is intended and that alone constitutes lying. "To signify by words something that is not in mind" is the formal object or the formal *materia circa quam* of lying. Third, if we intend the effect of deceiving a person, this intended effect does not belong to the species of lying, but is rather a perfection or an additional circumstance of the species. Only the formal object or the material object or the remote end of deception, determines the moral species of lying.[79]

This formal object is wrong because it is "unnatural and undue for anyone to signify by words something that is not in mind."[80] Its material object can be virtually any utterance whatever. The material thematizes or realizes the formal object, but the formal object is not itself purely thematic. Rather, the form's "matter" shapes the morality of any utterance whatever.[81] Thus, even if that external, material utterance be accidentally truthful, the formal object will make the utterance "essentially" a lie. That essence is derived from the formal matter or object accepted by the will and intended as such.

Thomas writes, "circumstances of human acts should be called their accidents."[82] He clarifies this immediately. Accidents can have two forms: as they are in a subject or as they are related to other accidents of the same subject. As it is the latter that pertains to circumstances, a circumstance is "an accident of an accident."[83]

Thomas gives us three concrete examples of circumstances. In theft a circumstance is not the fact that the stolen object belongs to another, but whether what is stolen is great or small. A circumstance is not the end that specifies an act, but an additional or a remote end.[84] For example, that a valiant person act valiantly for the good of the virtue of fortitude is not a circumstance. But to act valiantly for the sake of delivering the state or Christendom is accidental to acting valiantly. Finally, the act of pouring water over ourselves is not a circumstance of washing. That we should be chilled or scalded, healed or harmed is an effect and is, therefore, circumstantial to the act of washing. We notice that each circumstance is accidental to the object. The first is the size, the second is a remote (as opposed to a proximate) end, and the third is an effect. Being accidental to the object makes the circumstances accidental to one another.

Citing Aristotle, Thomas distinguishes the object or the *circa quid* from the *quid*.[85] The *circa quid* is the object from which the matter of the intention is derived; the *quid* is the matter of the realized or executed act or choice.

Thus, when Thomas argues that the *cur* and the *quid* are the most important circumstances, they have to be understood as circumstantial to the formal object or *circa quid*; that is, the *cur* is a remote end, the *quid* is the matter of the external act.[86] But the *cur* and *quid* are circumstances, not as accidental to the act, but as accidental to one another.

Apart from an actually intended, that is, specified act, the *cur* and *quid* remain as general concepts accidental to one another. Indeed, the entire notion of "end," from "last end" through "remote ends" to the "proximate end," represents a trajectory, or better, an inclination seeking an object. As inclination, the end, from "last" through "remote" toward the "proximate," remains formal. When an inclination becomes specific, that is, when an inclination accepts an object and therefore becomes an intention, then an end, the proximate end, gives species.

As a trajectory, however, the entire notion of the end as inclination recedes from the formal object or *circa quid* further and further into the person. Conversely the concept of *quid* moves from the formal object or *circa quid* into greater and greater specificity. The *quid* needs the further circumstances that provide a context for the realization of the *circa quid*. Further specificity results from more constricted notions regarding the matter itself. For instance, when Thomas talks of the species of lust, he writes that the sub-species are derived from differences in the matter, as e.g., was violence used (rape), was the person married (adultery), was the person a minor (seduction).[87] These further specifications, however, are only derivative of a first species, wherein the formal difference of the object gives that species. The more specifically we talk, the more remote we are from the formal object and consequently from the end. Thus, the trajectory of the object moves toward specificity, and the two trajectories move in contrary directions.[88]

The end that gives species, like the formal object itself, is not a circumstance to the species of the act. An end antecedent to the proximate end or more remote from the object itself is, however, a circumstance and does not give species. Only the proximate end that formally expresses the object in the intention pertains to the act itself. In an actually intended and realized action, the object is formally the *circa quid* and materially the *quid* itself. And—what is more important—the *circa quid* precedes absolutely the *quid*: we choose acts according to what we intend, not vice versa.

These insights into the circumstances of specific acts and the consequent proximity of end and object reveal two points. First, as general concepts the end and the object are not identities: one does not identify or restrict the other. This difference highlights the distinction between *exercitium* and specification. The will can will anything it wants other than that which it does not want. But whatever it wants must first be something, and that something is an object. In terms of the distinction between formal and final causality, the object gives the form of specification; it no longer gives the end. The end is no longer in the object, but in the will. Yet for Thomas any end other than the last end is unformed, that is, it has no particular object and therefore no determinative form. When it has a particular object, the object specifies the proximate end and the inclination becomes an intention. This intention, that is, an end specified by its object, gives the moral species to human acts.

Second, within the specifically intended act, the two terms (end and object) are undoubtedly interwoven. In the intention the proximate end meets the formal aspect of the object.[89] The former is the moving power; the latter provides through its matter the form of specification.

Thus, sins of commission and omission do not differ specifically, because the formal object of the intending will in both types of sin is the same. The sins are not specified by particular acts but by subject matters. The omission of moderate eating belongs to the same species as excess in eating: gluttony.[90] Thomas always derives the object that gives species to the human or moral act from the *materia circa quam* in the intention. Further, the species of sin are not derived from the various antecedent, remote active, or motive causes, but from that cause in which the end is the object of the will.[91] Nor, obviously, is the species of sin derived from the act, but from the object in the intention. The intention, wherein the inclination meets and accepts a specifying object, is the locus for Thomas's moral investigations.

Finally, the formal object or formal *materia circa quam* is in the intention; the material object or material *materia circa quam* is in the realized act.[92] Here rests the accidental relationship between *cur* and *quid*. The formal and material objects or *materia circa quam* are accidental in that what is wanted (*cur*) is not always that which is realized (*quid*). There is no necessary relationship between what one wants and what one realizes. For this reason, Thomas uses precise language to argue that the formal object gives species in moral matters or that the matter about which (*materia circa quam*) the will intends gives species. Thomas does not say that in moral matters either the material object or the realized *materia circa quam* gives moral species.

Thomas writes that the object or the intelligibility of the "external act can stand in a twofold relation to the end: first as being of itself (per se) ordained thereto . . . ; the other way as being ordained accidentally (per accidens)."[93] Examples of the first kind include the realized acts of an intended theft and of an intending adulterer. These external acts are of themselves ordained to the object of the intention. Examples of the second kind include accidental theft by a person intending to be just and theft by an adulterer who needs extra money to commit adultery. These external actions are not of themselves objects ordained to the agent's end.

The culpability of accidentally related external acts depends on whether they have been directly assumed by the agent. As the adulterer does directly assume the act of theft, the one external act has a twofold malice: the theft and the adultery. On the other hand, theft committed by the just person who does not directly assume the theft does not make that person culpable.[94]

In both cases, a voluntary act has two expressions, the internal and external acts. Each act has its own object, its own intelligibility, and so each object gives its own species. Thomas describes the two species this way:

> Now that which is on the part of the will is formal in regard to that which is on the part of the external action. . . . Consequently the species of a human act is considered formally with regard to the end, but materially with regard to the object of the external act.[95]

The object, species, or intelligibility of the act as internal is derived from the formal object, the object as it is in the will. This form, inasmuch as the will is active, precedes the external act in every way.[96] The object as it is in the will always occasions the first categorical movement of the will. This object, having been presented and accepted, is what the will wants to realize.[97] As Thomas writes, "it is from the end that we derive the meaning of the means."[98] This end or first object alone pertains to the moral species of an act.

Nevertheless, the *materia circa quam* for an end can be the same as the *materia circa quam* for a means or an external act because "all the objects of human acts are related to one another."[99] For this reason, any end can become a means for another end. The intelligibility of an end can be the same as the intelligibility of a means or vice versa.[100] Nothing about the *materia circa quam* of an internal or external action distinguishes them. They are distinguished only by their order of acceptance: if it is the first object, it is the intention; if the second, then the means.

In support of this argument, Thomas inverts the Aristotelian example of one who steals in order to commit adultery, and describes one who commits fornication in order to steal.[101] Fornication can be a means or an end; theft can be a means or an end. They are both objects. They can be the intelligibility of an intention or of an external act. The plasticity and indeterminacy between the end and the means is due to the concept of object, which describes the intelligibility of the act as either interior or external. A given object is an end, if the will has accepted the object as the intelligibility, explanation, or ground for its way of acting. Only this object, the formal object, or the *materia circa quam* of the internal act, gives moral species to actions.

In any given act, the relation between form and matter is the relationship between the internal act of the will and the external action, but not between an end and an object.[102] With uncommon precision Thomas describes the relation between form and matter without restricting the word "object" to either form or matter, because each internal and external act has its own intelligibility derived from its respective object.

The relation between form and matter is the relationship between internal and external acts, the end and the *quid*, the intention and the executed act, or the ends and the means. The term "object" or *materia circa quam* is applicable to any of these ten phrases insofar as the object gives intelligibility to any act, whether assumed formally in the will or realized materially in external action.

One is hard pressed to find anywhere in Thomas's writings an explicit derivation of an "object" from an exterior act. Rather, the end takes its intelligibility from the object, and once the end has this form it seeks to move other powers to attain the realization of this object. The form precedes the realized object, the external action, in all ways. The notion of object is a primary notion: it is not derived from the external act or from the end; rather, it gives meaning to both. It is the intelligibility, the *materia*, giving substance either to the intention or to the external action.

THOMAS'S CONCEPT OF THE OBJECT AND CONTEMPORARY ISSUES

The key concept for understanding Thomas's moral theology is object. The object, as Thomas describes it, concerns not so much what we do, but where we begin. The wrongness of lying has its origin, not in the act, but in the intention. We are not liars because we commit the act of lying; we are liars when we think it right to contradict in word what we have in mind. Being liars, we consequently commit the act of lying. For this reason formal objects precede the commission of acts.

In the same way, lust is not defined as intending to commit acts of rape, seduction, or adultery. Lust as a formal object appears when we allow venereal pleasures to overcome preferred ways of human acting.[103] One is not a person dominated by lust because one commits acts of rape, seduction, or adultery; one commits these acts because one is dominated by lust. Our disorder comes, not from assuming, intending, or committing these acts, but from our assumption of the object of lust, the unrestrained indulgence in venereal pleasures. This formal object is the matter of lust.

Thus does Thomas fix the locus of morality. Though the end gives species to moral acts, it is only the end as proximate to the formal object. As Thomas measures the formal object, so he measures the end. His primary interest is not in the further recesses of the acting person. Rather, he addresses the end most proximate to the object.[104] Where that proximity occurs, there the will intends an object. There subject and object meet and agents and their actions can be understood, because there the object is in the agent as intending. The end is a specific *hoc vel illud* (this or that thing), but it is not simply specific acts. It is specific matters about which a well-ordered will ought to be concerned.

These insights address four issues in contemporary moral theology. First, the entire discussion of objects and proximate ends occurs under the will's movement in specification which is measured as fitting to the reason, i.e., as right or wrong. Thus, the entire treatise on human acting is concerned with rightness. Does contemporary argument make the same presumption?

Certainly some contemporary authors fail to distinguish the two movements of the will (*exercitium* and specification) and continue to discuss the relationship between the will and reason without consideration for any historical development within Thomas's writings. So long as this ahistorical approach to Thomas continues, Klubertanz's earlier complaint that Lottin's discovery has gone unheeded remains valid. How many commentators, in fact, take note of this shift? Certainly, Thomas himself recognized that his treatise on the moral act occurs singularly under the will's movement *quantum ad specificationem* wherein the object gives intelligibility and species and is, in its turn, measured by its fittingness to reason. But one is hard pressed to find that recognition in the many commentaries on Thomas's moral theology, epistemology, anthropology, or natural law theory.[105]

Often even great contributors to moral debate presume that when Thomas talks of persons or intentions, he must be speaking of goodness as opposed to rightness. They, too, overlook both the centrality of the object and Thomas's decision to locate intention in the realm of specification. Louis Janssens, for example, argues that Thomas appropriated from Aristotle the insight that there are certain "actions whose very name implies wickedness." Curiously, however, Thomas raises this issue only once in an objection in which the issue is theft and never again refers to the Aristotelian category.[106]

But granting that Thomas could have determined some absolutely wrong actions, is Janssens correct in interpreting this to mean that the performance of these actions indicates not simply that the act is wrong but also that the agent is bad?

Janssens seems to presume that intending a wrong act is a sign of badness. For Thomas intending a wrong object means that the agent is already disordered, and whatever external act is realized from the wrong formal object will most probably be wrong as well. Janssens presumes that Thomas has another moral description for intention (badness) different from that which describes the external act (wrongness). But inasmuch as both are objects, both will be described as right or wrong. But whence Janssens' presumption? From Thomas? Certainly not.

Second, the insights in this chapter concern our contemporary efforts to describe the concept of object. During the last few decades, we have vigorously debated whether the object or the end gives moral species. In many cases, the proponents of the end consider the "object" to describe the external act or the choice. Janssens and Richard McCormick seem to equate the object with an external act.[107] Ironically, William May, in his campaign to demonstrate the centrality of "moral absolutes," holds a position similar to McCormick's.[108]

This debate, insofar as Thomas's writings are concerned, is unfounded. Both the end and the object give species; both the intention and the subject matter in the intention give species; both the "proximate end" and the "formal object" give species. These are not contradictory but complementary claims. The danger in the contemporary presupposition is the danger of defining the object too narrowly, that is, of equating it with clear physical or external acts. One or both sides may presume that the object fits this description, but the presumption overlooks Thomas's main concern with objects, that is, that they are first internal and formal. Thomas, unlike William May, is not primarily concerned with whether people perform lusty, treacherous, or slanderous acts. Thomas is concerned with the agents' thoughts, not with whether they are intending to commit lusty, treacherous, or slanderous acts but whether they are lusty, treacherous, or slanderous in their daily thinking. Thomas knows that people may eventually commit acts under these categories, but he is more concerned with their internal acts or thoughts and ruminations.

Third, this chapter concerns the contemporary description of the concept of an end. Thomas frames the end as the proximate one, excludes the last end from giving species, and identifies the proximate end with the formal object. The end as measured for morality is measured as the object is, not as the last end is: both pertain to the fittingness of reason. But contemporary arguments seem to suggest that the end conveys a certain degree of goodness and privacy. That presupposition of goodness involves "honest striving" or "meaning well"; it operates in phrases like "a good end does not justify a bad means."

When deontologists see the word "end" or "intention" they become fidgety and issue all sorts of reservations. Perhaps rightly so, because proportionalists sometimes use "intention" to express "goodness." Deontologists fear that the "end," unless it is well-framed or bracketed as "proximate," will fall into that receding trajectory and become thoroughly private. Such an "end" would be measured solely by the subject and not for its rightness but for its sincerity. The concept of "end" in giving species conveys a significant amount of goodness language in contemporary circles; in Thomas, it did not.[109]

Fourth, and finally, the insights in this chapter address a presupposition not held by deontologists or proportionalists; i.e., that an object, as form for an act, is only form in immanent, and not transient, operations. Immanent operations are those operations that address virtuous activity: the effect of an immanent act remains in the agent. No one seems concerned, however. Deontologists are more concerned with whether certain moral absolutes (actually, "absolute moral prohibitions") are being followed; proportionalists are more concerned with finding values that enhance the world. The writings of both schools suggest a certain transience to moral action. In the former, by acting this way one follows or breaks the order of nature or God; in the latter, by acting this way, values in the world increase or decrease. On the other hand, Thomas's objects are immanent and their first concern is not with nature or the world but with the agent. These objects first make the agent more or less right, before they make anything or anyone else more or less right.

Thus, in the famous case of Mrs. Bergmeier, who in order to gain release from a Soviet prison and return to her family, satisfies the condition for release by getting pregnant through intercourse with the jailer. In this much discussed case, deontologists analyzed the violation of a "moral absolute." Proportionalists tried to weigh values; at least one wrote that the act would be allowed "under two conditions: (1) that the absolute value of the welfare of the resultant child be protected; (2) that the absolute value of the warden's dignity not be violated."[110] Once again, this position is similar to the deontologists' position. Both are concerned about the possibility of harm to the law, the jailer, and the child. But neither side analyzes the effect this object would have on Mrs. Bergmeier herself. I think we can say, by a study of other cases, e.g., the sheriff and the lynch mob, that neither side of the debate treats the object as part of immanent activity. The object for both parties is transient. Its effect vis-à-vis the world or the law is the measure of its rightness. For Thomas, the formal object is primarily concerned with immanent operations. Therefore, as we shall shortly discover, it is precisely the formal object that gives Thomas the foundation to determine how specific actions are virtuous or vicious.

NOTES to Chapter Four

1. The following important works treat in one way or another the object or the end. Dominico Capone, *Intorno alla verità morale* (Rome: Pontificia Universitas Gregoriana, 1951). Karl Hörmann, "Die Bedeutung der konkreten Wirklichkeit für das sittliche Tun nach Thomas von Aquin," *Theologisch-praktische Quartalsschrift* 123 (1975): 118–192. Wolfgang Kluxen, *Philosophische Ethik bei Thomas von Aquin* (Hamburg: Felix Meiner Verlag, 1980). Odon Lottin, "Les Éléments de la Moralité des Actes chez Saint Thomas d'Aquin," *Revue Néo-Scolastique* (1921–22): 281–313, 389–429; (1923): 20–56. Dalmazio Mongillo, "L'elemento primario della legge naturale in s. Tommaso," *La Legge Naturale*, ed. L. Rossi (Bologna: Edizioni Dehoniane, 1970), 101–123. Brian Mullady, *The Meaning of the Term "Moral" in St. Thomas Aquinas* (Vatican City: Libreria Editrice Vaticana, 1986). Servais Pinckaers, "Autonomie et heteronomie en morale selon S. Thomas d'Aquin," *Autonomie: Dimensions éthiques de la liberté*, ed. Carolos Josaphat Pinto de Oliviera and Dietmar Mieth (Fribourg: University of Fribourg, 1978), 104–123, and "Le rôle de la fin dans l'action morale selon Saint Thomas," *Le Renouveau de la morale* (Tournai: Casterman, 1964), 114–143. Dietrich Schlüter, "Der Wille und das Gute bei Thomas von Aquin," *Freiburger Zeitschrift für Theologie und Philosophie* 8 (1971): 88–136. Franz Scholz, "Possibilità e impossibilità dell'agire indiretto," *Fede Cristiana*, ed. Klaus Demmer and Bruno Schüller (Assisi: Cittadella Editrice, 1980), 289–311. Antonin Sertillanges, *La Philosophie Morale de Saint Thomas D'Aquin* (Paris: Librairie Felix Alcan, 1922), 15–68. H. D. Simonin, "La Notion d'intention dans l'oeuvre de S. Thomas d'Aquin," *Revue des sciences philosophiques et théologiques* 19 (1930): 445–463. Gerhard Stanke, *Die Lehre von den "Quellen der Moralität"* (Regensburg: Friedrich Pustet, 1984).

2. The scholastic concept "measure" is equivalent to today's "evaluate." Because the concept appears with such regularity in the *Summa*, I will use it rather than the more accessible English term. See also Alfons Auer, "L'autonomia della morale secondo Tommaso d'Aquino," *Fede Cristiana e Agire Morale*, 32–61; Karl-Wilhelm Merks, *Theologische Grundlegung der sittlichen Autonomie* (Düsseldorf: Patmos, 1978), esp. 125–135, 163–170.

3. S.T. I.II.18.5c.: "Unicuique enim rei est bonum quod convenit ei secundum suam formam; et malum quod est ei praeter ordinem suae formae. Patet ergo quod differentia boni et mali circa obiectum considerata, comparatur per se ad rationem: scilicet secundum quod obiectum est ei conveniens vel non conveniens. . . . Unde manifestum est quod bonum et malum diversificant speciem in actibus moralibus: differentiae enim per se diversificant speciem."

4. I.II.18.5c.: "In actibus autem humanis bonum et malum dicitur per comparationem ad rationem."

5. I.II.9.1c.: ". . . uno modo, quantum ad agere et non agere; alio modo, quantum ad agere hoc vel illud."

6. I.II.12.1c: "Intentio, sicut ipsum nomen sonat, significat in aliquid tendere."

7. II.II.4.7c.: "Voluntas non fertur in aliquid nisi prout est in intellectu apprehensum."

8. I.II.27.2c. See also Joseph de Finance, *Être et Agir dans la philosophie de saint Thomas* (Paris: Beauschesne et Fils, 1945), 287–296.

9. S.T. I.82.4c.; II.II.98.1.ad3.; *De caritate* 3.ad12. See also Klaus Riesenhuber, *Die Transzendenz der Freiheit zum Guten*, 63–64.

10. See S.T. II.II.47.8.ad3.

11. II.II.4.7c.

12. I.II.12.1.ad1. and ad3.

13. I.II.19.1c.

14. I.II.19.1.ad3. See also I.II.19.3c.,ad1. and ad2.; 5c.; 10c.

15. I.II.19.2.ad1. and 1c., 2c., 3c., 5c., 7c.

16. I.II.19.3. ob1.and ad1.

17. I.II.19.3.ad2.

18. I.II.19.3.ob2. "Appetitus autem rectus est voluntas bona." See also I.94.1.ad2.: ". . . bona voluntas est ordinata voluntas."

19. On the question of the will's contents, see Wolfgang Kluxen, *Philosophische ethik bei Thomas von Aquin*, 30ff.

20. S.T. I.II.1.1c. and 3c.

21. See Herbert Kramer, *The Indirect Voluntary or Voluntarium in Causa* (Ph.D. dissertation, The Catholic University of America, 1935). Lucius Ugorji, *The Principle of Double Effect* (Frankfurt am Main: Peter Lang, 1985), 42–43.

22. S.T. I.II.74.1c., 2c., 3c. See also I.II.1.1c.; 18.6c. and 9c.

23. I.II.71.5.ad2. and 6.ad3.

24. I.II.18; 2c. and ad2; 4c.; 5c. and ad2; 6c.; 7c.; 8c. See also the Prologue to I.II.18.

25. I.II.19.1c.: "Unde voluntas bona et mala sunt actus differentes secundum speciem. Differentia autem speciei in actibus est secundum obiecta,

ut dictum est. Et ideo bonum et malum in actibus voluntatis proprie attenditur secundum obiecta."

26. I.II.19.1.ad3.

27. I.II.18.6c.; 19.1c.; 2c.; 3c.; 5c.

28. I.II.19.1.ad3.: "Bonum per rationem repraesentatur voluntati ut obiectum; et inquantum cadit sub ordine rationis, pertinet ad genus moris, et causat bonitatem moralem in actu voluntatis."

29. I.II.19.2c.: "Bonitas voluntatis ex solo uno illo dependet, quod per se facit bonitatem in actu, scilicet ex obiecto."

30. I.II.19.3c.: "Bonitas voluntatis dependet a ratione, eo modo quo dependet ab obiecto."

31. I.II.19.2.ad1.: "Unde quantum ad actum voluntatis, non differt bonitas quae est ex obiecto, a bonitate quae est ex fine."

32. I.II.1.3c. and ad3. Thomas adds that this end can be ordained to other ends, but his premise here is that: ". . . idem actus numero . . . non ordinatur nisi ad unum finem proximum, a quo habet speciem." Cf. I.II.1.5c.

33. I.II.19.1.ad2.

34. I.II.60.1.ad3.: "Moralia non habent speciem a fine ultimo, sed a finibus proximis."

35. In I.II.1.3c. Thomas presents the end as specifying for moral actions. The emphasis here is on "moral" species and though Thomas discusses the issue of specification in the article, he keeps the discussion purely formal.

36. I.77.3c.

37. I.77.3.ob1. and ad1.

38. I.II.18.2c.

39. I.II.18.6c.: "Actus interior voluntatis accepit speciem a fine, sicut a proprio obiecto."

40. I.II.18.6.ob1. and ad1.: "Etiam finis habet rationem obiecti."

41. I.II.19.2c., ob1. and ad1.

42. I.II.54.2c. and ob3.

43. I.II.54.2.ad1.: ". . . in distinctione potentiarum, vel etiam habituum, non est considerandum ipsum obiectum materialiter, sed ratio obiecti differens specie, vel etiam genere." See also I.II.18.6.ad1. In both instances, the English Dominicans translate *ratio* as "formally," obviously as a contrast to materially.

44. I.II.54.2.ad3.: "Sunt etiam ipsi fines obiecta actuum interiorum." We should note here the subtle use of the plural, another reminder that we are discussing proximate ends, not the last end, which is singular, both as the natural end and as the particular expression of it in each willing person. Cf. note 34 above.

45. I.II.60.1c. See also I.II.58.1-3; 54.2c.

46. I.II.60.1c.: "Manifestum est autem quod in moralibus ratio est sicut imperans et movens; vis autem appetitiva est sicut imperata et mota."

47. I.II.60.1.ob3.

48. I.II.60.1.ad3.: "Moralia non habent speciem a fine ultimo, sed a finibus proximis."

49. I.II.54.3c.; 63.2c.; II.II.Prologue.

50. I.II.72.1c. and ob1.

51. I.II.72.1.ad1.: ". . . finis principaliter habet rationem boni: et ideo comparatur ad actum voluntatis, qui est primordialis in omni peccato, sicut obiectum. Unde in idem redit quod peccata differant secundum obiecta, vel secundum fines."

52. Louis Janssens in "Ontic Good and Evil" (*Louvain Studies* 12 [1987]: 62–82), refers the reader to *Quodlibetum* III.27: ". . . cum actus recipiat speciem ab obiecto, non recipit speciem ab eo secundum materiam obiecti, sed secundum rationem obiecti. . . ."

53. I.14.2c.; 18.3.ad1; 23.2.ad1; 54.2c.; 56.1c; 85.2c; 105.3c and ob1; I.II.3.2.ad3; 31.5c.; 74.1c. and ad3. From Aristotle, *IX Meta* 8.1050,a23-b2. In these citations, Thomas often gives "velle" as an example of immanent operations.

54. S.T. I.II.74.1c.: ". . . tales actus sunt omnes actus morales, sive sint actus virtutum, sive peccatorum."

55. I.56.1c.: "Et ita se habet obiectum unitum potentiae ad huiusmodi actionem, sicut forma quae est principium actionis in aliis agentibus." See also I.14.2c. and 54.2c.

56. Thus, e.g., prudence, through operation, perfects itself. See I.II.57.5.ad1.

57. I.56.1c. Cf. 14.2c.; 54.2c.

58. I.II.18.2.ad2.: "Obiectum non est materia *ex qua*, sed materia *circa quam*: et habet quodammodo rationem formae, inquantum dat speciem."

59. I.II.18.2.ad3.: "Neque etiam potentiarum activarum obiecta semper habent rationem effectus, sed quando iam sunt transmutata: sicut alimentum transmutatum est effectus nutritivae potentiae, sed alimentum nondum transmutatum comparatur ad potentiam nutritivam sicut materia circa quam operatur."

60. On this *materia circa quam* giving species and form, see Klaus Riesenhuber, *Die Transzendenz der Freiheit zum Guten*, 24ff.

61. S.T. I.II.9.1c.; 18.2c.,ad2., ad3.; see also I.II.8.1c.; 12.1.ad1. and ad3.; 22.2c.; 26.2c.

62. I.II.18.2.ad2.; 18.5c.; 18.6c. and ad1.; 19.10.adsc.2; 54.2.ad1.; 57.2.ad2.; 72.1.ad3.; II.II.25.1c.

63. I.14.5.ad3; 14.6c.; 75.3.ad1; I.II.35.4c; 54.1.ad1; III.2.5c.; 6.4.ad2.; 72.4c.

64. See Klaus Riesenhuber, *Die Transzendenz der Freiheit zum Guten*, 10, 82.

65. Dominico Capone, *Intorno alla verità morale*, 28.

66. S.T. II.II.47.5c. and 11c.

67. II.II.59.2.ob1.; and ad1: "Obiectum per se et formaliter acceptum specificat habitum: non autem prout accipitur materialiter et per accidens."

68. II.II.59.2c.: "Propter defectum comparationis operationis ad proprium obiectum, quae quidem recipit speciem et nomen a per se obiecto, non autem ab obiecto per accidens. In his autem quae sunt propter finem, per se dicitur aliquid quod est intentum: per accidens autem quod est praeter intentionem."

69. Thomas held this position even before he achieved the synthesis; see DM 9.2.ad10.: "In moralibus obiectum constituit speciem, non secundum id quod est materiale in ipso, sed secundum formalem rationem obiecti." Thomas adds: "Differt autem obiectum inanis gloriae prout est veniale et mortale peccatum, secundum rationem formalem obiecti, id est secundum differentiam finis et eius quod est ad finem."

70. S.T. I.II.18.6c.; 19.2.ad1.; 34.4c.; 54.2.ad3.

71. I.II.18.7.ad2.

72. I.II.18.2.ad3.

73. II Sent.d.36.q.1a.5ad4: "Ad quartum dicendum, quod est duplex materia: ex qua, vel in qua, et materia circa quam: et primo modo materia dicta non indicit in idem cum fine, sed secundo modo est idem cum fine, quia obiectum finis actus est." See also S.T. I.II.18.2.ad2.

74. I.II.18.2.ad2. and ad3.

75. I.II.72.3.ad2.; 73.3.ad1.

76. I.II.8.1c.; I.II.18.2.ad3.

77. II.II.64.7c.: "Morales autem actus recipiunt speciem secundum id quod intenditur."

78. II.II.59.2c.; 43.3c.; 110.1c.; 186.1.sc.; and 186.2c.

79. II.II.110.1c., ad1. and ad3.

80. II.II.110.3c.

81. See I.II.75.4c. and ad1.

82. I.II.7.1c.: "Circumstantiae actuum humanorum accidentia eorum dicenda sunt." See also Giuseppe Pizzuti, "Natura, implicazioni e limiti del concetto di 'circumstania' in Tommaso d'Aquino," *L'Etica della Situazione,* ed. Pietro Piovani (Naples: Guida, 1974), 55–72; Franz Scholz, "Possibilità e impossibilità dell'agire indiretto," 292ff.

83. S.T. I.II.7.1.ad2.; and ad3.: "Accidens dicitur accidenti accidere propter convenientiam in subiecto."

84. Only remote ends are circumstances. In addition to I.II.7.3.ad3., see DM 2.7.ad8. DM 2.4.ad9 reads: "Duplex est finis: proximus et remotus. Finis proximus actus idem est quod obiectum, et ab hoc recipit speciem. Ex fine autem remoto non habet speciem; sed ordo ad talem finem est circumstantia actus."

85. In *Sententia libri Ethicorum* III.2.1111,a3-6. See also S.T. I.II.7.3c.

86. I.II.7.4c.

87. II.II.154.1c.

88. Klaus Riesenhuber, *Die Transzendenz der Freiheit zum Guten,* 117.

89. See DM 2.7.ad8.: "Similiter dicendum est de fine, quod finis proximus est idem quod obiectum, et similiter est de eo sicut et de obiecto. Finis autem remotus ponitur ut circumstantia."

90. S.T. I.II.72.6c.

91. I.II.72.3c. Thomas adds that because the object has been accepted, an end gives species to the act (ad1.).

92. I.II.22.2c.; 26.2c.

93. I.II.18.7c.: "Obiectum exterioris actus dupliciter potest se habere ad finem voluntatis: uno modo, sicut per se ordinatum ad ipsum; . . . alio modo, per accidens."

94. II.II.59.2c.

95. I.II.18.6c.: "Ita autem quod est ex parte voluntatis, se habet ut formale ad id quod est ex parte exterioris actus. . . . Et ideo actus humani species formaliter consideratur secundum finem, materialiter autem secundum obiectum exterioris actus." See also I.II.72.6c.

96. I.II.20.1.ad3.: "Omnibus modis prior."

97. See Dominico Capone, *Intorno alla verità morale*, 31–32.

98. *In Sententia libri Ethicorum* III.15.150: "Ex fine sumitur ratio eorum quae sunt ad finem."

99. S.T. I.II.73.3.ad3.: "Omnia obiecta humanorum actuum habent ordinem ad invicem."

100. I.II.13.3c. and ad2. See also Karl-Wilhelm Merks, *Theologische Grundlegung der sittlichen Autonomie*, 143.

101. S.T. I.II.75.4c.

102. From I.II.18.7. It is possible to misconstrue Thomas's use of "object" because Thomas contrasts "object" with end. But the object here is explicitly the object of the exterior act: "obiectum exterioris actus."

103. S.T. II.II.153.2c.; 3c.; 154.1c.

104. On this tension and the importance of understanding the object within the inner structure of the will, see Klaus Riesenhuber, *Die Transzendenz der Freiheit zum Guten*, 111.

105. E.g., Brian Mullady, *The Meaning of the Term "Moral" in St. Thomas Aquinas*, 60ff.; Laurence Dewan, "The Real Distinction between Intellect and Will," *Angelicum* 57 (1980): 557–593.

106. Louis Janssens, "St. Thomas and the Question of Proportionality," *Louvain Studies* 9 (1982): 40. Janssens cites S.T. II.II.66.7.ob2 and ad2.

107. See Louis Janssens, "Ontic Evil and Moral Evil"; Richard McCormick, *Notes on Moral Theology 1980 through 1984* (Lanham, Maryland: University Press of America, 1984), 166ff. See also Brian Mullady's critique of both Janssens and McCormick in *The Meaning of the Term "Moral" in St. Thomas Aquinas*, 26 and 38ff.

108. William May, "Aquinas and Janssens on the Moral Meaning of Human Acts," *The Thomist* 48 (1984): 582, 592. With certain improvements, though clearly highlighting the object as descriptive of external acts, see the same agenda in his *Moral Absolutes* (Milwaukee: Marquette University Press, 1989), 61ff.

109. Bernard Hoose comments on the confusion that surrounds this issue. He points out that sometimes the proportionalists have not been clear in considering intentions as right or wrong, but sometimes they get it right only to have the deontologists overlook the distinction (*Proportionalism: The American Debate and its European Roots*, 41–68).

110. See David Blanchfield, "Methodology and McCormick," *American Ecclesiastical Review* 68 (1974): 372–389, reviewed in Richard McCormick's *Notes on Moral Theology 1965 through 1980* (Lanham, Maryland: University Press of America, 1981), 536ff.

CHAPTER 5

The Moral Virtues

According to Thomas, we measure whether our intentions are right or wrong, i.e., whether the object we have in mind is fitting for human behavior. Contemporary language, however, treats questions of intention as questions concerning honesty or goodness, e.g., "Did you really mean well?" In Thomistic language, goodness questions concern remoter ends, even the last end, rather than the intended or proximate end. For Thomas, the question of intention is, "What did you want?" not "Why did you really do it?"

Again, according to Thomas, the object which gives moral species is the intended end. Because the object gives species as it exists in the subject matter of the intending agent, the object is the form of immanent operations. These operations are different from transient ones wherein the object passes out of the agent into something that is made. In an immanent operation, the agent is not maker, but doer. The agent's object gives form to the agent's activity, transforms the activity and, in turn, transforms the acting agent. In a manner of speaking, inasmuch as the agent cannot be distinguished from such activity, the object never really leaves the agent. An illustration of the difference between these two operations can be found in the poem, "Among School Children," in which Yeats asks "How can you tell the dancer from the dance?" The question refers to an immanent operation.

Thomas writes in the Prologue to the *Secunda secundae*: "We may reduce the whole of moral matters to the consideration of the virtues."[1] By virtue, does he mean rightness: that by virtue we are well-ordered and that our intentions and actions actually attain justice, temperance, or chastity? Or does he mean goodness: that by virtue we strive to intend and to act justly, temperately, or chastely? Or does Thomas combine goodness and rightness?

I intend to argue that the moral virtues are connected by one form, prudence, and that prudence alone, according to Thomas, establishes the virtues as "moral." Demonstrating that, I will contend that since the measure of a virtue is the measure of prudence, Thomas's description of the moral virtues singularly concerns rightness.[2]

This chapter is divided into five sections of which three are analytical, one is interpretative, and one practical. Thus, the first investigates the nature of virtue, including the distinction between the human and the infused virtues; the second develops the importance of the notion of perfection and the meaning of the word "good" in Thomas's writings; the third focuses on the virtues of prudence and justice. The fourth section critiques the notion of rightness in Thomas; the fifth and concluding section applies this material to contemporary concerns in moral theology.

THE NATURE AND KINDS OF VIRTUE

Virtue disposes through operation a matter or power to its perfection. It, therefore, perfects a power for its operation and is rightly called an "operative habit."[3] The notion of virtue stands midway between a power and an operation. In respect to operation, virtue is in a state of potentiality for its nature, like the power it perfects, is further ordained to an operation.[4] The ultimate perfection, therefore, consists neither in the matter, i.e., the power, nor in the form, i.e., the virtue, but in the end or the operation. Thus, the purpose or end of virtue is operation.[5]

Virtues make us "good" and likewise enable us to perform "good" operations (Thomas's terms).[6] These are not two distinct effects; rather, we are immediately made "good" by a "well-done" operation. Virtue, as principle of operation, perfects the power in which it adheres through the operation. In a word, as form, virtue disposes the matter or power for the power's operation, which is the end of the virtue and the power.[7]

Virtue is a nonsubsistent form and, therefore, does not have the *materia ex qua*, the matter out of which something is made. Rather, virtue resides in matter. The matter in which virtue resides is the power that "hosts" it. On occasion Thomas calls this power the material cause in a virtuous action.[8]

This power is, of course, in addition to another kind of matter: the matter through which a form has intelligibility. This *materia circa quam* belongs to the form and gives a virtue its specificity. Thus, the virtue's intelligibility is the matter about which a virtue is concerned.

There are three matters here. The first is the matter of a transient act as in art whose matter is external *materia ex qua*. The second is the matter or material cause of an immanent operation, i.e., the agent or the agent's power. The third is the matter as in subject matter or as in a form's very intelligibility: "The matter about which a virtue is concerned is its object and . . . [this object] fixes the virtue to a certain species.[9]

Distinguishing these three matters makes accessible the following central statement: "The object is not the matter of which, but the matter about which; and [the object] stands in relation to act as its form, as it were, through giving it its species."[10] Thus, an operation receives its species from the form, which is the proper object.[11] This object, or the specific form, provides the intelligibility through its *materia circa quam*. From this *materia* or object the operation is understood.[12]

Thomas writes in the Prologue to the *Secunda secundae* that, vices and sins, like virtues, are also different from one another according to their matter or object. Thomas adds, "Now the matter about which a virtue does right, and the opposite vice deviates from the right, is the same. Accordingly we may reduce the whole of moral matters to the consideration of the virtues."[13] Thomas gives examples of these matters in *De virtutibus cardinalibus*: the "needs of this life" for justice; "sexual pleasure" for temperance; "uncertainty" for prudence; and "danger" for fortitude.[14]

These various matters about which virtue is concerned specify the distinct virtues. They also provide a context, a measurability, to determine whether the matter is a virtue or a vice, a difference found by measuring whether the matter is or is not fitting to reason. Measuring the matter of a virtue and its opposite vice is the function of prudence. Prudence distinguishes the matter of justice from injustice. It does so, by appointing the mean, for the mean in "the needs of this life" is just, and the mean in matters of danger is bravery. In giving the mean, prudence gives the matter its form and makes the *materia circa quam* a "moral" virtue.

In the *Prima secundae*, Thomas distinguishes the acquired from the infused virtues, a distinction that requires a radical change in Augustine's definition of virtue as "a good quality of the mind, by which we live righteously, of which no one can make bad use, which God works in us without us." On the suitability of this definition Thomas notes the restrictiveness of the phrase: "which God works in us without us." He writes, "If we omit this phrase, the remainder of this definition will apply to all virtues in general, whether acquired or infused."[15] Thomas, therefore, explicitly rejects Augustine's assumption that all virtues are the work of God and distinguishes the human from the "superhuman" virtues.[16]

Since the superhuman virtues are above the human, the end that they attain differs from the end of human virtue. Human virtues attain a level of happiness that is imperfect, while the perfect happiness of the theological virtues is a participation in the Godhead. The end of each of the virtues is different, because the end of a human virtue is a proximate end, while the end of a theological virtue is always the last end.[17]

The end to which the human virtues direct us is attainable through human nature, but the last end is only attained by charity. Charity is the principle of all good works directed to our last end. Only with charity can our acts be "good" (Thomas's term) in the sense of being directed to God.[18] But we can have the acquired virtues without having charity, and, in fact, having the acquired or human virtues neither determines nor is determined by whether or not one also has charity.[19] Likewise, being in the state of grace or of mortal sin has no bearing on the acquired virtues; such conditions affect only those virtues that concern the last end, the theological virtues.[20]

The distinct ends of the theological and the human virtues mean, therefore, a difference of objects. Since habits are specifically distinct by the formal difference of their objects, the theological virtues differ from the human virtues in that the object of the theological virtues is God, while the object of the intellectual and moral virtues is "something comprehensible to human reason."[21]

The good or the perfection to which the human virtues are directed is defined according to the rule of reason, from which the objects are derived. The good or the perfection to which the theological and infused virtues are directed is the good as defined by divine law.[22] Thus, moral and intellectual virtues are produced in us by humanly reasoned acts, while the theological virtues, being beyond our capabilities, are produced in us by God. Not surprisingly, then, Thomas explicitly distinguishes the righteousness of virtue which pertains to the actions of life from the righteousness pertaining to the essence of the soul.[23]

The moral virtues have, therefore, the same context as their objects, as we saw in the previous chapter. First, the end that specifies virtues as moral is not the last end. Second, these virtues have objects presented by reason, comprehensible to reason, and measured by reason. Finally, these objects themselves give the virtues their species. Thus, the context of moral virtues as distinct from theological virtues excludes Thomas's concepts of the last end and charity and our concept of moral goodness.

This claim reveals the similarities between the intellectual and moral virtues. Just as their formal objects are the same, so also are their effects; both perfect us through the doing of "good" deeds. What distinguishes them is only the matter in us to be perfected. That which perfects the intellect is an intellectual virtue; that which perfects the appetite is a moral one.[24]

In summary, by human virtue "we live a good life." By infused virtue we live a "good life." But the "good life" in the former refers only to the "rectitude of life measured by the rule of reason."[25] The "good life" achieved by the moral virtues is the life of a rightly ordered person. Thomas himself provides us with a summary when he writes that by the theological virtues the mind is united to God; by the intellectual virtues reason itself is perfected, and by the moral virtues the appetite itself is perfected.[26] The "good life" of the infused virtues includes union with God; the "good life" of the human virtues signifies the attainment of a perfection.

THE IMPORTANCE OF PERFECTION AND
THE MEANING OF THE GOOD

Thomas attributes perfection to the human virtues, union to the infused or theological virtues. We will return to union and the virtue of charity in the next chapter, but first we must consider the importance of perfection and the meaning of the word "good" as they appear in Thomas's writings on the moral virtues.

Virtue is an operative habit. As a habit, virtue does something: it perfects a power for its operation. Thomas uses this assertion frequently and in various forms: virtue perfects the matter, the power, the intellect, the appetite, the person, the passions, and the soul.[27] Virtue as form perfects the power in which it resides, while power is the matter or subject that virtue perfects.

Thus, virtue perfects the person, making the agent good and the operations also good.[28] But what does it mean to say that the agent is good? The answer is simple: the good is the perfect. Admittedly, the good perfects, but the good perfects because it is perfect.[29]

The identity of the good with the perfect is continuous throughout Thomas's writings. In his *Commentary on the Sentences*, Thomas writes "goodness pertains to the communication of perfection."[30] In *De veritate* he tells us quite simply: "The relation implied in the word good is the status of that which perfects."[31] In the *Summa contra gentiles*, Thomas writes that the good for each thing is its action and perfection.[32] And, in the *Compendium of Theology*, he says that the "perfect signifies what is good, since the perfection of anything is its goodness."[33] Later in the same work he writes: "the term good signifies perfect being."[34] The good finds its definition in the perfect.[35] This identity becomes even more evident in *De malo*, a Roman work contemporary with the beginning of the *Summa theologiae*. Here, Thomas proposes three uses of "good" and each is a "perfection." Clearly, therefore, "the perfection of a thing is called good."[36]

That the notion of good is derived from the notion of the perfect is nowhere more clearly stated than at the beginning of the *Summa theologiae*. Notably, the discussion of God's goodness (question six) follows the discussion of God's perfection (question four). The bridge between these concepts (question five) is Thomas's discussion of goodness in relation to perfection.

Using the notion of the appetible, Thomas argues that the good is the appetible because the appetible is the thing's perfection.[37] Later in the same question he states that the good is that which all things seek, but that overly cited phrase derives its meaning from the earlier one, i.e., that the perfect is that which all things seek. Thus, even before the question of God's goodness, Thomas has established that something is called good insofar as it is perfect.

Thomas responds to the question whether essential goodness belongs to God alone, by stating: "God alone is good in essence." But to make this argument, he immediately returns to the previous question and argues that something is called good insofar as it is perfect. Thomas argues that perfection is threefold and that no created thing by its own essence is perfect in all three aspects. Thus, perfection belongs to God only, and God as this perfection is also the last end.[38]

Goodness is, then, the completion or fulfillment of some entity, i.e., its perfection, or, as Thomas calls it, its good. Should a being lack something that it ought to have, it would be imperfect. But God is good, for God is at once the perfection and fulfillment of God's self and all being. God is. Nothing about God waits for completion. God is the perfection of all perfections. In God is neither lack nor potency.

The "perfect" is, therefore, much like our term "right." The attainment of the due is what we call right. Conversely, in negative terms, failure to attain the due is what we call wrong. Thomas calls this attainment "good," but his meaning does not differ from our use of the word "right." Something is "good" (Thomas's term) or "right" (our term) because it is perfect.

In the eighteenth question of the *Prima secundae*, when Thomas introduces the fourfold goodness of a human action, the first goodness is of the genus, i.e., of the act itself. Insofar as an act is the end of potency, an act is a certain perfection. Thus, "being" itself is "good" (Thomas's term) or "right" (our term) because it is in act: it is what a potency should become.[39]

Thomas's fourfold goodness really concerns a fourfold perfection. The more fulfilling the act is, the better it is or, as we would say, the more right. The entire meaning of good in Thomas's writing turns on the notion of perfection. Similarly, our notion of right depends on the same concept. Virtues make us "good" (Thomas's term) or "right" (our term) because they perfect us.

Granted that they are "good making" because they perfect, since our perfection is twofold, we appear to be using the word good in two different ways. The first is that which our own natural human powers can attain. The second is that which is above our human powers.[40] The difference in the two perfections is the difference of the ends attainable by natural capacities, for naturally speaking, the second perfection is unattainable.

The perfection of the theological virtues is perfection essentially, whereas the perfection which applies to us as morally virtuous is perfection in an analogous sense.[41] This analogous understanding of perfection helps us to understand what Thomas means by describing the difference between the two as actually between the perfect and the imperfect. Thomas does not suggest some type of continuity between the perfect and imperfect. The former is not simple fulfillment of the latter, nor is the latter a stage toward the acquisition of the former. In the perfect (i.e., the theological virtues) we attain the true notion of happiness, but in the imperfect, i.e., the acquired virtues, we do not attain perfect happiness, but a "particular likeness of happiness."[42] Perfect happiness is attained through charity.

In the perfect happiness our minds will be united to God. That phrase, *mens hominis Deo coniungetur*, occurs frequently at the beginning of the *Prima secundae*.[43] Our perfect happiness consists not in that which perfects the intellect by some participation, but in that which is so by its essence.[44] Our happiness rests in perfection through an essential union with God.

Thomas calls the perfection through union, a union attained by the theological virtues, the essential perfection. There only are we perfect, insofar as we attain our proper last end. But perfection through union is accomplished through charity. Only through charity are we united to God, who is the last end of the human mind.[45] By charity we attain perfection, or the last end. Without charity, we do not.

The notion of perfection as applied to the theological virtues is distinct from the notion of perfection in the human virtues. The threshold separating the two perfections is the fact that union with God requires charity; the perfection of the moral virtues does not. The perfection found in union with God excludes amoral and immoral motivation precisely because it requires charity. But the perfection based on the moral virtues is a perfection that we can attain whether our motives are love or self-interest. The perfection without union is the completion attained by reason.

Prescinding from the issue of grace, we can have neither, either, or both perfections. We can have charity without the acquired virtues, and we can have the acquired virtues without charity. Thus, just as these perfections differ, so, too, do the uses of the word "good." The word "good" as used to describe the perfection of reason or appetite is measured by reason itself. The word "good" as used for the perfection through union with God is measured by charity. There are two measurements for the word "good," because there are two distinct perfections. Thomas himself provides the summary:

> According to the Philosopher, "the virtue of a thing is that which makes its subject good and its work good likewise." Consequently, wherever we find a good human act, it must correspond to a good human virtue. Now in all things measured and ruled, the good is that which attains its proper rule. . . . But, human acts have a twofold measure; one is proximate and homogenous, viz., the reason, while the other is remote and excelling, viz., God: wherefore every human act is good, which attains reason or God.[46]

The good of the acquired virtues attains the rule of reason; the good of the theological virtues attains the rule of charity. We must avoid the temptation to think that the latter good is somehow an extension of, or at least dependent on, the former. Rather, the two measures or rules are distinct, and the exterior acts of charity "must be measured both according to charity and according to reason."[47] All our actions can be measured as being perfect according to reason or perfect according to charity. The former concerns whether the action is right; the latter, whether the action expresses the agent's love or goodness.

Thomas's description of the good (perfection) of the acquired virtues does not differ from our understanding of the rightly ordered self. Identifying Thomas's good with our right is based on three grounds: the good is measured as attaining the rule of reason; the good of the moral virtues is applicable to bad persons or sinners; and the moral virtues can be called good without reference to charity. Moreover, the fact that the word "good" applies equally to intellectual and moral virtues provides further indication that it is closer to our concept of moral rightness than to our concept of moral goodness. The acquired virtues differ only in the matter, the intellect or appetite, that they make good or perfect. The perfection attained by reason through the moral and intellectual virtues Thomas calls good because through them we attain what we and our powers should become. The only perfection that the moral virtues require and attain then is a rightly ordered self.[48]

PRUDENCE AND JUSTICE

Among the intellectual and moral virtues, prudence stands in a category by itself.[49] First, the intellectual and moral virtues are distinguished by their subjects. The subject of the moral virtues is the appetite: justice is in the will; temperance and fortitude, in the concupiscible and irascible powers. As an intellectual virtue, prudence is in reason. Second, as the habit of an immanent operation, an acquired virtue perfects the subject in which it dwells as its matter. Thus, while a moral virtue perfects the appetite, an intellectual virtue perfects reason; therefore, prudence perfects reason. Third, though both the matter as subject and the matter as perfected by prudence are the same in prudence as in the other intellectual virtues, the "material difference of objects" distinguishes prudence from the others.[50] Prudence has the same object or matter about which the moral virtues are concerned.

The object of justice is life's needs, the object of bravery is daily danger, but the matter about which prudence is concerned is things to be done, i.e., the object of prudence is all immanent operations.[51] Since prudence's object concerns all immanent operations, it needs the specific moral virtues to provide the context for its activity. For this reason, prudence is the only intellectual virtue requiring the moral virtues. In other words, as all immanent operations are its object, prudence always engages the same objects as the moral virtues.

Just as prudence requires the moral virtues, the moral virtues require prudence. The mutual dependency between the moral virtues and prudence occasions Thomas's affirmation that prudence and the moral virtues are interconnected. Without prudence, this interconnection could not be posited and the three moral "virtues" would be "habits," i.e., "natural inclinations" lacking "the complete character of virtue."[52] In themselves, these habits are only inclinations. Acting through prudence, however, reason directs and forms these inclinations into the moral virtues.[53]

Without prudence, the moral virtues are not virtues but habits. The same cannot be said of charity, for without charity, though they would not be perfect in attaining the last end, they would still be virtues. Because the acquired virtues may be considered as perfections of the human natural powers, they can exist as Thomas notes independently of whether a person is wicked or good or in mortal sin. In addition, the virtues are defined without Augustine's limiting phrase that "God works within us without us," an omission compatible with the acquired virtues, but not compatible with charity. Finally, the good of virtue can be measured by its attainment, albeit imperfect, of the rule of reason, but this measurement is explicitly distinct from charity as the perfect measurement of virtue.[54] In themselves, therefore, the moral virtues are interconnected by some form other than charity.[55]

That the moral virtues and prudence can exist as virtues without charity stands in sharp contrast to the impossibility of any of the four virtues existing without the others. The interconnection of the moral virtues with prudence is their constitutive element because through it they participate in reason and, therefore, receive the title "virtue."[56] Without prudence, the moral virtues are merely "habits" or "inclinations."

The centrality of prudence in establishing the interconnection of the virtues is often underlined by Thomas in texts that parallel prudence to charity. Through prudence, "the moral virtues are united together" just as the gifts of the Holy Spirit are connected through charity.[57] In a word, "the connection among moral virtues results from prudence, and as to the infused virtues, from charity."[58] The moral virtues are interconnected through prudence.

It is not surprising that Thomas also refers to form in describing prudence's relationship to the moral virtues. Prudence unites the virtues because in defining the mean for each moral virtue it stands as "that which is formal in all the moral virtues."[59] If prudence stands as form to these virtues, then these virtues stand as matter to prudence. Thomas writes that the matter of the moral virtues relates the virtues to one another and that the "whole matter of moral virtues falls under the one rule of prudence."[60]

Concerning matter and form in virtue, Thomas argues that the formal aspect of the object is from reason and fixes the mean, while the material element is the power of the specified moral virtue. Moral virtue derives its goodness (Thomas's term) not from the matter, which consists of passions and operation, but from its formal element. Each habit has its own matter; the form, however, is derived from prudence, since in all human virtues the formal element is derived from the order of reason.[61] Each habit is specified by its own matter, e.g., justice by operations, fortitude by passions, but each is a virtue by prudence.[62]

Admittedly, Thomas writes that to be well-disposed to the end depends on the rectitude of the appetite, and similarly, that the truth of the practical intellect depends on its conformity to the right appetite. These affirmations do not, however, establish any precedence of the moral virtues over prudence.[63] Rather, Thomas consistently maintains that the desire of the appropriate end arises from the right apprehension of the end.[64]

Thomas writes that prudence not only directs the moral virtues in their choice of the means but also appoints the end, which in all moral virtues is the mean to be attained.[65] Later, Thomas modifies this by stating that *synderesis* (the base of practical reason), not prudence, appoints the end, but he adds that the moral virtues do not appoint the end. Furthermore, the end appointed by *synderesis* is not the proximate end that specifies a moral virtue, but the first principle, to do good and avoid evil. Thus, though *synderesis* appoints the general end of moral virtue, yet the moral virtues cannot tend to that end abstractly. Rather, they still need specific objects toward which to tend. They need prudence to "prepare the way," to present the right objects to the moral virtues. In this later modification, Thomas diminishes the role of prudence in relation to *synderesis*, but not in relation to the moral virtues. He concludes that prudence, because of its priority, is more excellent than the moral virtues.[66]

In presenting right objects to the virtues, prudence appoints the mean to moral virtues.[67] In the moral virtues the mean has the character of a rule and measure.[68] In order to attain its proper perfection or its end, a moral virtue must attain the rule of reason.[69] Thus, the rectification attained in justice occurs through attaining the mean. Thomas writes that through the moral virtues "we live a good life," namely, "the rectitude of life which is measured by the rule of reason."[70] The moral virtues derive their goodness by the attainment of this rule which is the attainment of the mean. The inclinations or moral virtues are, in fact, measured and ruled by this mean, insofar as they attain it. Prudence, on the other hand, is that measure and rule.[71]

Prudence in giving the mean stands as the formal element to the moral virtues, and the matter of all the moral virtues falls under its rule.[72] Without prudence, the habits would only be habits or inclinations, and, in fact, would not be virtues at all.[73] Prudence is the sine qua non for moral virtues.

Moreover, the very concept of "virtue" is derived precisely from prudence, because it appoints the mean, which is the rule and measure of moral virtues, their end.[74] The "rectitude of life" is measured as virtuous by this rule, because from this rule the moral virtues derive their "goodness." Insofar as prudence in appointing that mean is that measure and rule, prudence plays an essential role in the formation of habits as moral virtues.[75]

Finally, the moral virtues per se can exist without charity, not as perfect virtues but as virtues that are measured by a rule explicitly distinct from charity. As pertaining to a category distinct from the infused virtues, prudence parallels charity: they constitute the human and infused virtues respectively through unifying them.[76]

Therefore, though Thomas calls charity the form of the virtues, we should not overlook the relation of prudence to the moral virtues, which is the relation of the formal to the material. In the context of the acquired virtues per se, prudence alone has "goodness" (Thomas's term) or "rightness" (our term) essentially, while the other three have "goodness" (Thomas's term) or "rightness" (our term) only through prudence.[77] Prudence makes the habits virtues and in thus perfecting them makes them "good." We conclude, then, as Thomas did, that a moral virtue is a "habit of choosing the mean appointed by reason as a prudent man would appoint it."[78]

Yet, prudence needs the inclinations of justice, temperance, and fortitude as given matter already existing within the person. These inclinations are pre-existing; they exist inchoatively in the person, tending through the natural reason or synderesis toward the last end of moral virtues, which is to do good and avoid evil.[79] They cannot, however, move toward any proximate end, any right *hoc vel illud*, without prudence.

Prudence, on the other hand, does not pre-exist in us. Prudence is acquired by the exercise of right reason in the matters of the three moral virtues. Prudence needs matter, but the matter which it perfects is a matter already directed "athematically" by the first principle to its last end. As a form received into matter, prudence orders, directs, and moves the moral virtues. Insofar as prudence does this, it moves in the same way as a command does, as an ordered act of the reason.[80] To the simple tendencies of the various habits, prudence gives the order which constitutes them as moral virtues. For the moral virtues are not good by their material element, which as dispositions exist in each person in different ways according to different aptitudes, but by the formal element itself which is prudence. The principle of virtue is the good as defined by reason; the principle of moral virtue is the good as defined by prudence.

Among the virtues, a hierarchy exists. For instance, an intellectual virtue is greater or better than a moral virtue.[81] But the specific priority of prudence over the other virtues is manifold. First, according to principles, prudence puts order into the acts of reason, while justice puts order into the operations of external acts, and fortitude and temperance prevent the withdrawal or thwarting of reason.[82] Second, since the cause of human good or perfection is reason, the virtue nearest to the cause is more excellent than the others. Third, the virtues perfect the subjects in which they are found, and these subjects have their hierarchy: reason is higher than the will, which itself is higher than the concupiscible and irascible powers. Therefore, prudence, being in reason, is more excellent than the moral virtues.[83] Fourth, prudence is essentially good, whereas the moral virtues, by participation in prudence are good by what they effect. In itself and in relation to its subject, prudence supercedes the other virtues called moral.[84] Prudence simply is the principal of all the human cardinal virtues.

Prudence is the essential "goodness" of the moral virtues, the form that perfects or makes right the matter of the moral virtues. That essential "goodness" (Thomas's term) is "rightness" (our term). The moral virtues, by deriving their actual "goodness" (Thomas's term) from prudence, remain completely within the ambit of rightness in all of Thomas's discussions of the virtues as they are in themselves. The contemporary description of "goodness" as we understand it is not considered in these writings.

Though prudence is the essential goodness, justice is the chief of the moral virtues. Its matter is "our intercourse with others."[85] Justice is strictly concerned with rectifying operations or external acts, whereas the other two moral virtues rectify the subject's passions. The virtue of fortitude and temperance rectify (*sufficienter rectificantur*) our dealings with ourselves; justice rectifies our dealings with others.[86] Thus, the essential matters of justice are external operations or affairs, not passions. In fact, Thomas asserts that if the due measure of the external act is destroyed, justice is destroyed. In a word, justice is doing things right.[87]

Thomas writes: "since the good of the worker consists in the work, this fact also, that virtue makes the worker good, is referred to the work, and consequently to the power."[88] Just as an act is made good through attaining the rule whereby human acts are regulated, and just as it is through the matter of the passions that we are rectified in ourselves, through justice our operations are made good.[89] We, in turn, are called "good" (Thomas's term) through justice, because it is only through right or just operations that our wills are rectified.

The attainment of the rule by which actions are called just simply depends on prudence. Justice as a natural inclination to observe the due measure among persons cannot attain the rule of reason except as it is moved and directed by prudence, which provides the mean and is itself the form, rule, and measure of justice.

Contemporary notions of justice suggest that we are just when we want to be just, or when we love justice, or when we desire to be just and to act justly. In the *Summa*, however, concepts of desiring, wanting, or loving justice are conspicuously absent. There is no mention of a primary *exercitium* wherein we could be just or good (our term) either by seeking justice, by moving ourselves toward the prudent mean, or by moving reason toward finding the prudent mean. In the *Summa*, we are just when we act and live justly. We are just when we have attained just lives.

Thomas's overall presentation of justice concerns the rectification of our dealings with others and the consequent rectification of our wills. Simply put, the moral virtues concern attainment, not striving. They concern only the question of rightly ordered acts and rightly ordered lives; the question of goodness in the contemporary sense is not raised in this context. In the ambit of Thomas's discussion on the moral virtues, his goodness always means our rightness.

INTERPRETING THE DATA: THE NOTION OF RIGHTNESS

I had expected Thomas to present the virtues as expressions of moral goodness. I had expected them to be like primary *exercitia*, that is, like a just will moving the reason to find a prudent mean, or a temperate will to do the same. But I found no such position in the *Summa*. On some occasions, there seemed to be an exception, as when Thomas states that prudence needs the moral virtues and that through them, we are rightly disposed to the end.[90] But when Thomas compares the moral virtues and prudence he argues that prudence is simply better and that the moral virtues are "merely" more excellent "relatively" in moving the powers to act.[91] Thomas could have asserted this movement of the moral virtues as a distinct goodness, as a first *exercitium*. Instead, this movement is no more than Avicenna's *exercitium*, that is, a secondary one, not motivation but a habitual exercise leading to the attainment of the mean. The role of the moral virtues is nothing more than to be steps on the way to the perfection of prudence. The moral virtues are part of an order wherein matter precedes form and the imperfect precedes the perfect.

On another occasion Thomas asks whether when we perform an unjust act, we ought always be called unjust. Since an act cannot destroy the habit of a moral virtue, the question refers not to whether the habit is destroyed by acting unjustly, but whether the description, "I am at this moment unjust through doing an unjust act" is always true. Thomas answers that if we act in unintended ignorance, the act, though unjust materially, cannot be called an unjust operation, because the direct object of an unjust operation is lacking.[92]

Thomas has evaded the question. We have done a deliberate and intended act that is unjust but we have not intended the act as unjust. The act's formal and "unjust" object has been "accepted," but only from ignorance. But what actually was intended? To intend an unjust act is not the same as to intend an act as unjust. The former concerns wrongness; the latter concerns badness. Had Thomas used his own distinction, he might have said, "Yes, when we intend unjust actions our intention, like our action, is unjust. Thus, both are wrong." Instead, Thomas states effectively that when we intend an unjust act as unjust, we are bad; otherwise, we are not. Thomas does not answer the question "Are we unjust, i.e., wrong, when we intend an unjust object?" Thomas asked a question about wrongness, but answered a question about badness.

Consider the following scenario: we think that all men are inferior to women. Let us presume that we are always unselfish in following this fundamental principle. We would always have a wrong intention in our thoughts about men and women because the direct and formal object of our intention is that men and women should not be treated equally. That object or intention is wrong, and all the acts so intended are wrong. But we are not intending this object as wrong or unjust. As a matter of fact, we are intending these acts precisely because we hold the object (inequality) as right and fair. Thus, according to our distinction we are good because our motivation is good, though the object or intention of our acts is false or wrong.

Thomas does not come to the same conclusion. Thomas's formal object, the unjust object, remains in us, but the culpability for that intention is removed by ignorance. Ignorance as an excuse suggests that our intention was not our motivation: the formal object as unjust was not assumed as such by us. Thomas implicitly distinguishes intention from motivation.

This position is not unlike Thomas's position on the erroneous conscience.[93] Here Thomas argues that failure to obey our conscience is always evil, but obedience to an erroneous conscience excuses us from the consequently erroneous act.[94] Thus, according to Thomas, we are not bad.

Thomas appears in these instances to appreciate the fact that our wrong intentions or wrong consciences do not make us bad. He remedies both cases by an appeal to ignorance excusing. But we should also note that Thomas never asserts that we are good when we follow an erroneous conscience.[95] He does not suggest in such cases that our acts followed from goodness. Thomas could have said that we exercised our conscience, that is, that we sought to find the right. Instead, he posits that we acted out of ignorance. The order of precedence is important for Thomas: for ignorance to excuse, ignorance must precede the intention.[96] But does anything else precede the intention? Is it only out of ignorance that we intend? As Thomas has no concept of motivation, all that is antecedent to intention is ignorance. What, however, of the will's self-movement and movement of the reason? Was there not a primary *exercitium*? And did it not precede the mistaken object? Was there not an acting out of conscience that first prompted our willingness to adhere to the decision of conscience? Thomas had this concept of the primary *exercitium* available, but he did not use it.

Except in the theological virtues, Thomas has no description for goodness other than perfection through the attainment of the rule of reason. Since in the above two cases we do not attain the perfect, the word good (Thomas's term) would not be appropriate. The issue is not whether the action is perfect or good, for it is not. In one case, an unjust act is performed; in the other, an erroneous conscience has been followed. The issue is culpability, however, and Thomas excuses us from culpability in both cases. But the grounds for excusing from blame should raise the further question, namely, whether there are also grounds for praising.

In both cases, we are striving to attain right action. Though the action is wrong, we are "good" (our term). But, given that Thomas already judges the act as not good, he is unable to see that we deserve praise. Rather, he only judges that we do not deserve blame, because ignorance excuses. Lacking a proper definition of goodness (in our sense), Thomas refrains from asserting goodness. By his singular definition of the good as the attainment of perfection, Thomas excludes the possibility of entertaining this distinction.

Curiously, on one occasion, in the *Secunda secundae*, Thomas mentions false prudence. On seeing the category, I wondered if there was something antecedent to prudence itself that causes prudence to be false. With thorough consistency, however, Thomas knows of no moral concept that precedes prudence. Rather, he argues that false prudence results from taking counsel not for the whole of life, but for a particular end only. But why would we fail to consider the whole? Thomas does not entertain that question; instead he discusses the need for a rightly ordered appetite. Nothing in this article suggests any description of moral self-movement antecedent to the quest for prudence.[97]

Thomas, subsequently, raises other questions analogous to false prudence, e.g., in question fifty-one, "Of the virtues which are connected with prudence," and question fifty-five, "Of the vices opposed to prudence by way of resemblance." Again, Thomas never discusses a movement antecedent to prudence. Instead, he focuses the argument on the failure to consider prudently the entire scope of life. Do we fail to consider because we lack ability or because we fail to strive? Thomas gives us no answer, because he does not raise the question. Ironically, when Thomas has the opportunity to discuss the possibility of badness as a cause of false prudence, he does not do it. He merely asserts the wrongness of false prudence. The topic of motivation is never raised.

Thomas is surely correct in holding that the descriptions of the moral virtues concern whether our will and appetites are rectified. The virtues describe us as rightly ordered or not, but the attainment of being rightly ordered in the moral virtues is not a description of moral goodness. The description of moral goodness must include the notion of why we strive for such an attainment. Preceding the question of whether the will is rightly ordered comes the question of moral goodness: why does the will want to be rightly ordered? This question pertains to the moral aspect of the primary *exercitium*, that asks why the will moves reason? This question is not in Thomas's writings concerning the act or the moral virtues per se, yet it is the only question that concerns goodness. All other questions pertain, as the material in the last two chapters demonstrates, to rightness.

The discussion of human virtues is a description of reason perfecting the human, in which we are described not as good in essence but as good in reason.[98] The object of the will vis-à-vis the moral virtues is the good of reason. The statement that Thomas writes shortly before the ninth question of the *Prima secundae* is operative throughout Thomas's writings on the act and the moral virtues: "the good will is a well-ordered will."[99] Indeed, the statement is repeated in the *Prima secundae*: "The right appetite is the good will."[100] Inasmuch as "good" (Thomas's term) means "right" (our term and Thomas's), we have a simple definition of rightness: that which is well-ordered, but we do not have a definition of a good will in our sense of the phrase.[101]

Thomas himself offers us a conclusion. The essence of the virtues formed by prudence is simply rightness: "The essence of human virtue consists in safeguarding the good of reason in human affairs for this is man's proper good."[102]

CONTEMPORARY APPLICATIONS OF THOMAS'S MORAL REASONING

The importance of Thomas's position for contemporary moral theology may not be immediately evident. We tend to think of goodness and rightness in terms of good people and right acts. But Thomas's primary question for rightness is not about acting, but about thinking. Thomas places the locus of moral rightness in the intended or formal object, and by so doing prompts us to enlarge our understanding of moral reasoning.

Familiar with the contemporary uses of virtue language, we naturally associate that language with the language of goodness. Morally good people are virtuous people, we think. But Thomas's presuppositions are different and incline him to hold that the rightly ordered are the virtuous. The contemporary presupposition would make love or charity the form of the virtuous life. Thomas's presuppositions make prudence that form.

Inasmuch as contemporary thought identifies charity or goodness with the form of the virtues, it is not surprising that the role of the virtues themselves is secondary. Today, a virtuous person is one whose will is well disposed to find and follow guidelines of moral rightness. It is a commonplace to say that virtues provide the good moral character from which to execute right moral norms. In this model, the virtues do not provide the right guidelines or insight, but the good will. Good character is what we need to execute the right insight resulting from deontological, proportionalist, or consequential reasoning.

If, on the other hand, we identify prudence with the form of the virtues, then the virtues themselves will provide the guidelines to direct human or moral right action. The virtues are not simply formal exhortation or parenesis; they bear content and are, in fact, the context for moral reasoning. This form of moral reasoning is certainly different from post-Enlightenment forms of moral reasoning with their prescriptions and prohibitions; it is, after all, Thomas's own form of moral reasoning.

Furthermore, Thomas's entire agenda in the treatise on human action can now be seen as a prelude for his treatise on the virtues. Both concern rightness, and the importance of establishing the object as it is in the intention as the locus of moral reasoning is made clear when we understand that the right formal object is the virtuous or prudential object.

Thus, this study proposes, vis-à-vis the contemporary discussion about the virtues, an important shift in understanding how the virtues make the agent "good" and one's actions likewise. No longer can we presume (if we follow Thomas) that somehow the virtues make us good, loving, or holy people. Rather they make us rightly ordered, so that we may reason and act well in the practical order.

This shift prompts us, therefore, to renew our examination of the virtues as offering direction and guidelines. The virtues communicate right living to us. In and of itself, a virtue can give direction for what constitutes right action. This type of moral reasoning has appeared only in recent years. Thus, in her *Personal Commitments: Beginning, Keeping, Changing*, Margaret Farley finds guidelines for moral rightness in fidelity. In *Moral Theology: Dead Ends and Alternatives*, Antonio Moser and Bernardino Leers turn to the four cardinal virtues, humility, and patience for guides to right living in the context of liberation theology. Paul Wadell offers the guidance of friendship in his *Friendship and the Moral Life*; Jean Porter's article highlights courage and temperance; and Anne Patrick's theme is justice.[103] Even in a practical area like medical ethics, many authors, e.g., Leon Kass, Syndey Callahan, and Patricia Jung have turned to the virtues for moral direction.[104] Over the past five years, these authors have used the virtues in a new way, not as exhortations to be good, but as directions for living rightly. The present work contributes to those efforts by explicating the difference between goodness and rightness and by demonstrating that the best of the Christian tradition (as represented by Thomas) argues likewise. Further, Thomas's other positions on the intention, the object, and the distinction between *exercitium* and specification provide us with a vast and comprehensive program for moral reasoning in the context of the virtues. Indeed, the virtues as rightness are a context for developing a personal yet objective ethics.

NOTES to Chapter Five

1. On the meaning of the moral virtues in Thomas, see in particular, Guiseppe Abbà, *Lex et Vertus* (Las-Roma: Biblioteca di Scienze Religiose 56 [1983]). Josef Endres, "Anteil der Klugheit am Erkennen des konkreten Wahren und an dem Wollen des wahrhaft Guten," *Studia Moralia* 1 (1963): 221–153, and *Menschliche Grundhaltungen* (Salzburg: Otto Müller Verlag, 1958). Anthony Falanga, *Charity the Form of the Virtues according to Saint Thomas* (Washington, D.C.: Catholic University Press, 1948). Gerard Gilleman, *The Primacy of Charity in Moral Theology* (Westminster: Newman Press, 1959). Etienne Gilson, *The Christian Philosophy of St. Thomas Aquinas* (London: Gollancz Ltd., 1957). John Harvey, "The Nature of the Infused Moral Virtues," *Catholic Theological Society of America* 10 (1955): 172–221. George Klubertanz, "Ethics and Theology," *The Modern Schoolman* 27 (1949): 29–39; and "Une theorie sur les vertus morales 'naturelles' et 'surnaturelles,'" *Revue Thomiste* 59 (1959): 565–575. John Langan, "Augustine on the Unity and the Interconnection of the Virtues," *Harvard Theological Review* 72 (1979): 81–95. Odon Lottin, *Psychologie et morale aux XIIe et XIIIe siècles*, 3:99–535; 4:551–663. Paul Merken, "The Transformations of the

Ethics of Aristotle in the Moral Philosophy of Thomas Aquinas," *Atti del Congresso Internazionale* 5 (Naples: Edizioni Domenicane Italiane, 1974), 151–164. Dietmar Mieth, *Die neuen Tugenden* (Düsseldorf: Patmos, 1984), 11–59. Josef Pieper, *The Four Cardinal Virtues* (Notre Dame: Notre Dame University Press, 1980). Servais Pinckaers, "Virtue is not a Habit," *Cross Currents* 12 (1962): 65–82. Antonin Sertillanges, *La Philosophie morale de saint Thomas d'Aquin*, 160–530. Conrad van Ouwerkerk, *Caritas et Ratio* (Nijmegen: Drukkerij Gebr. Janssen, 1956). William van Roo, *Grace and Original Justice According to Saint Thomas* (Rome: Analecta Gregoriana, 1955), 127–152.

 2. On prudence constituting the virtues, see: Austin Fagothey, *Right and Reason* (St. Louis: C. V. Mosby Co., 1959), 227. Philippa Foot, *Virtues and Vices* (Oxford: Basil Blackwell, 1981). George Klubertanz, "Presidential Address: The Empiricism of Thomistic Ethics," *American Catholic Philosophical Association*, (1957): 15; "Ethics and Theology," 36–38; *Habits and Virtues* (New York: Meredith Publishing Co., 1965), 162ff.; John Langan, *Desire, Beatitude and the Basis of Morality in Thomas Aquinas* (Ph.D. dissertation, University of Michigan, 1979), 378; Odon Lottin, *Psychologie et morale aux XIIe et XIIIe siècles*, 3: 232–233; Jean Porter, "Desire for God: Ground of the Moral Life in Aquinas," *Theological Studies* 47 (1986): 62ff.; Antonin Sertillanges, *La Philosophie morale de saint Thomas d'Aquin*, 219–232; Janet Smith, "Can Virtue Be in the Service of Bad Acts?" *The New Scholasticism* 58 (1984): 357–373.

 3. S.T. I.II.55.2c.; 55.3c.; 56.1c.

 4. I.II.49.3. ad1. and 3c.; 49.4.ad1; 71.3c.

 5. I.II.56.1c.; 56.6c. III.34.2c.

 6. I.II.55.3sc.; 56.1.ob2.; II.II.47.4c.

 7. I.II.54.1c. and 4c.; 55.2c.; 56.1c. and ad2.

 8. I.II.55.4c.; 74.1c. and ad3.

 9. I.II.55.4c.: "Materia autem circa quam est obiectum virtutis . . . eo quod per obiectum determinatur virtus ad speciem"

 10. I.II.18.2.ad2: "Ad secundum dicendum quod obiectum non est materia *ex qua*, sed materia *circa quam*: et habet quodammodo rationem formae, inquantum dat speciem."

 11. I.II.54.1.ad1.; II.II.59.2c.

 12. I.50.5c.

 13. II.II.Prol.: "Est autem eadem materia circa quam et virtus recte operatur et vitia opposita a rectitudine recedunt. Sic igitur tota materia morali ad considerationem virtutum reducta."

 14. *De virtutibus cardinalibus* 4.ad5. Cf. In III Sent. d.15q.2a.2sol.3ad1.: "Passio timoris est materia circa quam est fortitudo."

 15. S.T. I.II.55.4c.

 16. Alasdair MacIntyre seriously overlooks this break in *After Virtue* (Notre Dame: University of Notre Dame Press, 1981), 167, and the same Augustinian assumption often appears in his description of Thomas in *Whose Justice? Which Rationality?* (Notre Dame: Notre Dame University Press, 1988). MacIntyre uncritically accepts Peter Geach's mistake in *The Virtues* (Cambridge: University Press, 1977). On the distinction of virtues, see S.T. I.II.58.3.ad3; 61.1.ad2.

17. I.II.60.1.ob3. and ad3.; 62.1c., 2c., 3c.

18. I.II.65.2c. and 3c.

19. I.II.65.2.ob1. and ad1.

20. I.II.63.2.ad2.

21. I.II.62.2c.

22. I.II.63.2c.; 63.4c.; 65.3c.

23. I.II.56.1.ob1. and ad1.

24. I.II.58.3c.; 68.1c. and 8c.

25. I.II.68.1.ad3.

26. I.II.68.8c.

27. I.II.54.4c.; 55.2c.; 56.1c.; 57.5c.; 59.5.ad1.; 64.4.ad2.; and 65.1.ad1.

28. I.II.55.3sc.; 56.1.ob2.; 58.3c.; 68.1c.; II.II.47.4c.

29. See Joseph de Finance, *Essai sur l'agir humain* (Rome: Gregorian University Press, 1962), 86.

30. IV Sent.d.46q.2a.1sol.2.: "Bonitas ergo respicit communicationem perfectionis."

31. DV 21.6c.: "Respectus autem qui importatur nomine boni, est habitudo perfectivi."

32. SCG I.37.307.: "Naturaliter enim bonum uniuscuiusque est actus et perfectio eius."

33. *Compendium of Theology* CIII.203: "Perfectum autem habet rationem boni, perfectio enim cuiuslibet rei est bonitas eius."

34. Ibid., CXIV.223: "Est igitur considerandum, quod sicut nomine boni intelligitur esse perfectum, ita nomine mali nihil aliud intelligitur quam privatio esse perfecti."

35. George Klubertanz rightly notes that any definition of Thomas's "goodness" must include the relationship between the appetite and the appetible object (*Habits and Virtues*, 68ff.). For us, the relationship is based on perfecting: the "good" object (Thomas's term) is what the appetite wants to perfect it; the truly good object actually does perfect or order the appetite.

36. DM 1.2c.: "Secundum praemissa ergo apparet tripliciter dici bonum. Uno enim modo ipsa perfectio rei bonum dicitur, sicut acumen visus dicitur bonum oculi et virtus dicitur bonum hominis. Secundo dicitur bonum res quae habet suam perfectionem, sicut homo virtuosus, et oculus acute videns. Tertio modo dicitur bonum ipsum subiectum, secundum quod est in potentia ad perfectionem, sicut anima ad virtutem, et substantia oculi ad acumen visus." See also Joseph de Finance's remark that the three instances from *De malo* are reducible to the first (*Essai sur l'agir humain*, 87).

37. S.T. I.5.1c.: "Ratio enim boni in hoc consistit, quod aliquid sit appetibile. . . . Manifestum est autem quod unumquodque est appetibile secundum quod est perfectum: nam omnia appetunt suam perfectionem."

38. I.6.3c.: "Ipse etiam ad nihil aliud ordinatur sicut ad finem: sed ipse est ultimus finis omnium rerum. Unde manifestum est quod solus Deus habet omnimodam perfectionem secundum suam essentiam. Et ideo ipse solus est bonus per suam essentiam."

39. I.5.3c.: ". . . omne ens, inquantum est ens, est bonum. Omne enim ens, inquantum est ens, est in actu, et quodammodo perfectum: quia omnis

actus perfectio quaedam est. Perfectum vero habet rationem appetibilis et boni, ut ex dictis patet. Unde sequitur omne ens, inquantum huiusmodi, bonum esse." For the same reason Thomas argues that it is more perfect to pursue the good than to avoid evil (II.II.157.4c.).

40. I.II.2.3c. and 3.2.ad4

41. II.II.161.1.ad4.: "Perfectum dicitur aliquid dupliciter. Uno modo, simpliciter. . . . Alio modo potest dici aliquid perfectum secundum quid: puta secundum suam naturam, vel secundum statum aut tempus. Et hoc modo homo virtuosus est perfectus."

42. I.II.3.6c.: "Oportet autem intelligere perfectam beatitudinem, quae attingit ad veram beatitudinis rationem: beatitudinem autem imperfectam, quae non attingit, sed participat quandam particularem beatitudinis similitudinem."

43. I.II.3.2.ad4.; 3.3c.; 3.7.ad2.; 3.8c.

44. I.II.3.7c.: "Perfecta hominis beatitudo non consistit in eo quod est perfectio intellectus secundum alicuius participationem, sed in eo quod est per essentiam tale."

45. II.II.184.1c.: "Caritas autem est quae unit nos Deo, qui est ultimus finis humanae mentis."

46. II.II.17.1c.: "Secundum Philosophum in II *Ethic*, 'virtus uniuscuiusque rei est quae bonum facit habentem et opus eius bonum reddit.' Oportet igitur, ubicumque invenitur aliquis actus hominis bonus, quod respondeat alicui virtuti humanae. In omnibus autem regulatis et mensuratis bonum consideratur per hoc quod aliquid propriam regulam attingit. . . . Humanorum autem actuum . . . duplex est mensura: una quidem proxima et homogenea, scilicet ratio; alia autem est suprema et excedens, scilicet Deus. Et ideo omnis actus humanus attingens ad rationem aut ad ipsum Deum est bonus."

47. II.II.27.6.ad3.: "Exteriores autem actus . . . sunt commesurandi et secundum caritatem et secundum rationem."

48. My claim that the moral virtues make us right as opposed to good is new in the States, although some authors, unlike Klubertanz, have equated goodness with rightly ordered selves. See, for instance, Joseph de Finance, "Autonomie et Théonomie," *Gregorianum* 56 (1975): 207–235.

49. See the study of the neo-Scholastics' debate over prudence in José Roque Junges, *Consciencia y discernimento* (STD dissertation, Gregorian University, 1986), esp. 175, 229–290, 340–382.

50. S.T. II.II.47.5c.: ". . . cum prudentia sit in ratione . . . diversificatur quidem ab aliis virtutibus intellectualibus secundum materialem diversitatem obiectorum."

51. II.II.47.5c. and ad1. Thomas often distinguishes prudence from art: the former concerns immanent operations; the latter, transient. See I.II.57.4c.; 58.2.ad1., 3.ad1. and 4c.; 65.1c.; II.II.47.4c. and ad2.

52. I.II.65.1c., ad1, ad3, ad4. See especially ad1.: "Si autem exercitetur bene operando circa unam materiam, non autem circa aliam, puta bene se habendo circa iras, non autem circa concupiscentias; acquiret quidem habitum aliquem ad refrenandum iras, qui tamen non habebit rationem virtutis, propter defectum prudentiae, quae circa concupiscentias corrumpitur. Sicut etiam naturales inclinationes non habent perfectam rationem virtutis, si prudentia desit."

53. See Frederick Crowe, "Universal Norms and the Concrete 'Operabile' in Saint Thomas Aquinas," *Sciences Ecclésiastiques* 7 (1955): 115–150, 257–292.

54. I.II.55.4c.; 63.2c.,ad2. and 4c.; 65.2c., ob1. and ad1.; and II.II.17.1c.; 23.7c.ad1. and ad3.

55. Janet Smith, in her article, "Can Virtue Be in the Service of Bad Acts?" rightly argues that the concept of virtue is founded on prudence and not charity. But her examples illustrate that her use of the word "bad" should actually be the word "wrong", that is, her article more properly asks "can virtue be in the service of wrong acts?" I agree with her conclusions: a virtuous act cannot be in the service of wrong acts; if acts are wrong, they are imprudent and therefore not virtuous. On the other hand, the virtues can be in the service of bad acts, as Kant demonstrates in his *Foundations of the Metaphysics of Morals*, trans. Lewis White Beck (Indianapolis: Bobbs-Merrill, 1969), 11ff.

56. S.T. II.II.47.5.ad1.: "In cuius definitione convenienter ponitur virtus intellectualis communicans in materia cum ipsa, scilicet prudentia: quia sicut virtutis moralis subiectum est aliquid participans ratione, ita virtus moralis habet rationem virtutis inquantum participat virtutem intellectualem."

57. I.II.68.5c.: "Unde sicut virtutes morales connectuntur sibi invicem in prudentia, ita dona Spiritus Sancti connectuntur sibi invicem in caritate." Based on this analogy, Thomas continues, "ita scilicet quod qui caritatem habet, omnia dona Spiritus Sancti habet; quorum nullum sine caritate haberi potest."

58. I.II.66.2c.: "Ratio connexionis virtutum moralium accipitur ex parte prudentiae, et ex parte caritatis quantum ad virtutes infusas."

59. I.II.66.2c.: "Ex parte prudentiae, quantum ad id quod est formale in omnibus virtutibus moralibus."

60. I.II.65.1.ad3.: "Tota materia moralium virtutum sub una ratione prudentiae cadit."

61. I.II.67.1c.

62. II.II.47.5c.

63. See I.II.57.4c. and 5.ad3. On the precedence of prudence, see Dominico Capone, *Intorno alla verità morale*, 19ff., 46ff. Interestingly, Capone argues that prudence requires charity because the latter provides a "finality" to prudence. This finality is similar to our concept of moral goodness. In effect, Capone argues that the virtues require prudence in order to be "right" and charity in order to be "good."

64. See esp. S.T. I.II.12.1c., ad1., ad3.; 19.3ad1. and ad2.; 27.2c.; 27.4.ad1.; II.II.4.7c.; 47.8.ad3.

65. I.II.66.3.ad3.

66. I.79.12c.; II.II.47.6c. and ad1, ad3, and 7c.;

67. I.II.66.3.ad3.; II.II.23.6c.; 47.7c. and ad2.

68. I.II.64.3c.

69. See I.II.63.2c.; 63.4c.; 71.6c.; 74.7c.; II.II.8.3.ad3.; 17.1c.; 27.6.ad3.

70. I.II.68.1.ad3.: "De rectitudine vitae quae accipitur secundum regulam rationes."

71. I.II.64.1c.ad1. and 3c. On the importance of prudence as measurement, see Karl-Wilhelm Merks, *Theologische Grundlegung der sittlichen Autonomie*, 125ff.

72. S.T. I.II.65.1.ad1. and ad3.; 66.2c.

73. I.II.58.4c.; 58.5c.ad1., ad2. and ad3.; 65.1c.ad1., ad3., ad4.; 65.2c.; 65.4.ad1.; II.II.47.4c.; 47.6c.ad3.; 47.7c.; 47.13.ad2.

74. I.II.63.2c., 4c.; 64.1c.; 66.2c., 3.ad3.; 68.5c.; II.II.47.5c., 7c. and ad2.

75. I.II.64.1c., ad1. and 3c.; 68.1.ad3.

76. See I.II.63.2c.; 63.4c.; 71.6c.; 74.7c.; II.II.8.3.ad3.; 17.1c.; 27.6.ad3.

77. II.II.123.12c.

78. I.II.59.1c.

79. I.79.12c. I.II.58.5.ad1.; 63.1c.

80. II.II.47.8.ad3.

81. I.II.68.8c.

82. I.II.61.2c., 3c. and 4c.

83. I.II.61.2c.; 66.1c.

84. I.II.66.2c. and 3c.; II.II.123.12c.

85. I.II.66.4c. and II.II.58.1c.

86. II.II.58.2c. and ad4.; 58.3c.

87. I.II.60.2c.; II.II.58.4c.

88. I.II.56.1.ad2.: "Cum bonum operantis consistat in operatione, hoc etiam ipsum quod virtus facit operantem bonum, referatur ad operationem, et per consequens ad potentiam."

89. II.II.58.8c: "Secundum autem interiores passiones consideratur rectificatio hominis in seipso." See also II.II.58.3c.

90. I.II.65.1c.

91. I.II.66.3.ad2.: "Per hoc etiam non probatur nisi quod virtus moralis sit melior secundum quid."

92. II.II.59.2c. and ad1.

93. See, e.g., Domenico Capone, *Intorno alla verità morale*, 54ff; Xavier Colavechio, *Erroneous Conscience and Obligations* (STD dissertation, Catholic University, 1961), 67–119; Eric D'Arcy, *Conscience and Its Right to Freedom* (London: Sheed and Ward, 1961); John Dedek, "Freedom of the Catholic Conscience," *Chicago Studies* 7 (1968): 115–125; Joseph Dolan, "Conscience in the Catholic Theological Tradition," *Conscience: Its Freedom and Limitations*, ed. William Bier (New York: Fordham University, 1971), 9–19; John Mahoney, *Seeking the Spirit* (London: Sheed and Ward, 1981), 50ff.; Aniceto Molinaro, "Coscienza e norma etica," *Vita Nuova in Cristo*, ed. Tullo Goffi and Giannino Piana (Brescia: Editrice Queriniana, 1983), 449–490; Antonin Sertillanges, *La Philosophie Morale de Saint Thomas d'Aquin*, 531–554.

94. S.T. I.II.19.5c. and 6c.

95. Odon Lottin, in "La valeur normative de la conscience morale" (*Ephemerides Theologicae Lovanienses* 9 [1932]: 431), argues that though the act

is "objectively bad" (Lottin's term), the person is good. He adds: "S. Thomas s'est toujours refusé à tirer cette conclusion." See also his *Principes de Morale* (Louvain: Éditions du Mont César, 1946), 1:186–187; 2:153–154.

96. S.T. I.II.6.8c.
97. II.II.47.13, especially 13c., ad2. and ad3.
98. I.II.55.4.ad2: "Bonum quod ponitur in definitione virtutis, non est bonum commune, quod convertitur cum ente, et est in plus quam qualitas: sed est bonum rationis." On reason as the root of human good, see Odon Lottin, *Psychologie et morale*, 3:567.
99. S.T. I.94.1.ad2.: "Bona voluntas est ordinata voluntas."
100. I.II.19.3.ob2.: "Appetitus autem rectus est voluntas bona."
101. See George Klubertanz, *Habits and Virtues*, 127–128; "Ethics and Theology," 38; and Paul Merken, "Transformations of the Ethics of Aristotle in the Moral Philosophy of Thomas Aquinas," 57. Merken sees much in Thomas's statement, "a man is called 'good' by the will" (*In Sententia libri Ethicorum* III.6.451). I ask, however, what does Thomas mean by "good"?
102. S.T. II.II.129.3c.: "Ad rationem virtutis humanae pertinet ut in rebus humanis bonum rationis servetur, quod est proprium hominis bonum." See also II.II.47.6c. and Karl-Wilhelm Merks, *Theologische Grundlegung der sittlichen Autonomie*, 167.
103. Margaret Farley, *Personal Commitments: Beginning, Keeping, Changing* (New York: Harper and Row, 1990); Antonio Moser and Bernadino Leers, *Moral Theology: Dead Ends and Alternatives* (Maryknoll, New York: Orbis, 1990); Paul Wadell, *Friendship and the Moral Life* (Notre Dame: University of Notre Dame Press, 1989); Jean Porter, "Perennial and Timely Virtues," *Changing Values and Virtues*, ed. Dietmar Mieth and Jacques Pohier (Edinburgh: T. & T. Clark, Ltd., 1987), 60–68; Anne Patrick, "Narrative and the Social Dynamics of Virtue," *Changing Values and Virtues*, 69–80.
104. Leon Kass, "Practicing Ethics," *The Hastings Center Report* 20 (1990): 5–12; Syndey Callahan, "Abortion and the Sexual Agenda," *Abortion and Catholicism*, ed. Patricia Jung and Thomas Shannon (New York: Crossroads, 1988), 128–140; Patricia Jung, "Abortion and Organ Donation," *Abortion and Catholicism*, 141–171. See also the present author's "What is Morally New in Genetic Manipulation?" *Human Gene Therapy* 1 (1990): 289–298.

PART 4

Being Good

CHAPTER 6

Charity: Moral Goodness?

In the last chapter, I noted that, faced with the mistaken unjust act or the erroneous conscience, Thomas develops an argument based on an ignorance antecedent to intending: these mistaken acts are excused because the ignorance was not intended. Thus, Thomas recognizes that something is antecedent to intention. But rather than giving it a positive description akin to that of the will's *exercitium*, Thomas remains with the object in the sphere of specification. We still have no moral description of the will's primary *exercitium*, that is, no explanation from the will for its self-movement toward specification.

Similarly, faced with the problem of false prudence, Thomas explains its "badness" as the failure to consider adequately the full scope of prudential judgment. Being irresponsible, we and our act are "bad" (Thomas's term) or "wrong" (our term). This position is no different from the inference mentioned earlier: an imprudential act leads us back to an evidently imprudent person. But why is that? Is it because a person in conscience was striving for the right but failed? If so, the person is good, according to our terminology. Or is the person's imprudence due to a failure to strive? If so, the person is bad. These antecedent questions are not raised by Thomas.

There is no evidence that Thomas measures human *striving* in any of his writings on the moral act and the acquired moral virtues. Instead, he restricts himself to the object and proximate end, wherein reason presents the former and measures both. Thus, Thomas employs no concept of moral goodness in these two areas of reflection. Thomas remains within the context of specification and never enters the context of the primary *exercitium* of the will.

"Good," then, in Thomas's contexts coincides with our "right," though a number of Thomists, overlooking the distinction between goodness and rightness, equate the terms. Austin Fagothey, for example, explains the word "moral" in his much cited *Right and Reason*:

> Morality is the quality in human acts by which we call them
> right or wrong, good or evil. It is a common term covering the

goodness or badness of a human act without specifying which of the two is meant. . . . Since the word *immoral* means morally bad, it indicates an act that has a definite moral quality (a bad one). When clearly opposed to *immoral*, the term *moral* means morally good.[1]

This passage makes perfect sense if Fagothey is discussing rightness and wrongness. But the passage makes no sense if he is discussing the goodness and badness of persons. Moreover, the passage assumes that if the object willed is "bad," the agent is "bad." But that inference from the act to the agent can only be made in issues concerning rightness or wrongness; that is, if an object willed is wrong, the agent is wrong. If the question is whether the agent is good or bad, we must ask not whether the object accepted and willed is right or wrong, but whether the agent is striving.

Issues concerning goodness and badness are distinguished by, and remain within, the context of an antecedent first movement of the will. In that context we can know the person before he or she wills a particular object. We do not need a description of whether a person or the actions are right or wrong. Rather, we must have a description of whether one strives "out of" (*ex*) or "on account of" (*propter*) love in order to realize "right order."

The issue that concerns us is this: does Thomas have a moral description for the first *exercitium*, for the will moving reason before reason presents the object? This is the question concerning human striving. Although Thomas does not use his own distinction of the *exercitium* to answer this question, his description of charity develops along the very lines of the ninth question of the *Prima secundae*. But is it fair to say that Thomas explicitly distinguishes goodness from rightness? To answer this question we will consider three issues: love, charity, and the different functions of charity as right making and as moral goodness.

LOVE, THE FIRST MOVEMENT

In the *Prima secundae* Thomas establishes love as the first movement.[2] He argues that the concupiscible precedes the irascible, both as first in intention and last in execution. Moreover, among the concupiscible passions, love is the first, preceding desire and joy; but desire, not love, is a tending toward an appetible object. Love precedes that tendency or desire; that is, love is the actual change in the appetite by the introduction of an appetible object. In this change, love rests as a complacency in the good, which complacency precedes all desire.[3]

As a resting in the appetible, love must be distinguished as either love simply or love relatively. Simple love rests in an object which is loved for itself. In relative love, the beloved is not loved for itself but for some good that comes from the beloved. The former is called the love of friendship; the latter, the love of concupiscence. In concupiscence, the lover actually loves for some reason other than friendship.[4]

Both loves are unions. Union must be distinguished between real and affective: the former belongs to an actual rest, the latter to an aptitude. Love belongs to the affective union. As an aptitude, love signifies that the lover is not yet in actual union with the beloved. Because its object is thus absent, love always requires a preceding apprehension of the beloved.[5]

Since all loves depend on a preceding apprehension, friendship and concupiscence are distinguished by their forms of apprehension. In friendship we apprehend the other as another self, and any subsequent apprehension of a good we wish for the friend, we wish as for ourselves. In concupiscence, we apprehend every good directly for ourselves. The primary apprehension in friendship is the friend as another self. In the love of friendship we apprehend the first good, the beloved, as likeness to ourselves; we apprehend subsequent goods for the union (of friendship) or for the friend as another self. In the love of concupiscence, we apprehend all goods for ourselves or for some other reason than the union itself.[6]

Since desire (*concupiscere*) follows love as a second movement, the two loves differ in that the love of friendship precedes desire as its ground.[7] In the love of concupiscence, because we desire the good for ourselves or for some other reason than union, there is no real love between us and the object.[8] In a manner of speaking, the love of concupiscence differs from the love of friendship in that the former is not seeking union. Without union as its ground, it has no real friendship as its ground.

How is this a moral description? Is love of friendship good? Is concupiscence bad? In answer to this question, we must not underestimate the fact that Thomas's writings on love in the *Prima secundae* occur within the context of the passions. Having first treated the acts that are proper to humankind, questions six to twenty-one, Thomas now treats the passions, i.e., acts that are common to humans and other animals.

At the beginning of his treatise on the passions, Thomas asks whether they are morally good or bad and answers that of themselves they have no moral description because goodness is derived from reason. When subordinate to or commanded by reason, the passions have moral goodness. Because the passions can be commanded by reason, the passions in us are different from those in animals, and when our passions are moderated by reason, we are perfected. Ordered passions enable us to be moved to the good; disordered passions are antecedent to judgment, obscure judgement, and diminish the goodness of the act. Judgments concerning the moral description of the passions depend, therefore, not on something intrinsic to them but on whether they are subject to reason.[9]

Further, a passion is only good when it turns to a true good. Not every passion is good simply because it tends to a good; rather, since a good may be only an apparent good, the good to which a passion turns must also be fitting to reason. Thus, insofar as an apprehension of reason precedes love, and love is a harmony with that which is apprehended, whether that harmony or complacency is "good" (Thomas's term) or "right" (our term) depends on whether the object is truly good or right.[10]

If we will anything, we will it under the aspect of "good" (Thomas's term). This is not a moral description but a natural one: the object of love is always good. For example, if we will suicide, we will it precisely as good. But suicide is an evil; not an evil as willed, but an evil as judged not truly good. If we were to apprehend suicide as evil, we would not will it. But if it is willed, it is willed as good. The moral question for Thomas is whether the good is truly good, that is, whether it is fitting to rational judgment.[11]

The question whether any love is morally good is the question concerning whether its object is truly good. Only if the appetite rests in that which is fitting to reason can we describe love as morally "good" (Thomas's term) or "right" (our term). Thus, for Thomas the "good" person takes delight in those objects that accord with reason.

But what if we love? Certainly, in contemporary language we think of the person who loves as morally good. Yet Thomas describes love not as a moral value but as a natural given. In fact, when Thomas delineates the two loves of concupiscence and friendship, he offers no moral description. Love of friendship is simply love. It is not of itself morally qualified. Admittedly, this love is the foundation in the *Secunda secundae* for understanding charity. But the moral qualification for the love of charity is that God is the beloved. Of itself, friendship is neither morally good nor morally right: it is amoral. It is not the love itself, but the object loved that determines the "goodness" (Thomas's term) or "rightness" (our term) of the lover's love. For Thomas, it is not that we love, but what we love.

Friendship and concupiscence per se are not comparable. Concupiscence is only relative to love in that every concupiscence is ultimately based on some love of friendship. Concupiscence is the secondary movement and describes loving an object not as likeness but for some other reason. Even a friendship can be based on some concupiscible pleasure, but if so, one will eventually discover some union antecedent to that particular concupiscence. A love of concupiscence will always have an antecedent love of friendship at its base. Insofar as the love of concupiscence is not comparable to the love of friendship, we cannot contrast the two as egoism versus neighbor love.[12] These are simply two descriptive categories and neither one is of itself better or more moral than the other.

In fact, even in contemporary thought, friendship alone does not necessarily imply moral goodness. For instance, a man who does everything out of love for his wife may actually be "good" (our term) in some matters. But if this love for his wife is exclusive of love for neighbor, then this man may well be bad: he loves his wife, but shuns his neighbor. Thus, only a general love for God or our neighbor, or both, can serve as an adequate description of moral goodness; friendship alone is insufficient. To know about moral goodness we must ask, out of what primary friendship do we act. In that question we find the fundamental love on which all other loves are based.

For Thomas the question is not whether we love, but what we love. Since love and desire (*concupiscere*) are each founded on friendship, that is, on love simply, the object that is loved as friend will also be the object loved as the final end. This friend will be the cause of all subsequent desiring, and thus a single friendship will determine the "goodness" (Thomas's term) or "rightness" (our term) of love.

Had Thomas raised the question of love as a general openness to the other as neighbor, he could have discussed our concept of goodness. He could have asked about loving. Then, instead of focusing on what we love, he would have focused on the quality of our loving. Thomas, however, asks only what specific (i.e., right) friend ought to be loved.

In order to determine the right friend, Thomas notes that the proper object of love is the good that causes love. This good must be apprehended, but the form of the apprehended good is the likeness it bears to the lover.[13] Likeness in itself does not make the lover good. Rather, the object's higher or lower relation to the lover determines which objects as likeness ought to be loved. Thus, the likeness with which we should seek union must be the likeness of which we are an image, not the likeness that is an image of ourselves. Insofar as union is the end of love, Thomas searches for an object as last end which is greater than we are and to which we bear likeness. This union alone will surpass the substantial union that we have with ourselves. To know, therefore, when love of friendship is good, we have to know whether the object with which the lover is complacent is the proper final end. For every act eventually proceeds out of love as out of a first cause.[14]

In Thomas's treatment of love we find four conclusions. First, love is the first movement of the will and love simply, friendship, precedes all desires. Second, there is no moral distinction between love of friendship and love of concupiscence. Rather, insofar as the second love is derived from the first, Thomas turns toward the object to discern what ought to be loved as ground of all desires. Third, relying not on the *exercitium*, but on love in specification, Thomas argues that whether any love is "good" (Thomas's term) or "right" (our term), depends on whether the object apprehended as "good" is truly fitting to reason. Fourth, notwithstanding this position, through friendship and its furthest recesses, Thomas comes to charity as that which unites us to the proper last end.

Before we proceed to charity, let us note two emerging functions that belong to it. First, inasmuch as the object defines the rightness of friendship, charity has a right making function: charity unites us with the most perfect, i.e., the right, end. The most perfect friendship is charity. Second, under the rubric of love, Thomas discusses only the object of love, not the phenomenon of loving. Under the rubric of charity, however, he does discuss loving itself. Indeed, as Thomas considers charity as loving as much as we can, he finds the measure of goodness.

CHARITY AS UNION

The key to understanding charity is union, which Thomas uses to distinguish charity from any form of love, including benevolence, because charity is benevolence based on union.[15] From its union with the last end, charity has three functions: form, command, and measure. Especially as command and measure, charity functions as moral goodness.

The existence of the theological virtues is established inasmuch as virtue is that whereby we are perfected to attain happiness and inasmuch as there are two happinesses, one proportionate to our nature and one beyond our capacities. The theological virtues exist necessarily for the attainment of the second happiness. They are distinct from the moral virtues in that their object is God, who is the last end; the object of the moral virtues is something comprehensible to reason. The theological virtues surpass human reason because they perfect the human mind supernaturally.[16] In a word, the object of the theological virtues is the last end. By establishing God as the object of the theological virtues, and by ascertaining the supernatural perfection of these virtues, Thomas presents us for the first time with the possibility of developing a moral description of the will as related to the last end. Rather than limiting the discussion, as he had previously, to proximate ends and objects proposed by reason, via the theological virtues, he enters the sphere of motivation, which is antecedent to intention, just as the last end is antecedent to proximate ends.

Having established the theological virtues in general, Thomas distinguishes three specific theological virtues: faith, hope, and charity. Faith directs reason; hope and charity direct the will. Hope is distinguished from charity in this: hope is for something to be attained, while charity is already a certain spiritual union in which the will is transformed into the last end. This union with the last end distinguishes charity from faith and hope.

The distinctiveness of charity as union with the last end appears again in the hierarchy of the three virtues. Since they have the same object, their rank is established according to their nearness to the object. Faith and hope by their very natures imply distance; that is, they are related to their object as to that which is not seen or possessed. Therefore, charity, which is a union already possessed (*iam habetur*), is the greatest of the theological virtues.[17] Only charity and not the other virtues has union with God.

Thomas emphasizes a sense of "alreadiness" or "immediateness" about the union of charity with God.[18] He writes that charity unites the soul to God *immediately* through union or a spiritual chain.[19] Again, he writes: "It belongs *immediately* to charity that man should give himself to God, adhering to him by a union of the spirit."[20] This immediacy is the actual union with the last end.

All virtues, natural and supernatural, have God as the last end insofar as they can be directed to the last end. Thus, any virtue can be referred to or attain to union with God through mediation. But only the theological virtues have God as their object, and among these only charity has God as the object already possessed. Charity mediates the will's union with God, even in faith and hope.

Charity needs faith, not for perfection, but for generation. Similarly, imperfect hope precedes charity. Faith and hope are its precursors, but they need charity to be in union with their object, God. Without charity, faith remains unformed, because it is not in union with that one in whom truth is believed to be. Without charity, hope unformed is simply concupiscible. But if hope is formed, charity precedes it by informing it to desire union not for reward but for friendship.[21] Through charity, faith and hope are in union with God. Thus, just as the theological virtues need charity to attain union, all the more so do the other virtues (whose objects are proximate ends and not the last end) need charity to attain the last end. Only charity is without mediation. Charity unites us to God, who is the last end of the human mind.[22]

Charity's union with God is not, however, an object or end to be attained; that is, the union that charity enjoys is not a *terminus ad quem*. Rather, the distinctive union that charity already has is its *terminus a quo*, that is, the end out of which it operates. Still, the end or term that charity seeks, its *terminus ad quem*, is everlasting union with the last end and this end, too, distinguishes charity from the other virtues. Faith adheres for the sake of truth; hope adheres in the expectation of receiving help to attain happiness. The adherence of faith and hope is, therefore, for another end. Charity adheres to God for the sake of God alone. Only charity has as its end that it may rest in God.

The point of departure, or the *terminus a quo*, for charity distinguishes it from and makes it the most excellent of the theological virtues. Further, the end it seeks, or the *terminus ad quem*, because it is not God's truth or a share in happiness, but God's very self, also distinguishes charity from and makes it the most excellent of the theological virtues. Thus, charity seeks its own perfection, that is, actual union, and therefore its relationship to the last end is simple: out of union with the last end, it seeks greater union. Charity seeks no other end.[23]

Charity has no other end but union with God. It seeks no other end, nor is there any other end out of which it acts. It acts *ex* "out of" union and *propter* "on account of" union. Charity, per se and propter se, is already united to God, the last end.[24]

Insofar as its beginning and its term are one, charity endures simply: through charity we adhere to God for God's own sake. Through charity, we merit, reject the world, and adhere to God.[25] A favorite phrase from the Psalms underlines this experience for Thomas: "Mihi autem adhaerere Deo bonum est" (Psalm 72:28). This adherence is our ultimate and principal good, our good simply, the end that the righteous seek.[26] Through charity, adherence to God is already present; nothing else is needed.

Since from beginning to end, charity is an adherence to God, the increase of charity along the way does not change it substantially. The virtue of charity in heaven will not differ from charity on earth. Perfect charity will remain the same in kind as imperfect, for imperfection does not belong to the specific nature of a thing. The imperfection of charity is accidental to it. Perfect and imperfect charity do not differ essentially but only according to states. In heaven, the imperfection of charity will be perfected, but what will be perfected is that which already exists: the union with God.[27]

The difference between the perfect and the imperfect in the moral virtues and the perfect and the imperfect in charity is incomparable. The moral virtues, ruled by reason, are constituted as virtue insofar as they are formed by prudence. The difference between perfect and imperfect moral virtue is the difference between virtue with or without charity. The person with perfect virtue is good simply because the person has charity. The person with imperfect virtue, being without charity, could be, as we saw in the last chapter, either good or bad.

On the other hand, the imperfection of charity does not describe a lack of goodness. Rather imperfect charity describes a pilgrim's charity. Until we have final beatitude, our charity remains imperfect. Yet, imperfect charity is union with God, though not union as final rest. Thus, the threshold concerning whether we are good is between the concepts of imperfect and perfect virtue, not between imperfect and perfect charity, for once we have charity, the threshold has already been crossed.

Thus, union is not only the key to charity itself, but also a key for understanding the hierarchy of perfection in charity. When Thomas distinguishes three degrees of perfection in charity, he argues that the lowest avoids anything contrary to God, the second seeks greater charity through increase, and the third seeks union itself, wherein we desire to be "dissolved and to be with Christ."[28] Admittedly, the perfect seek increase, but their principal aim is union. No concept better distinguishes charity than union: out of itself it seeks its own perfection.

The uniqueness of charity rests in its union with the last end, which is infinitely different from any other end. Charity is unique in that no other virtue can be its principle, because the principle of the entire moral order is the last end.[29]

Since charity alone tends to the last end as last end, and since the end has the character of principle in action and appetite, therefore charity above all other virtues is bound to the first principle. Charity is infinitely different from the other virtues because, as it is already in union with the last end, no other virtue can perfect it. Charity is the principle and end of all moral action: nothing precedes it as perfecting principle, and nothing succeeds it as perfected end. It perfects itself.

CHARITY AS FORM, COMMAND, AND MEASURE

In morality the form of the act is taken chiefly from the end.[30] Because charity is union with the first principle or last end, charity is already the most remote end in any human act. Thus, when Thomas discusses charity as form, he offers an extraordinarily restrictive statement: charity is not the essential or exemplar form and provides no material cause. Charity does not enter into the essential nature of a virtue itself.

Just as Thomas distinguishes the last end as distinct from specific ends, so, too, in speaking of the one virtue in union with the last end, he maintains that charity as form does not constitute a virtue's species, but rather directs the end of that species to the last end. Thus, charity as form of the virtues connotes solely that charity is the end of the virtues, for charity ordains each of the virtues to its end.[31]

Similarly, in the article concerning charity as the form of faith, Thomas argues: (1) the act of faith is directed by charity to its own end; (2) charity is the form of faith in that it quickens the act of faith; and (3) charity does not enter into the constitution of faith as an intrinsic form.[32] Charity as form is, if you will, essence-less, not essential form, but efficient form that directs the other virtues.

In *De caritate*, a work contemporary with the *Secunda secundae*, Thomas makes the same arguments: charity is the form of the virtues as mover. Charity as form does not belong to the species of a given virtue, nor does it enter into either the constitution or the essence of the virtues. Charity as form does not give intrinsic form, but it directs the virtues to the last end.[33] Only charity has union with God as its formal and final cause. The other virtues receive from charity this final cause, but not the formal cause. The formal cause in any elicited act is derived from the formal object of the specific virtue.[34]

Any statement that charity is the form of the virtues or of their acts signifies that charity is their end. Both statements mean that when charity commands, it provides the final cause that directs virtues from their own ends to charity's own end, the last end. In any act commanded by charity, therefore, there are two forms; the one derived from the virtue being commanded, i.e., the formal object of the act, which is prudent or not, right or wrong; and the other, which is charity, whose form does not enter into the essence of the act and which must therefore be measured by some rule other than prudence.

Command

In order to distinguish these two forms, we must understand the relationship between an elicited act and a commanded act. In any act, the formal object or the proximate end of a virtuous act is the proper elicited act of that virtue. Thus, eating moderately is an elicited act of temperance. But say that I am eating moderately because I want to be a just man and my reason for wanting to be a just man is because I wish to keep a promise I made to my wife in which I said I would become a just man. We note, then, that the temperate form or proximate end of the temperate act has a remote end, justice, and an even remoter end, fidelity. The function of these remote ends is to command: fidelity commands justice, which, in turn, commands temperance, which elicits a properly temperate object for eating.

Though nothing hinders the proper elicited act of one virtue from being commanded by another, charity itself cannot be commanded by another virtue, for the habit to which the end pertains always commands the habits to which the means pertain. Therefore, charity commands precisely because of its union with the last end and for this reason, it cannot be commanded.[35]

In *De caritate*, Thomas addresses the same issue. Since all the other virtues are ordered by charity to its own end, charity commands the acts of all the virtues. Similarly, since charity as form is not the essential form of the virtues, it does not elicit the acts of the other virtues, but rather commands them. This command is not as executing but as first movement.[36]

Thomas distinguishes two ways of commanding. In his treatise on the human act, command is an act of reason that presupposes an act of the will. Without discussing this presupposed act of the will, that is, the primary *exercitium*, Thomas simply discusses reason or prudence as the command that orders persons and acts. But when he speaks of charity as command, command becomes antecedent to all other movements. When the charitable will commands, it exercises a primary *exercitium*.

In the ninth question of the *Prima secundae*, in explaining the self-movement of the will, Thomas writes: "the will, through its volition of the end, moves itself to will the means.. . . Forasmuch as it actually wills the end, it reduces itself from potentiality to act, in respect of the means, so as, in a word, to will them actually."[37]

In both the *Summa theologiae* and *De caritate*, Thomas refers to charity as a mother. He writes, "charity is called mother because she conceives within herself from another, and here appeting for the last end, she conceives the acts of the other virtues by commanding them."[38] Here, finally, is Thomas's moral description of how the will in tending to the last end reduces itself to willing the means, that is, his description of the will moving itself into specification. Charity as commanding is a moral description of the will antecedent to any description of a will's act measured according to specification. Here, in the charitable will commanding, giving form through directing all acts to its own end, we have the "good will" (our term).

Measure

Just as form and command are derived from union with the last end, so, too, charity's measure is determined by union with the last end. In union with the last end, the measure and rule of charity is God: God alone measures charity. The intellectual and moral virtues perfect reason and the will according to a created rule and measure, i.e., the rational judgment. But charity, i.e., God, perfects the will not according to a created rule and measure.[39] Thus, the two measures are distinct: one is God; the other, reason.

The theological virtues, unlike the moral and intellectual virtues, are concerned with a rule not ruled by another rule. They have no means or extremes. The love of God is not subject to a measure because no mean is to be observed. Rather, the measure of charity is to love God above all.[40]

In the body of the article on the measure of charity, Thomas argues that since there is no mean to charity, there can be no excess in the love of God; the more the rule is attained, the better it is. In a word, the more we love God, the better our love is.[41]

Here, Thomas places a threshold between charity and the other virtues: that which is so by its essence takes precedence over that which is so through another.[42] Since charity has goodness itself, it is a measure. On the other hand, the other virtues are not goodness essentially, but are measured. But a question arises; when Thomas argues that the virtues are measured, is he suggesting that they are measured by reason or by charity? This is curious, since Thomas had stated earlier that reason is the measure of the moral virtues. Now, he suggests that the relationship between charity and the virtues is a relationship between the measure and the measured. Something new is emerging.

On two counts Thomas has already established that the moral virtues are not goodness essentially. First, citing Dionysius that "reason's good is the good of man," Thomas holds that prudence has goodness essentially while the other virtues have goodness only through prudence, because good and evil in human actions are predicated in reference to reason. But, second, this goodness, precisely because it is fixed by reason, is not the good that is convertible with being.[43] Thomas states that perfection in beatitude will be the perfection of the intellect effected not by a participation or likeness, but by an essential perfection of the mind, that occurs only through union with God, who alone is good essentially.[44] Thus, the perfection of the Christian life consists simply in charity and only relatively in the other virtues.

Thomas, therefore, never considers the moral virtues as good essentially. First, they are never considered the good as defined by reason except when formed by prudence; second, even then their goodness is only a relative goodness. Only charity in union with God as the last end has goodness essentially. Two measures are now emerging: essential goodness, which is charity, and goodness as predicated of reason. Thus, Thomas points to charity as the unique measure, which is to love God as much as God can be loved.

Finally, Thomas must distinguish the two measures, which he does by posing the problem this way: since reason measures the human will and external action, and since reason measures the external effects of charity, so, too, reason measures the interior act of the charitable will. He responds:

> An affection, whose object is subject to reason's judgment, should be measured by reason. But the object of the divine love which is God surpasses the judgment of reason, wherefore it is not measured by reason but transcends it. Nor is there parity between the interior act of charity and external acts. For the interior act of charity has the character of an end, since man's ultimate good consists in his soul cleaving to God, according to the Psalm [72:28]: "It is good for me to adhere to my God," whereas the exterior acts are as means to the end, and so have to be measured both according to charity and according to reason.[45]

Until this point, Thomas has spoken of two rules: the good as defined by reason, which measures the human virtues; and the good as defined by the divine, which measures the theological virtues. In general, Thomas has referred to these rules as proximate and excelling. The tone has been that one is the fulfillment of the other, that the two rules are somehow in continuity with one another, and that one is the more perfect in relation to the other. Now, however, Thomas distinguishes the external acts from the interior act of charity as adherence. Furthermore, he argues that external acts must be measured both as *ex caritate* and as fitting to reason. Measuring the same act with two distinct measurements is, as far as I can see, the distinction between goodness and rightness.

The interior act of charity is measured by no other mean but whether we love as much as we can. Since this interior act concerns whether charity commands or not, it is the measure of the first command, and so can only be measured by charity: this is the measure of one's last end. But this act, which concerns our most intimate end, is never exterior and can never really be measured by prudence. On the other hand, all activity is fundamentally exterior, since exterior is used here as a relative term. Except for the command of charity, each act with its proximate end, that is, its formal object, and any remote ends is subject to rational investigation and measurement. As such all acts are exterior to the one interior act that is measured as charitable or not. These exterior acts are not about the last end, but remote or proximate ends. Thus, quite apart from the one interior act, these exterior acts are subject to two measures: by the rule of reason to see if they are right and by the rule of charity to see if they are good. Unlike the one interior act of charity, the exterior acts can be measured by both reason and charity.

In the *Summa theologiae*, Thomas holds that any act commanded by charity is good essentially. He applies this position to the subject of grace to ask whether grace is the principle of merit through charity. He argues that merit has two causes, God's ordination and the human free will. Both causes pertain to charity. The charitable will is the fruition of the divine good; it is through charity that we merit. Furthermore, all the acts of the other virtues are ordained to this end, "insofar as the other virtues are commanded by charity."[46] Therefore, merit is attributed first to charity and secondarily to the other virtues, "insofar as their acts are commanded by charity."[47] Thomas completes the article arguing that charity in union with the last end commands, and that no act is meritorious unless done out of charity (*ex caritate*).[48]

The command of charity in union with the last end and thus antecedent to all other intended objects is the cause of essential goodness. All other dimensions of human acting, whether of the will or of the judgment, are called good or evil according to reason. They are only called good essentially when commanded by charity. Acting on that command, that is, acting out of charity, describes a distinct concept of goodness which parallels our own concept of goodness.

THE ORDER AND RELATIONSHIP OF CHARITY TO ITS OBJECTS

Earlier, I distinguished charity as right making, i.e., the gratuitous grace of attaining the last end, from charity as goodness, i.e., the human response of loving as much as we can. Here I will observe these two functions by considering first the order of charity as distinctly and formally in the will and second, the object of charity and the order of its extended objects, that is, the order among those things that are loved formally out of charity.

Charity is in the will. Specifically charity resides in the will, not reason, because charity is ruled not by reason but by divine wisdom. More important, charity resides in the will as it tends to the last end itself and not in the free will as it chooses things directed to the end.[49] This distinction demonstrates that charity resides in the will precisely as the will's self-movement, that precedes both reason and the specified actions of the will itself.

The end out of which charity acts is union with God. This end is not the end that the virtues seek, the *terminus ad quem*, because all virtues are referable to God. Rather, this end is the *terminus a quo*, the end "out of which" we act. This end is interior, already exists within us, and has the character of a principle in action and appetite. From this last end the will tends to the last end, the *terminus ad quem*, which is God, and this tendency commands subsequent movements of reason and the will. But, where there is a principle, there is order. Yet because the charitable will commands reason, the will must be ordered by something other than reason. Thus, Thomas argues that by charity the will is ordered.[50]

In contrasting the order of reason to that of the ordered will occasioned by charity, Thomas emphasizes the precedence of the charitable will by arguing that order flows from things into our knowledge. Order is more appropriate to charity than faith, because order proceeds from the charitable will into the believing person seeking understanding.

The order that charity provides is formal. This is not surprising, since we already know that charity as form does not enter into, or constitute, the subsequent virtues: the essence of each virtue is not derived from charity, but from the virtue itself. Thus, charity is the form of the virtues precisely in commanding and directing them and their acts to the last end. Similarly, it is called the end of the virtues because of the same formal function. Since it concerns the last end and commands the virtues which are about secondary ends, it commands and does not elicit the acts of the other virtues. Charity simply orders the acts of all other virtues to their last end.[51]

Charity works formally. The charity by which we are united to God and by which we love God *propter seipsum* is also the formal love by which we love our neighbor. The love of God commands us to love our neighbor. Beyond the general commands to love God, self, and neighbor, charity has no specific norms. As a measure without measure, charity works formally. The order of charity, unlike that of reason, is a formal order.[52]

The will ordered by charity prompts itself to strive as much as it can to perform virtuous acts. This order is not like the order attained by reason. The order of charity formally unites the will to God and makes the will willing to strive for right behavior in the concrete world. The order of reason, on the other hand, specifies the mean and through it attains right behavior.

Therefore, when Thomas examines the object of charity, he refers to it as that which is loved out of charity. The phrase, "out of charity" (*ex caritate*), is used sixty-six times in the question on object. In the parallel question in *De caritate*, the same phrase is used forty-nine times.[53] Loving "out of charity" is a description of motivation. The object of charity is the only object tied to a concept of motivation in the *Summa theologiae*.

In union with the last end, the first object of our love is God, who is loved *propter seipsum*. God is the first object of our love, because God's goodness is all perfect. Out of union with God we tend to greater union with God, seeking to love God above all.

Union with God is not simply the principle of charity, but also the principle of the order of charity. When Thomas asks whether one ought to love one's neighbor more than oneself, he argues that one ought to love oneself more. God is the entire good for each person and for each person the entire reason for loving: for this union one should love oneself more than all else after God. One loves oneself because, as partaker in the divine essence through charity, oneself abides in God's image. That image precedes and causes the likeness one has to the neighbor. In the order of charity, union with God precedes all other unions. Thus, one ought to love oneself more than a more upright neighbor because of the proximity of one's own union with God.[54]

The love for self is distinct from the love of the body. The former is a love for the rational nature of oneself to be further perfected. This love of the rational self is a love seeking integration in which there will be no conflicting desires.[55] This love for oneself is more important than the love for neighbor because it is the love that directs the mind to God. Love for oneself as object of charity is the willingness to submit to the rule of reason, and to turn away from the rule of reason is implicitly to turn away from God.[56]

That the union with the last end is a spiritual union also establishes the order requiring love of neighbor before love of one's body, because neighbor love is love by participation, in a fellowship of the human mind. Proximity in union argues that the soul of the neighbor is closer to one than one's own body is. The body is loved out of an overflow of spiritual union.[57]

Out of charity, this *terminus a quo* that is union with God, one is ordered to an object or end, the *terminus ad quem*, which is even greater union. Motivated by charity, one is moved to love God, oneself, the neighbor, and one's own body. Yet only the *terminus ad quem* of greater union with God is the ground for seeking greater union with oneself, one's neighbor, and one's body. Thus, one loves one's neighbor not for the neighbor's goodness but for the neighbor's own good, that is, for the neighbor to be in God. The end one seeks in loving the neighbor is union with God. God is loved as object, the neighbor is loved *ex caritate* on account of God.[58]

God is the reason (*ratio*) for loving the neighbor, as God is the entire reason for loving. One loves God as cause and the neighbor as recipient. The neighbor is the only object loved outside the end both as principle and as term, since the union with God refers to both. In fact, the "object" whom one loves in neighbor love is God in our neighbor.[59]

In the question concerning the order of charity, seven articles concern whether to love the person closer in union with God, or closer in union with oneself. Thomas generally sides with the one closer in union with oneself, because one will have more influence on such a one to better promote the fellowship of the mind with God. On the other hand, he concludes the question arguing that in heaven one will finally love those who at the end of their lives are closer to God.[60] The question of loving the neighbor and the order to be followed therein is based precisely on the concept of charity as union with the last end: in this life one loves that others may be in union with the last end; in heaven one loves those who are in union with the last end. The beginning and the end of charity is union with the last end.

When Thomas compares the love of God and neighbor, he establishes a particularly clear distinction. Primarily charity consists in love of God; secondarily, it consists in love of the neighbor, that is, in wishing well and doing good for the neighbor.[61] Thus, it would be reprehensible to love one's neighbor as the principal end (*principalem finem*), but not if one loved one's neighbor *propter Deum*. The ground for love of neighbor in charity is always the union one has with God: in charity, love of neighbor is subsequent to love of God.

Toward the end of the *Secunda secundae*, Thomas asserts not only that the love of neighbor is secondarily related to charity but also that it is accidental to charity. Earlier, Thomas had asserted that neighbor love belongs to justice and love of God to charity. Later, however, he argues that the end of charity is love of God and of neighbor; and, still later, that love of neighbor is an extension of the love of God. But finally, Thomas argues that the love of neighbor is accidental to charity.[62]

Thomas sees that even neighbor love can be enacted from another motivation. There are other reasons for neighbor love than charity. Thus, one can love one's neighbor without charity, just as one can honor one's parents without charity. No act but the love of God is essentially an act of charity. Love of neighbor is not an act of charity unless one loves God.[63]

If neighbor love is only accidentally related to charity, then neighbor love can belong to other virtues.[64] Thomas raises two instances. The first, mercy, relates to external works. When neighbor love belongs to mercy, it differs from charity: charity makes one like God by uniting one to God; mercy makes one like God only in a similarity of works. Charity's love of neighbor is motivated from union with God. Mercy is not necessarily so motivated.

The second instance concerns justice, specifically in the case of fraternal correction. If the correction is for social benefit, it belongs to justice; if for the spiritual welfare of the offender, then to charity. To correct someone in order to defend a wounded party is an act of justice. To perform the same act intending to bring the offender into closer union with the Lord belongs to charity.

There is no reason to suppose that acts of mercy or justice cannot be motivated by charity, insofar as charity commands. On the other hand, insofar as charity concerns the last end, it cannot be commanded by either justice or mercy. Only charity is without any antecedent motivation. Thus, in terms of the distinction between goodness and rightness, we can say that a merciful or a just act of neighbor love is a right act. Whether it is good, however, depends on whether the antecedent motivation is charitable. Thus, if neighbor love is accidental to charity, and charity is the sole concept of goodness in the *Summa*, then an act of neighbor love, though right, could actually be a bad act. Out of bad motivation, one could love the neighbor.

Thomas distinguishes three ways in which love of neighbor can be measured: first, the love of neighbor as contrary to charity, that is, when one places one's end in that love; second, the love of neighbor *propter Deum*, which is charity; and third, the love of neighbor on account of consanguinity or some other human consideration, which is nevertheless referable to charity. By charity one loves the neighbor, but without charity, one loves the neighbor by some other love.[65] The badness of that other love depends on whether its motive contradicts the love of God.

Neighbor love is only an act of charity when charity commands; i.e., when one acts out of union with God for God's sake. Charity makes one willing to strive to care for oneself and one's neighbor, but whether one's actions are right, i.e., whether they actually benefit oneself and one's neighbor, does not belong to the order of charity, but to the order of reason. Thus, neighbor love, like all exterior acts, has two measures: whether one strives to be loving and whether one attains that which is fitting to reason.

The order of charity is considerably different from the order of reason. The order of charity follows from a concept of union with the last end, wherein the "good" (Thomas's term) is measured by seeking the end. The order of reason considers proximate ends and means that are "good" (Thomas's term) or "right" (our term) insofar as they attain the mean. Indeed, for Thomas as we have seen, charity works formally, and of its measure, there is no mean. The measure of reason is not a formal measure: it determines, in fact, whether a person or an act is well-ordered. It is the measure of rightness.

That charity works formally to move one to loving God, to searching for a well-ordered personality, and to seeking to love the neighbor for the neighbor's own sake are the three facets of moral goodness. These three dimensions of Thomas's charity parallel exactly our contemporary concept of moral goodness. Whether we actually attain a well-ordered personality or perform actions that actually benefit a neighbor pertains to rightness. But that we strive out of charity to attain these ends belongs to goodness.

CHARITY, THE GOODNESS OF THE HEART

The union with the last end in charity is through the presence of the Holy Spirit. Since the Holy Spirit is itself the union of the Father and the Son, and since charity is present through the infusion of the Holy Spirit, one participates in the divine love, that is, the divine essence, when one has charity. In fact, charity is the divine essence itself: through charity the Holy Spirit dwells in a person.[66]

Thus, growth in charity is a greater participation of the Holy Spirit in the subject, intensifying the bond of unity.[67] Through one's inward spiritual growth toward greater union, one finally reaches the state of perfection, in which the potentiality of the mind is filled completely by God. As we shall see, precisely the Holy Spirit accomplishes one's attainment of the last end.

The distinction between goodness and rightness could be stated in this form: goodness measures whether out of love one *strives to attain* a rightly ordered self. Charity, for Thomas, is this measure.

Rightness, on the other hand, measures whether one *actually attains* a rightly ordered self. Thus, the order of reason determines whether proximate ends and means attain the mean. Charity, however, also attains the end, the last end; by charity alone we merit beatitude. This attainment of the last end is certainly a form of rightness, though in a specifically theological context. Given the difference between attaining and striving, we must distinguish charity as right making from charity as moral goodness.

Charity as right making does not function in the same way as the right making moral virtues do. Whereas the moral virtues need to be directed by prudence to be right making, charity is right making by directing prudence to the ultimate due end.[68] Aside from the order that charity gives to love God, self, neighbor, and body, charity also directs prudence to realize that what is to be done ought to be done for the last end, God. Charity directs by giving the proper moral motivation.

Charity does not direct by giving us actual insight into what to do in a specific act. Thomas argues that by charity the mind knows some spiritual truth, but this truth does not cast out dullness of the mind in other matters. In fact, the wisdom of charity is itself a participation in the union of the mind with God and hence is unlike knowledge, in which we know what we ought to believe. Like the new law, there seems to be no new information given by charity, beyond its fourfold formal order. What charity "teaches" us as new is completely interior and formal: to implore God's help, to strive to enter the narrow door of perfect virtue, and to be wary of being led astray.[69]

Thomas emphasizes that by charity one attains that which by nature is unattainable, the last end. By charity specifically, one attains the supernatural happiness that exceeds human capacity.[70] Thus, this union is completely gratuitous. As one only attains this state through God's gift of the Holy Spirit, the "rightness" of charity is completely derived from the divine life in each person. One may have dispositions for the reception of charity, but those dispositions themselves are derived from the Holy Spirit; the root of charity, grace, is always freely and completely derived from God.[71]

Against Pelagius, Thomas argues that one cannot fulfill all the precepts without fulfilling the precept of charity, and since that precept is fulfilled by the gift of grace, it is not possible to fulfill all the precepts without grace. Similarly, if by mortal sin the principle of the spiritual life, charity, is destroyed, God alone can repair it.[72]

The attainment of the last end through union with it in charity is completely by gift. Through the gift of grace, one attains that perfection which surpasses the perfection of reason. One attains what only

God can give us. But one attains it precisely through charity. In union with the last end, charity attains the ultimately right end.

Charity as gift from God and as presence of the Holy Spirit attaining for us union with the last end is distinguishable from our own efforts to grow in greater union. In this distinction we find the former as an expression of a gratuitous supernatural rightness and the latter as an expression of responsive moral goodness.

Though charity is attainment of the last end, it is not the attainment in which there is actual rest. Though God is always present in charity to make one good through God's own goodness, only in the perfection of charity in heaven is one's heart actually always borne toward God.[73]

Each person is called to goodness, that is, to love as much as one can. Yet this needs qualification. First, one is incapable of always bearing one's heart toward God. Even the endeavor to rid ourselves from all unnecessary attachments for the sake of God is itself an ideal, not often realized. More commonly, charity is the habitual giving of one's whole heart to God by neither thinking nor desiring anything contrary to the love of God. The goodness of charity is measured first by the refusal to go against charity.[74]

Given free will, one can lose charity because one's will is changeable. In heaven, the will of the blessed will not change, for there God will completely fill the mind's potentiality. On earth, as the will is not always in act, a motive for sinning may arise through which, were one to consent to it, one could lose charity. Acting out of charity one cannot sin, but acting out of something contrary to charity one sins and loses charity.[75] One remains in the goodness of charity by not falling into the temptation against charity.

Later, Thomas broadens his position and posits three levels in charity: resisting sin, striving for the increase of charity, and simply seeking union. Since this last level is occupied by few, the question concerning increase becomes particularly important: since the charity of the wayfarer can increase, the charity of the wayfarer should increase. Citing Gregory I, Thomas argues that to stand still on the way to God is to go back.[76] This position, like the call to grow in charity, highlights that the opposite of goodness, badness, is not deliberately willing the wrong, but failing to strive for the right, i.e., to grow in virtue.

Striving becomes operative in understanding charity. Charity increases not by a new essence being added, but by its deeper radication in us. It increases not by going from a state of absence to a state of attainment, but by having more presence or greater adherence in us. Charity increases in intensity, and that increase occurs not in the act itself, but in the striving (*conor*).[77] In striving, one grows in goodness.

The call to respond to grace in charity is the call to seek the increase of charity through striving to love God, oneself, and one's neighbor. It is a call to moral goodness and is measured not by what one attains, but that one strives to attain. The measure is not in one's acts, but in one's heart. As the intention is the locus for the measurement of the well-ordered person and act, the heart is the locus for the measurement of the charitable person who formally strives to become the well-ordered self and to perform well-ordered acts of neighbor love.[78]

The Holy Spirit gives spiritual life to the soul. In return, one turns to God with all one's heart. To love God with one's whole heart is the measure of charity. Thus, charity is perfect when one loves as much as one can. Though one is not always actually able to give one's whole heart to God, one can do so habitually through charity. Through that action, one's heart is enlarged.[79]

The importance of the heart is underlined when Thomas distinguishes between the perfect and being in the state of perfection. He argues that when one speaks of the state of perfection one is speaking of external actions in relation to the Church; when one speaks of perfection through charity one is speaking of one's inward disposition that only God knows. Here he cites (1 Kings): "Homo enim videt ea quae parent, Dominus autem intuetur cor" (16:7). The distinction embraces the contemporary one wherein the goodness of the heart is distinct from the rightness of our lives. Only God really knows the heart's goodness. Human law makes judgments that are distinct from the heart's law, which only God can measure. Thus, only God knows the goodness of the heart that makes public and private vows, and only God knows who has the baptism of desire.[80] These passages wherein the heart is measured only appear when treating the charity or goodness that only God can measure. The heart is reserved for the measurement of personal goodness as opposed to the measurement of human judgment, or what I call rightness.

The heart is also used for exhorting the practice of charity, that is, to move one toward more intense union with God, toward the perfection of one's rational nature, and toward greater bonding with one's neighbor in the fellowship of the mind. Thus, the commandment from *Deuteronomy* (6:5) becomes pivotal: "Diliges Dominum Deum tuum ex toto corde tuo. . . ." Thomas cites it to affirm one's ability to love God completely, to argue that God is loved as the end in loving one's neighbor, and to indicate the totality by which God is loved as last end. Taking this passage, he contrasts loving with one's whole heart, against loving with one's "whole mind, whole soul, and whole strength." Thomas argues that the heart denotes the act of the will and that just as the bodily heart is the principle of all movements of the body, similarly the will, in tending to the last end, which is charity's object, is the principle of all movements of the soul.[81]

The charitable will, by which one loves God with one's whole heart, precedes and commands all subsequent movements of the will and reason. Thus, linking the heart, which is only measured by charity, with the last end, Thomas returns to the precedence of the will, a precedence *quantum ad exercitium*, not *quantum ad specificationem*. Intending the last end, which is uniquely attributed to charity, corresponds to our concept of motivation: it unites one not with one's action but with one's self-determination to goodness or to badness. This motivation, described through the image of the heart, underlines not simply the interiority of the proper response to God's gift of union in the Spirit, but also the principle that to love with one's whole heart is to refer all things to God as last end. To love with one's heart precedes all subsequent actions and gives them their meaning, *formally*, of goodness.[82]

CHARITY AS GOODNESS ITSELF

Through charity, the human heart participates in the divine essence. This real participation highlights not only the union of one's spirit with the Holy Spirit, but also the response to God from one's own totality, the heart. The heart, measured only by divine judgment, is also the root of all subsequent movements, for only the heart is united to the last end. Insofar as the heart alone is united to the last end, we return to the question of precedence: first, as love which is the first movement; second, as will which when intending the last end precedes the movement of all specified actions of reason and the will itself.

This is a new moral description different from the other descriptions in the preceding chapters. Whereas earlier we saw goodness as fitting to reason and the attainment of the mean; here we see it fitting to union with God and striving for the end. Whereas earlier we saw goodness derived from the object presented by reason, the proximate end, here we see goodness as striving to maintain and to increase union with God, the last end. Whereas earlier the will was ordered through reason, here the will is ordered and subsequently orders. Whereas earlier the intention of the proximate end was founded on the object presented by reason, here the intention of the last end is antecedent to any such presentation.

Whereas earlier, virtue was measured by reason, here this virtue is not so measured. Whereas earlier goodness is known through reason, this goodness is known by God. Whereas earlier the virtues were not essentially good, this virtue is goodness itself. Whereas earlier virtues were in the good and bad alike, this virtue is only in the good. Whereas the former can be referred to the last end, here the virtue is already in union with the last end. The differences continue. But the distinction between moral acts and virtues and charity cuts across the same lines as that between rightness and goodness.

I find, therefore, no reason to refrain from stating that charity, which unites one to the last end, describes the self-movement of striving to grow in greater union with God, to integrate oneself better, and to seek the good of one's neighbor. These strivings, or formal interior acts, are antecedent to questions concerning specification, that is, they are antecedent to questions of intention and choice, or to questions pertaining to the proximate ends intended and the actual objects realized. In a word, the contemporary phrase, "moral motivation," best expresses the charitable person who loves self and neighbor formally out of union with God.

We have already seen instances in which writers from Fagothey to MacIntyre overlook the distinctive description Thomas gives to the moral virtues. The same problem faces charity, that is, the presumption that there is only one moral description, and that the measure of charity is an extension of the measure of the virtues. For thus, charity is often described today as perfecting the virtues.[83]

The irony in describing charity under this rubric is that this function is singularly a divine act and not a human act. Gratuitous charity perfects us in attaining the last end, and thus makes us right, but this is solely God's action, not ours. Curiously, this emphasis on charity leads to assertions by Christian ethicists that their system is superior to non-Christian ones precisely because it supernaturally perfects prudence. But, as this chapter demonstrates, our response in charity is another function of the virtue and provides a distinctive moral description for how we humans strive. Charity as the response to gift is an expression of moral goodness, not rightness.

Treating charity as human response and focusing on charity as a distinctive moral description has five major effects for moral theory. First, it enables us to see that Thomas's classification of the virtues was not under a single rubric, as it was for Augustine. Thomas, who distinguishes his treatment of the virtues from Augustine's very definition of virtue, offers us a new way of understanding moral description.

Second, in doing this he establishes charity as singularly the description of moral goodness. But, since charity is the singular description, Thomas provides (as we shall see further) no description of moral motivation for the non-Christian. Certainly, Karl Rahner appreciated this dilemma; it prompted him to discuss the morally good non-Christian as having charity, but anonymously so.[84] In any case, a contemporary description of moral goodness would do well to reflect on charity and on Thomas's thorough presentation of its growth in the person.

Third, Thomas argues that in all external activity there are two measures. Therefore, as every act bears two descriptions, the distinction between goodness and rightness is not between person and act, but between the heart and reason.

Fourth, although some contemporary moral theologians have contributed greatly to develop the notion of fundamental option, that notion only provides a conceptual understanding of the moral person pre- or a-thematically.[85] Charity, on the other hand, provides a description for thematic or categorical description. Whereas fundamental option describes our abiding condition as either good or bad, charity as striving describes our daily living as good when we strive and bad when we fail to strive. Thus, charity rescues fundamental option from the recesses of the human person.

Finally, charity as distinctive of our striving provides us with an understanding of love per se. Thomas's description of charity as moral goodness provides a moral account for love that does not, in my opinion, have an equal in contemporary thought. On that serious note, let us turn to Thomas's discussion of sin.

NOTES to Chapter Six

1. Austin Fagothey, *Right and Reason* (St. Louis: C. V. Mosby Company, 1959), 112–113.

2. S.T. I.II.4.3c. The following works pertain to charity: Frederick Crowe, "Complacency and Concern in Saint Thomas Aquinas," *Theological Studies* 20 (1959): 1–39, 198–230, 343–395; Anthony Falanga, *Charity the Form of the Virtues According to St. Thomas*; Gerard Gilleman, *The Primacy of Charity in Moral Theology*; George Klubertanz, "Ethics and Theology," and *Habits and Virtues*; John Langan, "Beatitude and Moral Law in Saint Thomas," *Journal of Religious Ethics* 5 (1977): 183–195; John Mahoney, *Seeking the Spirit* (London: Sheed and Ward, 1981); Servais Pinckaers, "Eudämonismus und sittliche Verbindlichkeit in der Ethik des heiligen Thomas," *Sein und Ethos*, ed. Paulus

Engelhardt (Mainz: Matthias-Grünewald, 1964), 267–305, and "Der Sinn für die Freundschaftsliebe als Urtatsache der thomistischen Ethik," ibid., 228–235; Jean Porter, "Desire for God: Ground of the Moral Life in Aquinas," *Theological Studies* 47 (1986): 48–68; Karl Rahner, "The Commandment of Love in Relation to the Other Commandments," *Theological Investigations* 5 (Baltimore: Helicon Press, 1966), 439–459, and "Reflections on the Unity of the Love of Neighbor and Love of God," *Theological Investigations* 6 (Baltimore: Helicon Press, 1969), 231–252; Hans Reiner, "Beatitudo und Obligatio bei Thomas von Aquin," *Sein und Ethos*, ed. Paulus Engelhardt (Mainz: Matthias-Grünewald, 1964), 306–328, and "Wesen und Grund der sittlichen Verbindlichkeit (Obligatio) bei Thomas von Aquin," ibid. 236–266; Conrad van Ouwerkerk, *Caritas et Ratio: Étude sur le double principe de la vie morale chrétienne d'après S. Thomas d'Aquin* (Nijmegen: Drukkerij Gebr. Janssen, 1956).

3. S.T. I.II.25.1c. and 2c.; 26.2c. and 2.ad.3.; 27.1c. See also Frederick Crowe, "Complacency and Concern in the Thought of St. Thomas," 1–39.

4. S.T. I.II.26.4c.; 27.3c.; 28.1.ad2. On friendship and *benevolentia*, see Klaus Riesenhuber, *Die Transzendenz der Freiheit zum Guten*, 57, 92–95.

5. S.T. I.II.25.2.ad2.; 27.2c.; 28.1c.; 28.2.ad2.; 29.1c.

6. On friendship and concupiscence, see Gerard Gilleman, *The Primacy of Charity in Moral Theology*, 107ff.

7. S.T. I.II.23.4c.; 25.2c.; 26.2.ad3.

8. I.II.26.4.ad1. and 4c.

9. I.II.24.1c. and ad1.; 3c., ad1. and 4c.

10. I.II.24.4.ad2.; 34.2c and ad3. and 4c.; 28.2.ad2.; 29.1c. and 2.ad2.

11. I.II.29.4c. and ad2.; 29.5c. See also 31.8.ad1.

12. Gilleman writes: "Love is love of concupiscence or of friendship depending on whether it takes its object as a means or as an end. Both forms of love can be egocentric or altruistic" (*The Primacy of Charity in Moral Theology*, 124–125).

13. S.T. I.II.26.1c. and 2c.; 27.1c., 2c., 3c.

14. I.II.28.1c. and ad2.; 6c. and 6.ad2: "ex amore, sicut ex prima causa."

15. I.II.65.5c.; II.II.23.1c.; 27.2c.ad2, ad3.

16. I.II.62.1c; 62.2c., 2.ad1. and ad2.

17. I.II.66.6c. See also II.II.24.12.ad5.

18. See Conrad van Ouwerkerk, *Caritas et Ratio: Étude sur le double principe de la vie morale chrétienne d'après S. Thomas*, 22ff.

19. S.T. II.II.27.4.ad3.: "Caritas est quae, diligendo, animam immediate Deo conuingit spiritualis vinculo unionis."

20. II.II.82.2.ad1.: "Ad caritatem pertinet immediate quod homo tradat seipsum Deo adhaerendo ei per quandam spiritus unionem." See also II.II.23.6.ad3.

21. I.II.65.5.; II.II.17.8c.;

22. II.II.184.1c.

23. II.II.26.3.ad3. Here Thomas explicitly contrasts the love of concupiscence, which seeks God for enjoyment, with the love of friendship, which seeks God alone. In light of this text, who can argue a eudaemonistic root to

Thomas's morality? See also I.60.5.ad2.; Gerard Gilleman, *The Primacy of Charity in Moral Theology*, 123; Klaus Riesenhuber, *Die Transzendenz der Freiheit zum Guten*, 158–159, 326ff.

24. On the relation between *propter* and *ex*, see Conrad van Ouwerkerk, *Caritas et Ratio*, 34.

25. S.T. II.II. 17.6c.; 23.6c.; 104.3c.

26. I.II.109.6c. and 114.10c. II.II.27.6.ad3.; 23.7c.

27. I.II.67.6c. and ad1.; II.II.19.8c.

28. II.II.24.9c. and ad3.

29. I.II.72.5c.: "Principium autem totius ordinis in moralibus est finis ultimus." See also I.II.87.3c; 88.1c.

30. II.II.23.8c.: "In moralibus forma actus attenditur principaliter ex parte finis."

31. II.II.23.8.ad1., ad2., ad3.

32. II.II.4.3c.; 3.ad1., ad2.

33. *De Caritate* 3c. and 3.ad1., ad4., ad16. and ad18.; 5.c.

34. *De Caritate* 5.ad2. Here Thomas uses *propter* to designate final cause.

35. S.T. I.II.114.4.ad1.; II.II.23.4.ad2.; II.II.32.1.ad2.

36. *De Caritate*, 3c. and 5.ad3. See also S.T. II.II.33.1.ad2. in which Thomas argues that in fraternal correction, charity commands and prudence executes.

37. S.T. I.II.9.3c. and ad1.

38. II.II.23.8.ad3.: "Et quia mater est quae in se concipit ex alio, ex hac ratione dicitur mater aliarum virtutum, quia ex appetitu finis ultimi concipit actus aliarum virtutum, imperando ipsos."

39. I.II.64.4c. and ad2.

40. II.II.17.5.ad2.: "Virtus autem moralis est circa ea quae regulantur ratione sicut circa proprium obiectum: et ideo per se convenit ei esse in medio ex parte proprii obiecti." See also II.II.26.2c. and 3c.;184.3c.

41. II.II.27.6c.

42. II.II.27.6.ad1.: "Illud quod est per se potius est eo quod est per aliud."

43. II.II.123.12c.: "Bonum autem rationis est hominis bonum." See also I.II.18.5c. and 55.4.ad2.

44. I.II.3.6c., 7c., and 8c.

45. II.II.27.6.ad3.: "Affectio illa cuius obiectum subiacet iudicio rationis, est ratione mensuranda. Sed obiectum divinae dilectionis, quod est Deus, excedit iudicium rationis. Et ideo non mensuratur ratione, sed rationem excedit. Nec est simile de interiori actu caritatis et exterioribus actibus. Nam interior actus caritatis habet rationem finis: quia ultimum bonum hominis consistit in hoc quod anima Deo inhaereat, secundum illud Psalm. 'Mihi adhaerere Deo bonum est.' Exteriores autem actus sunt sicut ad finem. Et ideo sunt commensurandi et secundum caritatem et secundum rationem." See also the parallel passages in III Sent. d.27q.3a.3sol.ad1.,ad2., and ad4.; In Rom. 12.1.964; *De Caritate* 2.ad13.

46. I.II.114.4c.: "Secundum quod aliae virtutes imperantur a caritate." Cf. I.II.62.4c; 65.2; II.II.23.7 and 8. The English translation reads *secundum*

quod as "since." But, as we saw in Chapter Five, the virtues can exist according to Thomas without charity. Cf. II.II.184.1.ad2.

47. I.II.114.4c.: "Secundum quod eorum actus a caritate imperantur." Here the English translation reads *secundum quod* as "inasmuch."

48. I.II.114.4.ad1. and ad3. Odon Lottin rightly notes that Thomas separates the question of goodness from merit by placing the two articles on merit (I.II.21.3 and 4) after the entire treatment of goodness. Furthermore, Thomas places the issue of merit with the issue of the last end, not with the goodness of the act which is found in the object exclusive of the last end (*Psychologie et Morale aux XIIe et XIIIe siècles*, 1:599 and 4:475).

49. S.T. II.II.24.1c., 1.ad2. and ad3.

50. II.II.26.1c. and ad1.

51. II.II.23.8c. and ad1. Brian Mullady appears to overlook charity when he writes that "the will is not a directive principle in man" in *The Meaning of the Term "Moral" in St. Thomas Aquinas*, 62.

52. S.T. II.II.23.2.ad1., ad3. and 5.ad2. The centrality of charity's formality is found in Gerard Gilleman, *The Primacy of Charity in Moral Theology*, 164; Klaus Riesenhuber, *Die Transzendenz der Freiheit zum Guten*, 112ff. See also Conrad van Ouwerkerk's *Caritas et Ratio*, p. 47, for its criticism of Antony Falanga's failure to observe the formality of charity's command in his (Falanga's) *Charity the Form of the Virtues according to St. Thomas*. For a different interpretation entirely, see Lawrence Dewan, "The Real Distinction of Intellect and Will," *Angelicum* 57 (1980): 573ff.

53. S.T. II.II.25; *De caritate*, 7.

54. II.II.26.1c.; 2.ad1.; 4c. and 4.ad1.; 13.ad3.

55. II.II.25.4.ad3.;7c.;12.ad2.

56. I.II.73.7.ad3.: "Hanc autem aversionem a regula rationis, sequitur aversio a Deo, cui debet homo per rectam rationem coniungi." The English translation wrongly translates the passage: "This turning aside from the rule of reason results from man's turning away from God, to Whom man ought to be united by right reason." Karl-Wilhelm Merks rightly translates it: "Die Abkehr von Gott in der Sünde 'folgt' (d.h. ist begründet in) der Abkehr von der regula rationis" (*Theologische Grundlegung der sittlichen Autonomie*, 170, note 251).

57. S.T. II.II.26.2c.; 2.ad3.; 4c.; 5c.; 5.ad2.

58. II.II.23.5.ad1.; 25.1c.

59. II.II.1.3.ad1.: "Unde non refert ad caritatem utrum in isto sit Deus qui propter Deum diligitur."

60. See II.II.26.6–13, especially 13c.

61. II.II.66.6c.

62. *De virtutibus in communi* 5c.; S.T. I.II.56.6c.; II.II. 3.2.ad1.;25.1c. and ad3;l84.3c.

63. II.II.103.3.ad2.

64. E.g., S.T. II.II.30.4.ad2.; 33.1c.

65. II.II.19.6c.; 18.2.ad3. See also II.II.27.8.ad2.

66. II.II.23.2c. and 2.ad1.; 3.ad3.; 24.11c. and 2c.

67. II.II.24.5.ad3.; 24.7c. and 11c.

68. I.II.65.2c.ob1. and ad1.

69. II.II.8.4c., ad1. and ad2.; II.II.9.2.ad1.; I.II.108.2c. and ad1.; 3c.

70. II.II.23.6c.: "Caritas attingit ipsum Deum." On the alreadiness of charity's attainment, see I.II.62.3c.; II.II.23.3.ad3.; 27.4c. and ad3.; 184.1.ad2. On charity as union with the last end, God, see I.II.72.5c.; II.II.9.2.ad1.; 17.6c.; 24.4c.; 24.12.ad5.; 27.4c and ad3.; 30.4.ad2.; 184.1c.

71. I.II.109.6c. See also II.II.24.3.ad1.

72. I.II.109.3c., 4c. and ad3., 5c.; I.II.88.1c.

73. II.II.24.8c. and 11c.

74. II.II.24.8c.: ". . . habitualiter aliquis totum cor suum ponat in Deo: ita scilicet quod nihil cogitet vel velit quod sit divinae dilectioni contrarium. Et haec perfectio est communis omnibus caritatem habentibus."

75. II.II.24.11c.,ad3. and ad4.

76. II.II.24.6.ob3.: "In via Dei stare retrocedere est." This quote actually belongs to Bernard: "In via vitae non progredi regredi est" (Serm. II in festo. Purif., n.3: ML183,369C). In III Sent. d.29a.8qla.2., Gregory does make a similar remark using the concept of striving: "In hoc quippe mundo humana anima quasi more navis est contra ictum fluminis conscendentis: uno in loco nequaquam stare permittitur, quia ad ima relabitur, nisi ad summa conetur" (Reg.Past. p.III,c.34: ML77,118c). See also S.T. II.II.24.9c. and ad3., and 4c.

77. II.II.24.4c., 5c., 6c. and ad1.

78. See John Mahoney, *Seeking the Spirit*, 57, 67, 73.

79. S.T. II.II.24.7.ad2.; 24.8c.

80. I.II.100.9c.; II.II.184.4c.; III.68.2.ad1.

81. II.II.44.5c.: "Dilectio est actus voluntatis, quae hic significatur per cor: nam sicut cor corporale est principium omnium corporalium motuum, ita etiam voluntas, ex maxime quantum ad intentionem finis ultimi, quod est obiectum caritatis, est principium omnium spiritualium motuum." See also II.II.27.5sc and c; 44.2.ob2 and ad2; 4sc and c.

82. I.II.100.10c. and ad2. For a concrete example of charity as first mover, see II.II.83.1.ad2. For an example of charity as first mover in commanded and elicited acts, see III.85.2.ad1.

83. Stanley Hauerwas, *A Community of Character* (Notre Dame: University of Notre Dame Press, 1981), 123.

84. Karl Rahner, "Reflections on the Unity of the Love of Neighbor and Love of God," 231–252.

85. E.g., Josef Fuchs, "Basic Freedom and Morality," *Human Values and Christian Morality*, 92–111; John Mahoney, *The Making of Moral Theology*, 32, 221, 332; Richard McCormick, *Notes on Moral Theology: 1965 through 1980*, 70–71, 426–427, 685.

CHAPTER 7

The Evaluation

I began this work asking whether, and if so, how Thomas Aquinas distinguishes goodness from rightness in the *Summa theologiae.* I have answered that question: Thomas proposes two distinct moral descriptions that parallel our own. But does Thomas evidence an appreciation for the distinction or does he establish the distinction for some other purpose?

An examination of Thomas's positions on the human act and the acquired virtues presents us with descriptions of actions and dispositions solely within the ambit of moral rightness. The good by which such acts and virtues are called is the good as predicated by reason, that is, as "right." These actions and dispositions are measured not by the will moving itself and reason toward rightness, which is the will's movement *quantum ad exercitium.* Rather, these actions and dispositions are measured as "right" or "wrong" through the objects or *materia circa quam* which are presented by reason and accepted for the will's movement *quantum ad specificationem.*

Charity as descriptive of God's action in a person also describes the "right," insofar as by charity one attains the "right" end for being human. On the other hand, charity is descriptive of one's formal striving toward the right realization of self and society. This concept of charity measures whether one loves God as much as one can and formally parallels our concept of moral goodness. It also parallels the description Thomas provided of the will's own formal *exercitium.*

Charity measures not the object accepted by the will but whether the will strives to move itself and reason as much as it can to love God. Like *exercitium,* charity precedes any question of specification. On the grounds that Thomas saw this measure as distinct from the good as descriptive of acquired virtues and human acts, I argue that Thomas has two measures of goodness akin to the contemporary distinction of goodness and rightness. These two measures parallel the distinction between *exercitium* and specification.

Now I ask in light of these two distinct measures, which appear in the treatise on charity, does Thomas use them for his moral theology? Does he evidence an appreciation for two specific moral descriptions? Does he establish the uniqueness of this measure of charity solely to describe charity or does he apply the distinction to other questions of morality?

The question can be answered by turning to the treatise on sin. Here I ask one question: if charity as moral goodness is formal (that is, if it is free of content) and measured solely as the striving out of love of God for rightness, is sin as moral badness formal and measured solely as the failure to strive out of love for rightness? As charity is the good will *quantum ad exercitium*, is sin the bad will *quantum ad exercitium*? In other words, does the description of sin treat the will *quantum ad exercitium*, that is, as failed motivation or heart for realizing the right? Or does sin treat the will as *quantum ad specificationem*, that is, as intending objects that reason says are wrong? If sin, like the human act and the acquired virtues, is only in the ambit of specification, then sin only considers wrongness, and the distinction present in Thomas's writings on charity is not present throughout his moral writings. Again, the question is this: does Thomas's concept of sin mean "wrongness" as in specification, or "badness" as in *exercitium*, or a combination of the two?

To answer this question, I will first examine the centrality of the specified object and the procession from the object to other considerations in the treatise on sin. Second, I will discuss the differences between mortal and venial sins and their motivations. Third, I will argue that as the formal concept of charity is not used in the writings on sin, the distinction between goodness and rightness fails to become a controlling concept in the moral writings of Thomas Aquinas. Fourth, and finally, I will discuss the case of the lying midwives to demonstrate the limitations in Thomas's description of moral acts.

CENTRALITY OF THE OBJECT IN THE TREATISE ON SIN

The order of specification has its point of departure in the object. The order of *exercitium* has its point of departure in the will moving itself. In addressing sin, Thomas clearly chooses the order of specification. Thomas's starting point is what we today call a "wrong" act: sin is an inordinate act, which derives its significance first and foremost from an object. From wrong acts, Thomas comes eventually to a position regarding a person's will. In a manner of speaking, Thomas begins with the act and recedes into the person.[1]

In the *Prima secundae*, having established the morality of human actions in questions eighteen through twenty, Thomas turns in question twenty-one to the "consequences" of human actions by reason of their goodness or malice. This question, consisting of four articles, has no parallel in Thomas's other writings. In it Thomas describes the grounds for naming human actions "right" or "sinful," "laudable" or "culpable," "meritorious" or "demeritorious" before God.[2] The grounds are always from the same source: the object accepted by the will.

Thomas argues that human action is called right or sinful on account of being good or evil. Because the will is free, the will's acceptance of objects indicates the goodness or badness of the will. Thus, all praise and blame is derived from the good or evil of one's actions. This same argument is used in reference to the other categories of moral description. Because the will is free, the objects accepted by the will indicate its moral state. Thus, "evil, sin, and guilt are one and the same thing."[3]

As opposed to Thomas's implicit presuppositions, however, the acceptance of a wrong object indicates at most a disordered will. Such acceptance does not indicate that the will is, in fact, sinful, i.e., failing to love as much as it can. I argue that acceptance only indicates what the will finds fitting: accepting a "bad" object (Thomas's term) or a "wrong" one (our term), the will displays only its disorder, not its badness. Thomas presupposes the opposite, however, based on a rather simple notion of human freedom: one either has freedom or one does not. Since one does, anything the will accepts as "bad," reveals the heart. Thus, when Thomas begins his treatise on sin, his starting point has already been established. Sin is so-called because it is an inordinate or a "bad human act" (actus humanus malus).[4] Sin is a bad act because it is the will's acceptance of an "inordinate object."

Thomas writes that external acts pertain to the substance of sin (pertinet ad substantiam peccati) because they are those acts commanded by the will.[5] The "badness" (Thomas's term) of sin is found in the "wrongness" (our term) of the object intended. This wrongness is the substance of the act. The substance, then, refers to the object that the will intends.[6] The substance of sinning is not in the formal exercitium of the will, but in the formal or specified object.

Thus, just as virtuous acts are acts in accord with reason that enable one to grow more rationally integrated, so sins are acts contrary to reason that make one less rationally integrated. Through sin, therefore, the reason becomes more obscured because, as Thomas often notes, sinful acts are contrary to reason.[7] Thomas draws a parallel between moral theology and moral philosophy: in theology sin is contrary to God; in philosophy sin is contrary to reason.[8] But, the former is derived from the latter. Thus, though sin is a transgression of the divine law, an aversion from God, that transgression or aversion is *subsequent* to the fact that sin is contrary to reason. To follow God one is obliged to follow one's reason and on that ground, any straying from the rightness of reason is an offense to God.[9]

According to Thomas, sin's contrariety to reason is not a formal one. Sin is not the willful act of contradicting reason. Rather, sin as contrary to reason is the *consequence* of choosing something that is contrary to the right. A sinner does not intend ever to depart from reason. The "evil" (Thomas's term) or the "wrong" (our term) of sin is beside the intention, because one does not intend it for its own sake. One does not turn away from the "good" (Thomas's term) or the "right" (our term) as the intended end. Turning away from the good is a consequence of turning toward some other object. For this reason, Thomas insists that sin does not take its species from that from which the will turns away, but from the object that the will intends.[10] Thus, in sin one turns away from the rightness of reason because one seeks something else. That which one seeks is itself contrary to reason, though one seeks it not at all for that ground.

Thomas calls the intention's turning to an object the "conversion," and the turning away, "aversion." The latter is generally consequent, but never antecedent to the former. By adhering to a mutable good, we contemn God.[11] Thus, though conversion is the substance of the act, the aversion is the fault of sin. The aversion from the right is what accounts for the privation or the actual evil of sin.[12] All sins are sins because they are a turning away or aversion from God, in the case of theology, or from reason, in the case of philosophy.[13]

The origin of sin is taken from the inclination to the end, while the gravity comes from the aversion. The end or the formal object is taken from the conversion, the gravity from the aversion. Conversion to the temporal good is the materiality or substance of the sin. Aversion is the perfective notion of sin. Sin, therefore, is composed of the substance of the act and the subsequent privation.[14]

This aversion never precedes the conversion, as it is impossible to wish to turn away from the good precisely as such. One turns away from the due end first by placing one's end in something undue, and thus by cleaving to an apparent and not the true good.[15]

Thomas suggests, however, that sins against the theological virtues are different from sins against the acquired virtues precisely along the lines of conversion and aversion. Sins contrary to the theological virtues are more grievous than others, since God is their object. Writing on despair, for example, Thomas argues that whereas sins against the theological virtues signify principally aversion from God and subsequently conversion to a mutable good, other sins are always first conversion and then aversion. A little later, he writes that sins opposed to the theological virtues signify aversion from God directly and principally. It is not that aversion precedes conversion, but that the aversion is directly related to the conversion: heresy is at once a conversion to a false opinion and, at the same time, an aversion from God.[16] Thus, in all sins but those against the theological virtues, conversion precedes aversion. In the sins against the theological virtues the conversion or substance of the sin is at once the aversion from the finally right.

After having established sin as an act contrary to virtue or reason, Thomas turns to the distinction of sins. The question naturally begins with whether sins differ in species according to their objects. The temporal or mutable object known is the principle of sin.[17] This object is understood always as the "formal" object, and this object as it is in the intention determines the species of the sin.[18] The species of the sin, as that to which the will tends, constitutes the substance of the sinful act.[19]

Certainly the reader wonders where the voluntariness of sin enters into Thomas's understanding of sin. As in question twenty-one of the *Prima secundae*, so, too, in the subsequent questions on sin, Thomas insists on the freedom of the will. The will is the first mover in sin. Because the will is free, one can attribute all guilt to voluntariness. Sin comes from the will. The will turns to what it wants, that is, to the "good."[20] But the good intended in sin is only an apparent one.[21] Thus, sin is the will's acceptance of something not truly good; it is nothing other than the deficiency of some "good" (Thomas's term) or "right" (our term) object that would be fitting to our nature.[22]

Thomas attributes sin to a defect in the apprehensive power: the will has not accepted a truly good object, only an apparent good. But the defect in the apprehensive power must be subject to the will, or there is no sin. Thus the will, which has for its object the real or apparent good apprehended by reason, chooses an object only apparently good because of some interior disorder.[23]

The interior disorder is any desire for a mutable good (or less right object in our terminology) which leads one to aversion from the real good or right object. This disordered self-love is at the root of each sin, because a well-ordered self-love would desire a fitting good. Just as the prudent or virtuous act arises from an ordered will, so the sinful act arises from a disordered one. The disordered act results, Thomas argues, from the lack of direction in the will.[24]

When ignorance is culpable, the defect is in reason. When passion is the cause of sin, the defect is in the sensual power. In both cases, the source of culpability is derived from the command of the will. But when malice is the cause of sin, the defect is in the will simply. In malice the will loves the lesser good; the will does not intend evil per se, but knowingly chooses the lesser right over the more right. This will is clearly disordered.[25]

The source of disordered actions in all forms of sin is a disordered will. I agree with Thomas on two points. First, one does not choose or intend deliberately the "wrong" per se. To intend the wrong per se is thoroughly irrational. Similarly, one does not choose to be "bad." Badness is the failure to strive to do the right. Moral "badness" is quite literally "failure," a failure to will.

Second, if sin is intended wrong action, then the will that sins is indeed wrongly ordered. But sin and the disordered will are concepts appropriate only to rightness and wrongness. In all this material Thomas never describes sin as derived from a will that fails to strive to love as much as it can. Nor does Thomas ever describe the cause of the disordered will. Thus, even in the sins contrary to the theological virtues, we can say that heresy is certainly wrong and that the will is not rightly ordered, but Thomas has not asked whether the heretic has failed to strive in her or his freedom to find the truth. Thomas does not leave the realm of specification to ask the question about goodness or badness.

I do not find, therefore, Thomas's concept of sin as the will's acceptance of inordinate objects to be a satisfactory description of "badness." The question of why the will is inordinate does not arise. The antecedent question of the *exercitium*, the question that precedes the question of specification, is not raised here. Certainly Thomas distinguishes the two questions in his section on human freedom, and certainly Thomas is right to argue that intended wrong actions evidence a wrongly ordered will; but the actual question of "badness" as it pertains to the *exercitium*, that is, the will's failure to move itself and reason to realize loving behavior and actions, is not raised here.

*   *   *

Thomas consistently uses specification as his point of departure and thus, remains within the ambit of rightness. Yet, specification and rightness are questions subsequent to the questions of *exercitium* and goodness respectively. Nonetheless, Thomas begins with specification and tries to show how these specified acts are blameworthy. From this problematic point of departure, Thomas determines the degree of blame through the two concepts: excuse and perfection.

Thomas establishes that the object alone is that which determines the gravity of a sin. The greater the wrongness, the greater the gravity.[26] The more harm caused, the greater the gravity. Thus, murder which concerns human life is a graver matter than theft which considers external things.

Given human freedom, one is more culpable for a grave sin, less for a lesser sin. But there are extenuating circumstances that ought to be taken into account. These circumstances concern the level of freedom one enjoys. Culpability is diminished to the extent that one's freedom has been constrained. To that extent, Thomas argues, one is excused.

The issue of excusing intended inordinate objects highlights the significance of Thomas's point of departure in moral discussion. The questions concerning whether ignorance, passion, drunkenness, or fear excuse someone from sin demonstrate the centrality of the object in Thomas's discussion.[27] Given that an inordinate act has been intended, Thomas asks whether the agent is excused. Thomas begins not with the agent but with the inordinate object.

Later moralists developed the distinction between objectively "sinful" and subjectively "excused." Like Thomas, they begin with descriptions of objects and deal with the agent by referring to this concept of being excused. Their concept of sin, like Thomas's, is simply a reference to a "wrong" act. We hold, however, that sin originates in a "bad" motivation and that wrongness is incidental to sin.

The differences between the two positions include the following. First, we begin with the person; other moralists, with either the formal object (the intention) or an external act (the choice). Second, we conceive of sin as arising from a bad motivation; they conceive of sin as an unfitting or disordered object. Third, we can conceive of sins actualized in the form of right actions, e.g., truth-telling; they conceive of sins as wrong acts. Fourth, we argue that goodness is striving to grow in freedom to serve the Lord; they argue that goodness is accepting right objects both in the intention and in the choice. Fifth, we distinguish between whether the person strives to the extent of her or his freedom from whether the person is well-ordered; they identify the well-ordered, which we call the rightly ordered, as "good." Sixth, we distinguish motivation from intention and choice; they distinguish between intention and choice. Seventh, we argue that morality is based on two moral descriptions, goodness and rightness; they have only the rightness of actions to go by and use the concept of being excused to account for various levels of human freedom at particular moments. This concept leaves them, however, with no moral description for the agent who has been excused.

The insight is central. According to these moralists a moral agent is excused for committing a "bad" action (their term) when (1) the person with an erroneous conscience labors to find and execute the right in fidelity to and love of God, (2) the person is unknowingly drugged into doing something wrong, or (3) the person is severely handicapped by particular passions. In each case their only moral assessment is "excused" or "not bad." This description is unsatisfactory because, in fact, the morality of the agents in each case is different. The difference is not found in the object at all, but in the agent.

The advocates of the "objectively sinful" but "subjectively excused" position create these difficulties because they do not distinguish between goodness and rightness. They cannot use the term "good" to describe the good agent in the first case because the term already has been used to describe the external, "objective" act. Calling the act "bad," they can hardly call the agent who did it "good." With only one descriptive phrase, they have no descriptive phrase for the agent. Thus, in these three cases they have no real moral description of the agent and can only treat each agent the same: "excused."

The difference, then, between Thomas's position and ours is fundamentally a question of order. We argue that sin is antecedent to action: we are sinners in our failure to strive to love as much as we can. Any acts or omissions resulting from this failure are sinful, whether they are right or wrong. On the other hand, Thomas argues that sin is wrong action and those who perform wrong actions are sinners. Only extenuating circumstances excuse completely or to some extent the sinners. Yet, when speaking of charity, Thomas's point of departure was just the opposite and similar to our own. The question concerning whether we love as much as we can is not found in the treatise on sin, or in any other section of the *Summa* except in the treatise on charity.

The concept of perfection also requires that the beginning point be the specified object. Thus, Thomas says that aversion is both subsequent to conversion and a perfective notion of sin.[28]

Starting with the object, Thomas asks whether a sin is more perfect by asking questions about the agent. The questions concerning more perfect sins are questions about a person's status and disposition.[29] Very late in his life, Thomas asserts that sin is also perfected by the consent of the heart.[30] Thus, after asserting that a wrong object has been performed, Thomas turns to the agent and asks, "how bad are you?"

In our distinction, however, the fact that one performs disordered actions only indicates the degree to which one lacks personal freedom or suffers disorders in various dimensions of one's personality. These actions do not indicate that one fails to strive to love as much as one can.

One particular perfection is noteworthy: malice, the perfection of sin.[31] Malice is sinning without any excuse, on purpose (*ex industria*), in full control. Here Thomas approximates a notion of "badness," yet the notion is not distinct, because he presumes first that the act must be "wrong." He contrasts malice with passion and argues according to the notion of perfection that the sin is aggravated through malice, diminished through passion. Beginning with a "wrong act" Thomas recedes into the person.

Through malice, Thomas argues that "wrongness" is perfected into "badness" by being performed deliberately, that is, by the disordered will choosing the lesser good. Certainly, in this instance we can talk of one's having deliberately and knowingly assumed and executed a wrong object. We, too, see this as sin, that is, badness. But insofar as malice is the perfection of a wrong act, we disagree. Why must the act of malice be a wrong act? Cannot malice take the form of a right act?

To some extent, we must agree with Thomas on malice as badness, but because he begins with wrongness, he presents a certain image. Consistently Thomas takes the acceptance of the object as descriptive of the intending person. Thus, if we assume a just object, we intend justice. Similarly for sin, if we assume an unjust object, we intend sin. But, where does the sin come from? Is the disordered object making us sinful, or is the sin in us already? Consider a merciless killing. Does the act of a merciless killing make us bad? Or were we already bad and out of that moral failure considered and executed a merciless killing? The order is important insofar as malice is the cause.

Is not malice as a cause antecedent to the sinful act? Is not the person acting with malice as a cause disregarding the invitation to be moral and doing whatever he or she wants to do? Certainly the person does not directly intend to go against God or morality; indeed, Thomas notes that no one intends to be bad or wrong. Nonetheless, I think that a person who fails to strive to love, or who willfully refuses the invitation to grow in freedom, is the one who is malicious. Being malicious, the agent will probably act maliciously. For Thomas, however, the objects arise first; the malice is subsequent: wanting the object so much, the agent disregards any consideration of the object's illicitness.

The concept of sin's perfection is misleading. It arrives at conclusions similar, in some cases, to our own. But it diverges, primarily because it begins with wrong acts and attempts to arrive at badness. Indeed, such a sequence is problematic because in reality badness precedes actions whether right or wrong ones, just as goodness precedes actions whether right or wrong. Thomas's concept of perfection takes, however, the opposite order.

The concepts of "excusing" and "perfecting" enable Thomas to describe the agent who performs "bad" actions (Thomas's term) or "wrong" actions (our term). Using the concept of excusing, Thomas diminishes the agent's culpability for the action. Using the concept of perfection, Thomas accentuates culpability. The sequence of both concepts is the same. In the long run, however, Thomas's moral description is still derived from objects. Charity excepted, Thomas's question is always, "what is one's relation to these objects?" If one does not intend bad objects as bad, the agent is excused. If one intends bad objects knowing that they are contrary to God, the act is perfected and the agent is culpable of malice. Thomas does not ask the antecedent question of whether the agent is striving out of love to find the right. Nor does he avoid the mistaken assumption that we can derive the moral description of persons from objects.

VENIAL AND MORTAL SIN

The concept of perfection helps us understand the distinction between venial and mortal sin. Venial sin is something imperfect in the genus of sin, whereas mortal sin is the perfect meaning of sin.[32] As imperfect and perfect, the sins are related precisely at the point of conversion. Through specific objects, Thomas determines generically venial and mortal sins. Often Thomas proposes an idle word as an example of a generic venial sin. Similarly, he proposes sins that are generically mortal. Sloth, for instance, is generically mortal, though only so when consented to by reason.[33] For the most part, mortal sins involve matters that contradict the order of charity. Something against the love of neighbor, e.g., murder or adultery, or something against the love of God, e.g., blasphemy or perjury, are matters that contradict elicited acts of charity. That they contradict charity, *materially speaking*, places them in the generic class of mortal sins.[34]

The relation between these two types of sin enables Thomas to note that through "addition" (*per additionem*) a generically venial sin can become mortal. The addition is of a deformity from the genus of mortal sin. The deformity or end of a venial sin is then subsumed by another deformity or end belonging to the genus of grave matter; e.g., an idle word uttered for the sake of fornication becomes a mortal sin. Not simply is the act of fornication itself mortally sinful, but the utterance of the idle word is now mortally sinful as well.

Similarly the perfect, mortal sin becomes imperfect, through a particular "subtraction," namely of the deliberate reason.[35] If a sin generically mortal is entertained by an agent, but the agent uses reason to combat this nascent passion, then through this "subtraction," the perfect becomes imperfect, and mortal sin becomes venial.

Mortal and venial sins, then, are related on the point of conversion: the objects to which these sins turn are related as perfect and imperfect. On the point of aversion, however, the two sins are absolutely and fundamentally unrelated. Besides requiring deliberate consent for objects generically belonging to mortal sin, mortal sin must also be an aversion from God. Thus, the two types of sin differ infinitely in respect of their aversion: mortal sins turn away from the last end; venial sins turn away from objects that may be referred to the last end.[36]

Because the two sins differ infinitely, Thomas argues that their relation to one another is "analogous."[37] In that mortal sin cleaves to its object as to its last end, it turns away from the last end; venial sin does not. Mortal sin destroys charity, but venial sin does not. In mortal sin, only God can repair the agent; but in venial sin the agent can be repaired because the order to the last end has not been damaged. Their debts of punishment distinguish the two infinitely.[38]

The two sins do not differ infinitely in conversion; they differ by aversion.[39] Thus, they are related analogously: venial sin is only analogously sin because its aversion is not from the last end. But both mortal and venial sin imply a defect in the due order. They are related, therefore, in this: they are both concerned first and foremost with wrong objects.[40]

Starting, therefore, with sin as inordinate objects Thomas now distinguishes the two types of sin. It remains to be seen whether mortal sin is wrongness and badness, while venial sin is wrongness and goodness. I note, however, that Thomas's distinction of venial and mortal sins does not anticipate any "right" actions as sin, for the point of departure in sin is the disordered object.

Thomas's concept of venial sin is, I think, best understood as wrongness enacted by a generally good person. It is unclear, however, whether the agent's motivation is actually good or actually bad. I say that the person is generally good because venial sin is committed by one who has charity habitually and yet performs an act not referred to God. Notwithstanding the wrong action, the agent's holiness is not destroyed, and her or his charity is undiminished by it.[41] Thus, generally speaking the person is good.

But, the wrong action is not simply error; it is personal wrongness somewhere in the passions or even in the will. Somewhere a disordered attachment continues, notwithstanding a habitual love for God. One cleaves to something, but not as the final end. In short, venial sin is an inordinate conversion without aversion from God. When one acts inordinately but habitually wishes never to be contrary to the love of God, one sins venially.[42] Venial sin always presumes wrongness, precisely by its specification as sin in the first place, that is, as an inordinate act. But when sinning venially, is the person actually, as opposed to generally, good or bad? Is venial sin goodness or badness? Here Thomas thoroughly causes confusion: some venial sins proceed from a good motivation; others do not.

On several occasions, Thomas presumes that a person can commit a sin with a good motivation. For instance, Thomas raises the question of one who steals to give alms. His response is the famous citation from Dionysius that good results from the entire cause, evil results from any particular defect.[43] Thus, that one steals proceeds from a good motivation, but that one's action is wrong means that one has sinned venially.

Later, when Thomas asks again about the case of one who steals in order to give alms, he describes the agent as acting from a good intention (ex aliqua bona intentione), but also as sinning from a good intention (ex bona intentione).[44] His central position is that though the motivation is good, the wrongness of the act does not permit us to call the act or the agent good.

Thomas proposes whether the act of fornication could be performed by a person who intends a good end. He asks whether such an act would be permissible, or if not, whether it could be excused. His answer invokes Dionysius: if the end of an act is disordered, the intended end does not suffice to excuse the act.[45]

Officious lies are by definition morally good: one lies out of love for a neighbor, either in order to help the neighbor or to protect the neighbor from harm. But Thomas declares that an action is only good when it is good in every respect. Therefore, because a lie is an inordinate act, an officious lie is never good; it is always a sin.[46]

In these instances, people whose motivation is at the moment actually good commit venial sin. Thomas, using Dionysius, precludes, however, the possibility of declaring the agent or the act good: the sinful acts as evil in themselves cannot become good.[47]

On other occasions, venial sin arises from people whose actions clearly do not result from a good motivation. For example, one may fail to provide fraternal correction on account of fear or covetousness.[48] Given that fear is the cause of this sin, does it arise from a person who has failed to strive? Is the covetousness something the agent could have overcome? Almost every venial sin cited in Thomas's writings refers to a momentary failure by the agent.[49] But, what is never clear is whether the failure results from a failure to strive, or from the simple limits of one's history and freedom, in which one strives but fails to overcome those limits.

Consider, for instance, (1) the case of a husband who for reasons of self-pity or jealousy decides to withhold his love from his wife for a few days. Or consider, (2) the friend who out of anger tells her friend the truth, namely, that a mutual acquaintance thinks poorly of the friend. Consider (3) the priest who after a tiring week takes out his frustration on his community by upbraiding his parishioners at the Sunday Mass. In each instance, a person has failed to strive to love, either (1) by not acting, (2) by right acting, or (3) by wrong acting. Clearly, in contemporary language, there is sin in each of these instances, and the sin originates in the failure, not in the action. But in his writings, Thomas simply considers venial sin as wrong action without considering whether the one who has committed it is bad or not. For Thomas, venial sin is any wrong action that is not a mortal sin.

There are, of course, valid reasons for holding that venial sin is any wrong action that is not a mortal sin. Odon Lottin points out that Thomas was, from the beginning, faced with a particular difficulty: either venial sin is in agreement with the last end and is, therefore, not sin; or it is against the last end, and is, therefore, mortal sin.[50] Thomas sees this. He writes in the *Commentary on the Sentences* that venial sin comes from one whose habitual though not necessarily actual disposition remains in God as the last end.[51] And, in later writings, as we have seen, he uses the same argument.

What distinguishes venial sin from mortal sin is that a wrongness has been committed by one whose act does not destroy union with God. Venial sin is committed by one in grace. Yet, in order to achieve this, Thomas has to avoid the actual motivation. When one asks, "but what is the motivation of the person who commits a venial sin?" Thomas simply responds that the motivation is not actual charity. Charity does not command in a venial sin. What, then, is the motivation for a venial sin?

I argued in the previous three chapters that the last end is the proper locus for understanding motivation. Yet, in order to ascertain the uniqueness of venial sin, Thomas precludes any discussion of motivation or the last end. He cannot argue that the one who sins actually acts out of that which is contrary to charity, for then he would have mortal sin. He cannot argue that one who sins actually acts out of that which is in union with the last end, because he has already described the activity as sinful.

To overcome this difficulty Thomas posits the distinction between actual charity and virtual or habitual charity and argues that the person who sins venially is not in the state of sin, because charity is habitually present. Thus, instead of answering the question whether venial sin comes out of a good or bad motivation, Thomas argues that in general, though not in this instance, the person acts out of charity. But what, then, is the actual motivation? Is the motivation good, and, therefore, not sin, or is it bad, and, therefore, sin? Thomas gives no real answer because he entertains differing possibilities. He simply argues that such an act is not an act of charity. Whether venial sin is really sin remains an open question.

If Thomas had faced the question more squarely, he may have found the distinction. If an inordinate action is performed out of charity or out of some other good motivation, e.g., benevolence, then the action is not sinful. We call it "good," though "wrong." If it is performed out of a bad or selfish motivation, then the action is sinful, that is, "bad." Following Thomas's order of presentation we begin with an inordinate action, yet our question concerns the person. Whether the act is inordinate or not is unimportant, for if the action were ordered or right, it could still be sinful. If Thomas had faced the actual last end of venial sin, this contemporary distinction might have surfaced. Instead, the question remains on the periphery and the inordinacy of the act, not the badness of the person, holds the center stage in Thomas's treatise on sin.

The difficulty of beginning with the inordinate act is found in the debate that flourished in moral theology during the 1920s and 1930s, concerning what should be said about imperfect actions. Consider for instance that we could choose between two right actions, one imperfect and the other more perfect. Thus, a teacher with ample time and ease could prepare a satisfactory lesson or a very fine one. A priest could visit a sick person or administer the Eucharist as well. A policeman could simply arrest a person or also treat the person with some dignity in the process.

Lottin argued that one who in conscience fails to perform the more perfect act sins, though venially, because the person knowingly performs the less perfect. He called the action subjectively, formally bad.[52] On the surface, this argument is a form of the distinction between goodness and rightness. Of itself, the action is not wrong, in fact, it is right. But, the agent demonstrates in fact, that he or she does not love as much as one can. Thus, here the motivation is "bad."

Interestingly, however, the debate is still posed from the context of the act and does not yet consider the person as the starting point. For that reason, the moralists do not really consider whether a "right" act can be a sin, but only whether a lesser right act can be a sin. Their question is not whether a right act can be a venial sin. Such an apparent paradox did not yet enter theological discourse. Therefore, the question was limited to this: between two acts that can with equal ease be performed, may one choose the lesser act without culpability? Despite its narrow scope, the debate demonstrated a movement toward the interiority of the person in order to find the decisive issue for sinfulness. Thus, it produced a significant insight: sin does not have to be a "wrong" action. The debate demonstrates that sin ought to be considered from a vantage point other than the inordinate action.

At most, Thomas describes venial sins as wrong actions and disordered inclinations of the agent, but not as acts of bad or selfish temporary motivation. In short, the venial sins that we commit every day by not striving as much as we can are not represented here. Only wrong actions are.

On the subject of mortal sins, curiously, Thomas does mention instances in which a right action is performed from a bad motivation. Arguing, for example, that something can be mortal by its cause (*ex sua causa*), Thomas cites the case of a person who gives alms hoping to lead another into heresy. In other instances he says that one could perform virtuous deeds out of vainglory or pride, or even make a lying pretense of one's good deeds. The same insight appears in his discussion of the relationship between guile and craftiness. Thomas does not take these central points and ask whether the apparent paradox has any significance; yet he seems to appreciate the insight common to each instance: one cannot know the actual motivation out of which another works.[53]

The question of appearances arises also from cases in which apparently bad acts are performed by good people. Osee's intercourse was not fornication, nor was Abraham's or Jacob's.[54] These cases though they appear sinful are not, and demonstrate that human actions cannot be known as "good" or "bad" by observation.

Though Thomas appreciates the hiddenness of the heart when he writes on charity, the question of the heart remains on the periphery when he writes on sin. Reflecting on the heart Thomas argues that one can only conjecture whether one is in the state of grace and has charity. On the other hand, he argues that one certainly knows whether one sins.[55] Certainly there are exceptions, like those above, in which Thomas recognizes the distinctive role of motivation but he never makes it part of his overall theoretical presentation of mortal sin.

Thomas begins his investigation concerning mortal sins by asking whether certain objects are contrary to charity. Rather than starting formally as he did in charity, Thomas starts materially. Rather than starting with the subject in union moving out to objects, Thomas starts with objects and moves into the subject. For Thomas one does not first stop moving toward God and subsequently do what one wills; rather, one performs certain acts and subsequently breaks a relationship.

Thus, in considering the first condition that makes a sin mortal, Thomas provides us with a fairly exhaustive list of objects that he considers generically, mortally sinful. First, he classifies those that are always mortally sinful: blasphemy, sloth, envy, sedition, injustice, theft, cursing, perjury, disobedience, and fornication. Then, he classifies those which are often generically, mortally sinful, but which are sometimes generically venial, especially when the matter of the action is not particularly serious. These issues are contention, scandal, negligence, railing, backbiting, derision, ingratitude, lying, hypocrisy, boasting, flattery, covetousness, fear, vainglory, gluttony, drunkenness, anger, pride, and false testimony.

These lists are particularly remarkable when we remember that the issues are determined according to whether their matter is contrary to charity.[56] As we saw in the last chapter, charity works formally, and as form it does not enter into the essence or substance of the virtue it commands. Charity as form, is simply charity as command, issuing from union with God and seeking greater union. Thus, for the most part, Thomas hesitates to speak of any elicited act that belongs to charity immediately, though he names these sins as acts that are contrary to charity.

In only four instances does Thomas present a particular type of action or behavior as an elicited act of charity. In each instance, Thomas remains aware of the difficulty of inducting the form of charity from an action per se. First, Thomas writes that beneficence, which is the act whereby one wishes one's friend well, is not a special virtue but belongs itself to charity, since both will the common aspect of good. If, however, one wills the friend well for any other reason than this, then beneficence belongs to another virtue.[57] Thus, beneficence per se is charity. But, the description of the behavior remains thoroughly formal: beneficence is performing an action of wishing one well. Like charity, it is a description of motivation. We have no description of a specified intended action. Once content is given, the act of beneficence belongs to a new species.

A second elicited act of charity is almsgiving. Almsgiving, however, more directly applies to mercy: it is an act of charity through the medium of mercy.[58] Still, one could perform almsgiving for the sake of leading another into heresy. Almsgiving is, then, derived from mercy, but it is only so derived when one specifically seeks the end of almsgiving itself. Otherwise almsgiving belongs to another species.

Third, Thomas describes fraternal correction from two perspectives. If one exercises it out of love for the offender's well-being, then fraternal correction is an act of charity. If one exercises it to protect the victim or the common good, then fraternal correction is an act of justice.[59] Only in the former, when the motivation of charity is attached to the action of fraternal correction, does Thomas argue its immediacy to charity. Like almsgiving, fraternal correction expresses a matter capable of being immediately expressive of charity.

Finally, at the end of his life, Thomas describes a fourth elicited act of charity: penance. Thus, if a penitent acts out of displeasure for her or his sins, then the act of penance belongs to charity immediately. If, on the other hand, the act aims at the destruction of past sin, then the act belongs to another virtue.[60] Only a purely expressive act of penance is an elicited act of charity.

I find no other instance in Thomas's work of an act belonging immediately to charity. On the contrary, Thomas holds that charity does not elicit the acts of other virtues, but commands them.[61] Charity remains formal in most of Thomas's writings. Of the four instances of immediate acts of charity, two, beneficence and penitence, are taken formally, and two, fraternal correction and almsgiving, still require the motivation of charity within their description. In effect, even when he describes elicited acts of charity, Thomas maintains a formal description of charity.

THE METHODOLOGY IN THE WRITINGS ON SIN

Quite differently, as the lists concerning mortal sin illustrate, Thomas considered ten instances in which the matters always belonged to mortal sin generically, and nineteen instances of matters that may, when serious, belong to mortal sin generically. Whereas in charity Thomas begins with the union of God and the agent and barely touches on the object; in mortal sin Thomas begins quite clearly with objects and from them recedes into the person to ask whether deliberate consent and known aversion are evident.[62]

His methodology on sin is, then, the opposite of that which he employed in the treatise on charity. Instead of speaking of the contrariety of mortal sin to charity formally, he speaks of that contrariety materially. Whereas in charity, Thomas writes that the "goodness" of an act (our term) is derived formally from charity; in mortal sin, the original gravity is first derived materially.

If Thomas can assign so few acts to charity immediately, how can he assign so many to its contrary? If Thomas realizes that the only way an act is "good," that is, charitable, is if charity commands it, where is the "bad" command in mortal sin? Thomas achieves "badness" (our term) only by arguing for deliberate consent to grave wrongdoing. In that, he finds the "bad" command implicitly evident.

In the process, however, Thomas makes a rather important presupposition. Thomas argues that when one chooses something contrary to divine charity, one shows that one prefers the former to the love of God and that one loves it more than God.[63] Alone, however, such an induction would not be possible: the performance of wrong action does not prove badness. Thus, when Thomas argues that a generically mortal sin when performed with deliberate consent is a mortal sin, he demonstrates an appreciation of the problem of inducting badness from wrongness. What, then, is deliberate consent? To understand deliberate consent, we turn again to the difference between venial and mortal sins.

Inasmuch as venial sin is an inordinate act that does not engage the last end per se and mortal sin is an inordinate act that does engage the last end per se, Thomas rightly argues that they are only analogously related. But the former does not describe whether the inordinate act comes from a bad motivation. Thus, as we have seen, venial sin is not clearly, and certainly not primarily, a manifestation of "badness," but only "wrongness." On the other hand, the object of mortal sin is of such significant scope that it engages the person's motivation and destroys the principle of goodness, when performed with clear consent.[64]

Thus, Thomas is placed in a particularly odd predicament. Since venial sin does not actually engage the agent's relation to the last end, it cannot affect charity. But since mortal sin engages the last end directly, it immediately destroys charity. Therefore, Thomas holds that nothing diminishes charity.[65] Thomas is, at least, consistent, but if charity is the principle of goodness, then charity can, in fact, be diminished. The problem for Thomas is that insofar as venial sin is only "wrongness," it is not a device for diminishing charity. He has no concept of lesser ordinary sins or "badness," those frequent sins wherein we fail to strive. If Thomas had conceived of sin, not as the "inordinate act," or "wrongness," but as failing motivation, or "badness," he would also have conceived of the diminishment of charity, and of whether that diminishment could ever become the destruction of charity itself. Having placed the fundamental definition of sin in the inordinate object, however, Thomas must logically argue that charity does not diminish.

To destroy charity, that is, to commit a mortal sin, Thomas sets three conditions. First, the action must generically belong to an action that is contrary to charity. Indeed, were the action generically venial it would still have to be used for the purpose of a generically mortal sin in order to be considered mortal. Second, one must deliberately consent to that generically mortal sin. Third, the aversion from God as last end must be accepted.[66] But must this aversion from God be explicit?

Every mortal sin takes its principal malice and gravity from its aversion from God. Does, however, turning to some mutable end require an act of the will to turn from God? Thomas answers no. When one chooses something contrary to charity, one proves that one prefers it to the love of God.[67] When one argues against having known that the given behavior is sinful, one is not only not excused, but slothful as well.[68] Thomas poses the objection that one who commits fornication unaware that the act is a mortal sin, sins venially. Thomas responds that if the person is an imbecile or madman, then the act is excused entirely. If not, then ignorance is vincible and the ignorance itself is a sin, and contains within it the defect of divine love, because one has not safeguarded oneself in the love of God.[69] The aversion from God is found not in an explicit intention but in intending an object that is generically mortally sinful.

Finally, does deliberate consent at least have to be explicit? I noted earlier, the contemporary preference for beginning discussions of goodness or badness with motivation. Thus, to determine sin I ask whether one strives or fails to strive for right living. The description of goodness or badness is then established, regardless of the rightness or wrongness of the consequent action. But when starting from the opposite end of things, that is, when attempting, as Thomas does, to induct badness from wrongness, one must first ascertain that the agent has failed to strive to realize virtuous or right action. Thomas's addition of deliberate consent justifies the description of a wrong act as a bad act: to do a generically mortal sin with deliberate consent expresses the agent's will to turn toward something wrong. By adding deliberate consent, Thomas ascertains the "badness" of the wrong action. Yet that deliberate consent would have to be explicit rather than inducted, as I hope to show, or else Thomas does not engage the badness of the agent.

What happens if one performs a generically mortal sin out of fear? Since the object has been willed, albeit out of fear, can the act be described as having the deliberate consent sufficient for description of mortal sin? Thomas proposes the objection narrated in Pope Leo's *Sermon on the Passion*, that Peter's denial of Christ was not an averted love. Thomas also cites Bernard or, more accurately, William of St. Thierry, who argues that charity was not lost in Peter's denial, but merely cooled.[70] Thomas responds that charity may be lost in two ways. First, directly, by actual contempt and in this way, Peter did not lose charity. Second, indirectly, as when a sin is committed against charity, through some passion or fear. Here Peter sinned against charity and lost charity, yet he soon recovered it.[71] The same position is taken in an earlier work, *Quodlibetum nonum* and in the later *De caritate*. In the latter Thomas argues that the objection does not hold unless we understand that after being lost charity was soon resurrected.[72]

There seems, therefore, to be two descriptions of deliberate consent: one is malicious, the other implicit. The latter is inducted from the case of one who fails to check intending a seriously sinful object. Describing this as deliberate consent is disturbing: it means that any generically mortal act, even if not committed maliciously, can still be a mortal sin. That is, in fact, Thomas's position. As in the case of Peter's denial, Thomas holds consistently that one who commits a generically mortal sin on account of a passion not rescued by the deliberate reason commits a mortal sin. Because, however, it is not committed maliciously, the sin's culpability diminishes though not as a venial sin, but as a mortal sin. Thus, the principle of goodness, charity, is destroyed, but there remains some grounds for its being redonated by God.

The implicit deliberate consent inducted from one who fails to check a seriously sinful action is found in several places in the *Summa*. For Thomas the only way an act lacks deliberate consent is if the act is checked before being executed. An executed act is still an act held as deliberated, though not maliciously so.

Thomas argues that a mortal sin is only venial when it is a sudden act as, for example, a sudden movement of unbelief, such as doubting the resurrection. Once one realizes, however, that divine law requires assent, were the movement (the doubt) to remain, it would be mortally sinful.[73] In another instance Thomas asks about morose delectation and argues that there are two ways that reason can fail: first, by deliberately provoking oneself to inordinate movements of passion; second, by failing to check in oneself the unlawful movement of passion. In the latter he again argues that failure to check is deliberate consent.[74]

Later, Thomas proposes the objection that a sin committed through passion cannot be mortal, because weakness is a motive for being pardoned.[75] Thomas replies that anything contrary to the last end is always a mortal sin, unless the deliberating reason is unable to come to the rescue. But, in proceeding from a passion to an act, the deliberating reason can come to the rescue. Thus, in these actions there is mortal sin. On this account, writes Thomas, many homicides and adulteries are committed.[76] In response to the objection, Thomas distinguishes between the veniality of an action, when it has cause to be forgiven and which lessens the sin, from the veniality of genus. He responds that only the latter is opposed to mortal sin.[77] A generically mortal sin committed out of passion is not venial but mortal, though its gravity is diminished.

Like the issue of aversion, the question of whether deliberate consent must be explicit is answered in the negative. Intending the sufficiently grave object is sufficient reason for attributing mortal sin to an agent. That intention is at once an implicit aversion from God and deliberate consent to an object. Thus, rather than add conditions for making wrong actions bad, Thomas only extends the ramifications of what it means to intend a generically mortal sin. One who intends such an object implicitly averts from God and deliberately consents to the sin committed.

The problem here is the result of an unjustifiable induction. Thomas has inducted from weakness, disorder, or wrongness to badness. Thomas has inducted a bad motivation from some wrong inclinations that have accepted seriously wrong matter. Certainly he admits that badness in these instances is less bad than in malicious consent. Still, the badness is mortal in that the principle of goodness, charity, is destroyed. Since charity is the only description of moral goodness in the person, the person bereft of charity has no goodness remaining. This person acting out of weakness is in the state of sin.

THE CASE OF THE LYING MIDWIVES

In the writings on charity Thomas treats the last end formally and similarly to his concept of *exercitium*. In the writings on mortal sin, Thomas treats the last end materially and similarly to his concept of specification. In charity Thomas describes the relation to the last end as a response of the heart and speaks of the subject in union with the last end. In mortal sin he speaks of objects. In charity, he maintains a threshold between agents and objects, between charity and virtues, between the command of charity and the right intended object. He offers only four elicited acts and yet maintains the purity of charity's formality. In mortal sin, he presents twenty-nine categories of generically mortal sins, presumes, to a large extent, deliberate reason, and often inducts badness from wrongness.

Thomas has here two different orders: the order of the person in union with God and the order of the object. In the treatment of the virtues, he carefully distinguishes the last end from any question concerning objects. By establishing this threshold he arrives at the peculiarity of charity wherein our union with the last end remains formal, seeking expression in rightly ordered selves and in actions. In sin, he materializes that last end. In charity, Thomas has a concept of motivation antecedent to any action. In sin, he has objects antecedent to any persons. The methods conflict.

For this reason, I argue that Thomas does not use the difference between charity and reason, developed in his treatise on charity, as a distinction between goodness and rightness. Though the difference between these two concepts is clear in the treatise on charity, they are not thematized in his moral writings. The result is that the conditions and the method for determining goodness are not comparable to the conditions and the method for determining badness.

If we do not thematize the distinction, we may forget that even that which is wrong may not be a sin. Certainly an act is not a sin if we do it out of goodness, that is, as striving to live and act rightly. Thomas is sensitive to this issue and often describes a good motivation that diminishes the wrongness of an act. But the difficulties that arise in these cases do so because he does not distinguish the two concepts. Consider, for example, the moral dilemma posed by the following story. The problem, of course, is to distinguish goodness and rightness.

Exodus 1:15-21 is the story of the midwives ordered by Pharaoh to kill all Hebrew male newborns. Fearing God, two midwives did not do as the king commanded and let the children live. Pharaoh learns of this and demands to know why they have let the children live. The women answer, "Because the Hebrew women are not like Egyptian women; for they are vigorous and are delivered before the midwife comes to them." The story concludes that God dealt favorably with the midwives, rewarding them because they feared God.

The story caused particular consternation for the medieval reader. On the face of it, God rewards someone for lying. Since lying is a sin, how could God reward these women? Thomas discusses this story on six occasions.

In his *Commentary on the Sentences*, Thomas uses this story to ask whether every lie is a sin. According to the second objection, it would seem that not every lie is a sin, because no sin is rewarded by God, but the Egyptian midwives were rewarded by God. But, Thomas responds, the women were rewarded for the act that saved the boys, not for the act of lying. Thomas has resolved the problem by distinguishing two different actions.[78]

Thomas returns again to the issue in the same article to answer an objection concerning the presence of lies in the Scriptures. On the one hand, Thomas says, the testimonies of scriptural writers are never lies, but must be taken figuratively. On the other hand, the words of other people reported in the Scriptures may well be lies. Within the second category, Thomas proposes three classes. First, the words of malicious ones, and here Thomas cites the crowds blaspheming Christ. Second, the words of those who are commended by the Scriptures not for their perfection of virtue but for the source of their virtue ("aut alicuius qui commendatur non perfectione virtutis sed de profectu"), and here Thomas cites the midwives who lied not to cause injury but to worship the Lord. Third, the words of those who are commended for the perfection of virtue but whose words must also be taken figuratively. Here Thomas proposes no example.[79] This time Thomas distinguishes not between actions but between the motivation or source (*profectus*) of the act and the act itself. Nevertheless, like the first occasion, this time, too, the lie is excluded from commendation.

Thomas also discusses the lying midwives in the next article that asks whether all lies are mortal sins. In the first *sed contra*, Thomas argues from Jerome that God does not build spiritual houses on account of mortal sins, and since the midwives received these houses, they did not sin mortally by lying.[80]

In the same article, however, Thomas presents the objection that if lies were excused from mortal sin, that would especially be evident in the case of officious lies. But officious lies are commuted from receiving eternal reward to receiving only temporal reward, as Gregory had demonstrated in the case of the midwives: by the guilt of the lie, their heavenly reward became a temporal reward. Thus, for Gregory, the reward was actually a punishment and all lies are mortal sins.[81] In response, Thomas notes a variety of opinions. Some argue that the midwives' desire to save the children's lives made the sin officious and therefore venial. But as the lie was also to save their own lives, it was therefore mortal. Thomas calls this position unreasonable, since one ought to save one's own life, just as one ought to save the lives of others.

He argues three issues. First, the tradition of Jerome shows that to the degree they wanted to save the boys' lives, their act was meritorious. Second, regarding the lie they sinned venially and, according to Augustine, are commended not for the perfection of justice but the source of justice ("non perfectae iustitiae, sed profectus ad iustitiam"). But, third, as they omitted to confess the divine truth before Pharaoh, they sinned mortally, and their reward has been commuted. Thomas, evidently uneasy with this third position, adds, if they did not sin mortally, still their goodness was not informed by grace, and for this reason, they receive a temporal reward, grace being necessary for an eternal one. Thus, Thomas leans again to the second distinction and calls the act a sin despite its good *profectus*.

This early work makes several noteworthy points. First, all lying is a sin, but not necessarily a mortal sin. Officious lies are a case in point: lying to help or to protect someone from being harmed is a sin, but not a mortal one. Second, in the case of the lying midwives they are commended for the source (*profectus*) of virtue, not the perfection of virtue. Third, they merit because they wanted to save the children from harm, but their action is sinful though venially so. Finally, Thomas hints at some difficulty with the severity of Gregory's judgment.

Roughly two years later, at Paris during Christmas 1257, Thomas again discusses whether lying is always a sin. In the *Quodlibetum octavum*, Thomas raises the objection that the Scriptures commend people who lie, e.g., the midwives, Jacob, and Judith. Therefore, lying is not always a sin. Thomas responds to the objection exactly as he had in the *Sentences*. The midwives are praised not for lying but for the pity that led them to fall into lying ("propter misericordiam ex qua in mendacium inciderunt"). Thus, they are commended for a certain characteristic, namely, the source of virtue, not its perfection.[82] The source of their act was good, but its result was not; the lie itself proceeded from goodness. Here is Thomas's first direct association between the lie and goodness. The earlier arguments asserted that the women's motivations were good; here even the motivation for the lie itself is good. The lies do not come from ignorance but from mercy.

Twelve years later, in the last article of the *Prima secundae*, Thomas argues that temporal gifts in themselves are not an indication of an agent's goodness. He argues, too, that some agents without the right intention (*rectam intentionem*) are moved to undertake works in relation to the divine will. He cites two instances: one clear, the other ambiguous. First, the king of Babylon besieges Tyre not for the service of God but to take dominion. Second, the midwives want to save the children, on the one hand, and, on the other, frame lies. Thomas does not say why they receive a reward; and whereas no goodness is attributed to the king, the ambiguity of the second case highlights Thomas's own ambiguity.[83]

Finally, in the *Secunda secundae*, Thomas again asks whether every lie is a sin and whether every lie is a mortal sin. Here Thomas establishes the various categories of lying, including the officious lie, and specifies their order of gravity: "the greater the good intended, the more is the sin of lying diminished in gravity."[84] As always,

Thomas begins with the object before the person. As the object is sinful, so the agent intending it is sinful. But, to the extent that the more remote or even final end is good, though there is sin, the sin is less grievous.

Suitably, when Thomas asks whether every lie is a sin, he raises the objection that no one is rewarded by God for a sin, but the midwives were rewarded; therefore, a lie is not a sin. Thomas responds that they were rewarded not for the lie (*pro mendacio*) but for their fear of God and their benevolence, out of which their lie proceeded. Afterwards, Thomas adds, the subsequent lie was not meritorious: "mendacium vero postea sequens non fuit meritorium."[85]

Thus, in two instances Thomas states not simply that the midwives have the source of virtue but also that the lie itself came out of that goodness. Earlier Thomas had attributed their lie to mercy; now he attributes it to fear of God and benevolence and distinguishes the lie from its source temporally. Their reward is for their fear of God, not for what they did afterwards, that is, their subsequent lie.

In the next article Thomas asks whether every lie is a mortal sin. His objections include Gregory's position that by lying the women forfeited the heavenly reward of kindness and received instead a temporal reward. Thomas argues that if the end intended be not contrary to charity, as in the officious lie, then the lie is not a mortal sin. Responding to the objection, he distinguishes the character of virtue found in the women's benevolence to the Jews and their fear of God, which deserves eternal reward, from the external act of the lie itself ("quantum ad ipsum exteriorem actum mendacii"). The lie, Thomas argues, could merit a fitting temporal reward, though it could not merit an eternal reward. Thomas adds that Gregory's position ought to be understood in this way, not as if the lie caused the loss of the reward won by the preceding affection.[86]

Thomas comes extraordinarily close in these discussions to our distinction of goodness and rightness. He distinguishes the agents who, for their fundamental benevolence and fear of God, merit eternal reward from the inordinateness of their action. The action, moreover, is judged in the temporal real rather than in the eternal, or spiritual, realm. Other points, however, must not be overlooked. First, in both articles Thomas refers to the difference in time: they are rewarded for their prior fundamental disposition, not for their subsequent act. Second, instead of pointing out that the act as measured by charity is good, but wrong as measured by reason, Thomas distinguishes their character from their act.

Thus, instead of using distinct measures for each object, Thomas uses one measure for the person; another for the act. In fact, he uses the measure of charity only analogously by applying the two constitutive elements of charity, benevolence and fear of God, to the case of these non-Christian women. As a result—and this is our third point—he cannot call the act "good." In a manner of speaking, Thomas has not exercised two measures; rather, he has measured two objects: the persons and the lie. Thus, the women are meritorious but their act is not; or, to use a phrase from the treatise on the virtues, the act is not referable to God.

If the act is commanded by benevolence, charity, or fear of God, if it is commanded by some final end as descriptive of one's fundamental motivation, why is it not called "good"? And why can it not be referred to God? In this case of the lying midwives, two presuppositions effectively block Thomas from thematizing this distinction. First, as I have pointed out repeatedly, Thomas has only one concept for moral description. Lacking our concept of "right," Thomas has only the concept "good," which generally means fitting to reason. Faced with an officious lie, which has benevolence as its motivation, i.e., a motivation that is by definition already morally good, Thomas refuses to call it good. He argues that for an act to be good it must be good in every respect, whereas evil comes from one single defect.[87] Thus, though Thomas argues that two measures of goodness exist and that external acts are subject to both measures when commanded by charity, he himself measures the external act by reason alone. Because the act is not "good" by the measure of reason, that defect means presumably that the act is not "good" by the measure of charity. But is the defect in one measure applicable to the other?

In the ambit of rightness or specification, any defect generally prompts the judgment that an act is wrong: if there is a defect in the intention, the choice, or the circumstances, we will generally hold that the act is wrong. An examination of our ordinary judgments will prove that. Similarly, only when the three elements converge correctly do we call the act right. Indeed, as we have said, rightness bears great resemblance to perfection. On the other hand, insofar as goodness is simply the question of one's self-movement, it is not subject to the dictum that concerns ends, objects and circumstances. This statement describes judgments pertaining to moral rightness, not moral goodness. The defect in rightness does not affect the description of goodness.

Second, though Thomas begins with the inordinate act, he diminishes the gravity of the sin by adding the good out of which the act is done. We, on the other hand, begin with persons and argue that people with charity and acts commanded by charity are good, though not necessarily right. This same judgment can be inferred from Thomas's position on the two measures of charity and reason. And Thomas, in fact, argues similarly in answer to Gregory's objection. He argues first that the two women are worthy of merit and only then that their act is not, though it does not remove the eternal merit won by the women's preceding dispositions. Starting with the person and proceeding to the act, Thomas is at least able to argue against Gregory that eternal merit is not lost by a subsequent act.

Yet, we cannot overlook the fact that Thomas employs two methods here. In answer to Gregory, he started with the women and proceeded to the act. On the question of sin, however, in which this answer occurs, he had already started with the act and proceeded to the person. Thomas does not argue that sin comes from sinful people, as we do in our distinction, that is, that bad acts come from bad motivations; Thomas argues from the inordinateness of the act. Having taken inordinateness or wrongness as the point of departure, he must diminish the culpability through the person's goodness, and in the process confuses the two measures. Having stated that all lies are sin, he must now try to resolve how those who perform sins are still worthy of merit. He must at least separate the agents temporally from their acts. Arguing that the motivation was good though the subsequent act was not, Thomas cannot argue that the women were also good when they acted. Starting with acts, instead of persons, Thomas cannot thematize the distinction.

The case of the lying midwives develops two points. First, Thomas works with only one measure, not two, though he measures two objects: persons and their external acts. That measure is "good," usually meaning right, even of persons. Only when he writes on charity does he expressly have two measures. Rather, and here is the second point, starting with the goodness or badness of acts (Thomas's terms), he then proceeds to persons. When, however, he is faced with an obvious difficulty, e.g., persons commended in the Scriptures though their acts are not commendable, Thomas must reverse the order of procedure.

The contemporary distinction between goodness and rightness represents these two movements. Goodness is the measure of persons, their habits of conduct, and their acts as proceeding from one who strives openly out of love to realize right living. It is the measure of the source itself, of whether the *profectus* is love or selfishness. Rightness is the measure of acts and the proximate sources of acts, that is, choices, intentions, and virtues, according to their fittingness to reason. Rightness is the measure of the execution, the attainment, the *perfectus*, in short, of whether the behavior has been properly realized.

Thus, the *profectus* and the *perfectus* are not two different poles of one moral description, but two different descriptions. If the source is oneself motivated by goodness, the agent and act are good. If the act is properly realized and fitting to the agent, the agent and the action are right.

Finally, we must ask ourselves at this point why the distinction made in the treatise on charity is not made in the treatise on sin. I offer a few possible reasons. First, treatises on sin have a long history stemming from the fifth-century penitentials. These works apply the same method that Thomas did; that is, beginning from a determined object, they attempt to determine the seriousness of the sin. Thus, Thomas's treatise on sin is simply an extension of a long tradition. Second, and more immediately, the Dominicans themselves, as I noted earlier in this work, were trained in the habit of specifying sins according to objects. As a second generation Dominican, Thomas was not inclined, I think, to doubt a habit assumed by all his contemporaries and predecessors. Third, living in a culture that focused so completely on sin leaves as "self-evident" a number of premises which, I think, could and should be questioned and examined. Again, John Mahoney makes the same point when he talks about the tradition's "careless familiarity" with sin that has been "domesticated and trivialized." Mahoney comments, "moral theology has not always appeared to take sin itself seriously enough." [88]

Thus, there were no stimuli available to Thomas to prod an examination of the presuppositions of the penitentials and the earlier treatises on sin. On the contrary, Thomas's treatise on sin is perhaps the least satisfactory part of his moral writings. Unlike his writings on reason, the will, the human act, virtues, and charity, Thomas's writings on sin do not exhibit any new critical insights. The only time newness arises is in the discussion of cases like that of the midwives, which discussions were themselves open to question. The more general topic of sin and its specifications was not an open subject. If Mahoney is right that the Church and its theology was preaching with too great ease on sin, Thomas, the evidence shows, must be included in this evaluation.

NOTES to Chapter Seven

1. On sin, see Frederick Copleston, *Aquinas* (Baltimore: Penguin, 1955), 199ff.; John Dedek, "Intrinsically Evil Acts: The Emergence of a Doctrine," *Recherches de théologie ancienne et médiévale* 50 (1983): 191–226; "Intrinsically Evil Acts: An Historical Study of the Mind of St. Thomas," *The Thomist*

43 (1979): 385–413; "Moral Absolutes in the Predecessors of St. Thomas," *Theological Studies* 38 (1977): 654–680; Th. Deman, "Péché," *Dictionnaire de Théologie Catholique* (Paris: Librairie Letouzey et Ané, 1933), 12:col. 140–275. A. Festugière, "La notion du péché présentée par S. Thomas," *New Scholasticism* 5 (1931): 332–341; Pierre Gervais, "Péché," *Dictionnaire de Spiritualité* (Paris: Beauschesne, 1984), 12: col. 790–853; Justo Laguna, "La doctrina de Santo Tomás sobre el pecado," *L'Agire Morale* (Napoli: Edizioni Dominicane Italiane, 1974), 499–509; John Langan, "Morality, Egoism and Punishment in Thomas Aquinas," *Heythrop Journal* 22 (1981): 378–393; Odon Lottin, *Morale Fondamentale* (Tournai: Desclée et Cie, 1954), 471–505; John Milhaven, "Moral Absolutes and Thomas Aquinas," *Absolutes in Moral Theology*, ed. Charles Curran (Washington, D.C.: Corpus Books, 1968), 154–185; Dalmazio Mongillo, "L'esistenza cristiana: Peccato e conversione," *Vita Nuova in Cristo*, ed. Tullo Goffi and Giannino Piana (Brescia: Queriniana, 1983), 491–552.

   2. S.T. I.II.21.1–4.
   3. I.II.21.2c.: ". . . in quibus idem malum, peccatum, et culpa."
   4. I.II.71.1c.: ". . . nam peccatum proprie nominat actum inordinatum"; I.II.71.6c.: "Peccatum nihil aliud est quam actus humanus malus."
   5. I.II.71.6.ad2.
   6. I.II.87.5.ad1.
   7. I.II.85.1c., 2c., 3c. See also I.II.21.1c.; 59.1.ad2.; 73.2c.; 94.3.ad2.; 98.1c.; II.II.153.2c.; 183.4c.
   8. I.II.71.6.ad5.: "A theologis consideratur peccatum praecipue secundum quod est offensa contra Deum: a philosopho autem morali, secundum quod contrariatur rationi."
   9. I.II.73.7.ad3. See also I.II.109.4c. and I.94.1c.
   10. I.II.72.1c.ad1. and ad2.; 72.6.ad2.; 72.8.ad2.; 72.9.ad1.; 73.1c.; 79.2.ad3.; II.II.39.2c.
   11. II.II.104.3c.
   12. I.II.85.5.ad3.; 87.5.ad1.
   13. See I.94.1c.; II.II.19.2.ad5.; III.8.7.ad3.
   14. I.II.84.3.ad2.; 85.5.ad3. See also I.II.73.3.ad2. and II.II.148.5.ad2.
   15. II.II.29.3.ad1. "A gratia gratum faciente nullus deficit nisi propter peccatum, ex quo contingit quod homo sit aversus a fine debito, in aliquo indebito finem constituens. Et secundum hoc appetitus eius non inhaeret principaliter vero finali bono, sed apparenti." See also I.94.1c.; II.II.9.4c.
   16. II.II.20.1.ad1. and 3c.; 10.5.ad1.
   17. I.II.112.5.ad3. ". . . peccatum habet pro principio et pro obiecto bonum commutabile, quod nobis est notum."
   18. I.II.72.1.ad3.; II.II.10.5ad1. Precisely because the object is formal, Thomas can argue that the difference between sins of commission and omission concern only the external act or material object. The sin is the same as it is in the will: the formal object, not the material object, specifies sins.
   19. I.II.72.5.ad1. "Ex parte conversionis, per quam respicit obiectum unde peccatum speciem habet." See I.II.87.5.ad1.
   20. I.II.74.2.ad1. and 5.ad2.; 75.3.ad3.; 80.1c. and ad3. and 80.3.ad1.; 83.3c. and ad3; 87.2c.

21. I.II.74.1.ad1.: "Malum dicitur esse praeter voluntatem, quia voluntas non tendit in ipsum sub ratione mali. Sed quia aliquod malum est apparens bonum, ideo voluntas aliquando appetit aliquod malum. Et secundum hoc peccatum est in voluntate." See I.II.74.1.ad2.; 75.2c.; 75.4.ad1.; 77.2c. and ad2.; 80.1c.; II.II.29.3.ad1.

22. I.II.109.2.ad2. "Peccare nihil aliud est quam deficere a bono quod convenit alicui secundum suam naturam."

23. I.II.77.1c., 2.ad2., 6.ad1; 80.1c.

24. I.II.75.1c. "Provenit enim defectus ordinis in actu, ex defectu directionis in voluntate." See I.II.75.1.ad3.; 78.1c.

25. I.II.78.1c: "Est autem voluntas inordinata, quando minus bonum magis amat." See also I.II.78.1c and ad2. On commands by the will and elicited acts of other powers, see I.II.74.2.ad1.; II.II.10.2c.

26. I.II.73.2c.: "Et ideo multum interest ad gravitatem peccati, utrum plus vel minus recedatur a rectitudine rationis. Et secundum hoc dicendum est quod non omnia peccata sunt paria." See also I.II.73.3c. and 8c.

27. I.II.76.3.; I.II.77.7.; II.II.125.4c; 150.4.

28. I.II.73.3.ad2.: "Ex ipsa indebita conversione ad aliquod bonum commutabile, sequitur aversio ab incommutabili bono, in qua perficitur ratio mali." See also I.II.73.5c.; II.II.162.6c.

29. I.II.88.2c.; II.II.6.2.ad2.; 100.1.ad7.; 142.3c.

30. III.90.2.ad4.: "Et ideo, licet peccatum perficiatur in consensu cordis."

31. I.II.78.2.ad2.: "Actus qui procedunt ex habitibus, sunt similes secundum speciem actibus ex quibus habitus generantur: differunt tamen ab eis sicut perfectum ab imperfecto. Et talis est differentia peccati quod committitur ex certa malitia, ad peccatum quod committitur ex aliqua passione." See also I.II.78.1c., 4c., and 4.ad3.

32. I.II.74.3.ad3: ". . . peccatum veniale, quod est quidam imperfectum in genere peccati." I.II.88.1.ad1: "Et ideo perfecta ratio peccati, quam Augustinus ponit, convenit peccato mortali."

33. II.II.35.3c. See also I.II.77.8.ad1.; 88.2c. and 6c.

34. I.II.88.2c.: "Cum enim voluntas fertur in aliquid quod secundum se repugnat caritati, per quam homo ordinatur in ultimum finem, peccatum ex suo obiecto habet quod sit mortale."

35. I.II.88.6c.ad1.: "Per subtractionem quandam scilicet deliberatae rationis."

36. I.II.74.10c.; I.II.87.5.ad1.; II.II.20.3c.

37. I.II.88.1.ad1.: "Divisio peccati venialis et mortalis non est divisio generis in species, quae aequaliter participent rationem generis: sed analogi in ea de quibus praedicatur secundum prius et posterius."

38. I.II.72.5c.ad1. and ad2. See also I.II.89.1.ad2. and ad3.; 88.1c.

39. I.II.87.5.ad1.: "Peccata non differunt in infinitum ex parte conversionis ad bonum commutabile, in qua consistit substantia actus; differunt autem in infinitum ex parte aversionis."

40. I.II.88.3.ad2.: "Peccatum veniale non est simile mortali in specie: est tamen simile ei in genere, inquantum utrumque importat defectum debiti ordinis, licet aliter et aliter."
41. I.II.87.5.ad1.; II.II.24.10c.; II.II.122.4.ad3.
42. II.II.44.4.ad2.: "Alio modo, ut habitualiter totum cor hominis in Deum feratur: ita scilicet quod nihil contra Dei dilectionem cor hominis recipiat. Et haec est perfectio viae. Cui non contrariatur peccatum veniale: quia non tollit habitum caritatis, cum non tendat in oppositum obiectum: sed solum impedit caritatis usum."
43. I.II.19.7.ob3. and ad3. See also I.II.19.6.ad1.
44. I.II.84.4.ob5. and ad5.
45. DM 15.1.ad3.
46. S.T. II.II.110.2c., 3c., and 4c.
47. II.II.33.2c.: "Actus autem peccatorum sunt secundum se mali, et nullo modo bene fieri possunt."
48. II.II.33.2.ad3.
49. I.II.77.8.ad1.
50. Odon Lottin, *Morale Fondamentale*, 492.
51. See I Sent. d.1q.3ad4.; In II Sent. d.42q.1a.3ad5.
52. Odon Lottin, *Morale Fondamentale*, 502. An ample bibliography on the debate itself appears in the same work (pp. 498–499).
53. S.T. II.II.111.2.ad1.; 132.3c.; 154.4c.; 162.6.ad1. See also II.II.55.4c. and ad2.; 104.2.ad3.
54. II.II.154.2.ad2. and ad3.
55. I.II.112.5c. and ad3.
56. See I.II.72.5c.; II.II.24.12c.; 35.3c.; 105.1c.; 112.2c.; 115.2c.
57. See II.II.31., especially 1c. and 4c.
58. II.II.32.1c.
59. II.II.33.1c.
60. III.85.2.ad1.
61. II.II.23.4.ad2.; *De caritate* 5.ad3.
62. S.T. II.II.35.3c.; II.II.36.3c.
63. I.II.88.2.ad1.: "Ex hoc ipso quod aliquis eligit id quod repugnat divinae caritati, convincitur praeferre illud caritati divinae, et per consequens plus amare ipsum quam Deum."
64. I.II.74.10c. See also I.II.88.2c.; 88.6.ad1.; II.II.35.3c.; III.90.2.ad4.
65. II.II.24.10c.
66. See I.II.74.10c. and II.II.20.3c.
67. I.II.88.2c. Alexander VIII in 1690 condemned the argument that one who sins against reason without sinning deliberately against God does not sin mortally (Denz.1290). Here we have Thomas's far earlier rejection of the same argument.
68. S.T. I.II.84.4.ad5.: "Potest tamen dici quod omnia peccata quae ex ignorantia proveniunt, possunt reduci ad acediam, ad quam pertinet negligentia qua aliquis recusat bona spiritualia acquirere propter laborem: ignorantia enim quae potest esse causa peccati, ex negligentia provenit, ut supra

dictum est. Quod autem aliquis committat aliquod peccatum ex bona intentione, videtur ad ignorantiam pertinere: inquantum scilicet ignorat quod non sunt facienda mala ut veniant bona."

69. I.II.88.6.ad2.: "Si sit talis ignorantia quae peccatum omnino excuset, sicut est furiosi vel amentis, tunc ex tali ignorantia fornicationem committens nec mortaliter nec venialiter peccat. Si vero sit ignorantia non invincibilis, tunc ignorantia ipsa est peccatum, et continet in se defectum divini amoris, inquantum negligit homo addiscere ea per quae potest se in divino amore conservare."

70. II.II.24.12.ob2.

71. II.II.24.12.ad2.: "Caritas amittitur dupliciter. Uno modo, directe, per actualem contemptum. Et hoc modo Petrus caritatem non amisit. Alio modo, indirecte: quando committitur aliquod contrarium caritati propter aliquam passionem concupiscentiae vel timoris. Et hoc modo Petrus, contra caritatem faciens, caritatem amisit: sed eam cito recuperavit."

72. *Quod.* 9.7.1.ad2. and *De Caritate* 6.ad2.

73. S.T. I.II.74.10c.

74. I.II.74.6c.

75. I.II.77.8.ob1.

76. I.II.77.8c.: "Cum autem ex passione aliquis procedit ad actum peccati, vel ad consensum deliberatum, hoc non fit subito. Unde ratio deliberans potest hic occurrere: potest enim excludere, vel saltem impedire passionem, ut dictum est. Unde si non occurrat, est peccatum mortale: sicut videmus quod multa homicidia et adulteria per passionem committuntur."

77. I.II.77.8.ad1.

78. See III Sent. d.38q.1a.3c.ob1. and ad1., ob2. and ad2.

79. Ibid., ob4. and ad4.

80. III Sent. d.38q.1a.4sc.1. The RSV replaces Jerome's "spiritual houses" with "families."

81. III Sent. d.38q.1a.4.ob3. and ad3.

82. *Quod.* 8.6.4.ad2.

83. S.T. I.II.114.10c. and ad2.

84. II.II.110.2c.: "Patet autem quod quanto bonum intentum est melius, tanto magis minuitur culpa mendacii."

85. II.II.110.3.ob2. and ad2.

86. II.II.110.4.ob4; 4c. and ad4.

87. II.II.110.3c.: "Quia ad hoc quod aliquid sit bonum, requiritur quod omnia recte concurrant." Then Thomas quotes Dionysius (De div. nom. 4. MG 3.729C.): "bonum est ex integra causa, malum est ex singularibus defectibus."

88. See John Mahoney, *The Making of Moral Theology* (Oxford: Clarendon Press, 1987), 32. The context for this remark is his discussion of the penitentials (pp. 1–36).

The Dialogue Concludes

Before 1270 Thomas held that the source of all movement was found in the object that reason presented to the will. Later, however, he presented two sources and distinguished the will's formal movement from its specification informed by objects. In his last distinction between the *profectus* and the *perfectus*, however, we again find only one source of movement instead of two.

The distinctions between the *profectus* and the *perfectus* and the *terminus a quo* and the *terminus ad quem* are not satisfactory. In those distinctions there is only one source and, therefore, one "good." They do not carry forward Thomas's 1270 finding that the will's movement *quantum ad exercitium* is not the will's movement *quantum ad specificationem*. These two movements have two sources: the source of all formal movement found in the will's movement *quantum ad exercitium* and the source of all material movement found in the will's movement *quantum ad specificationem*.

The will's movement *quantum ad specificationem* has its own source. Its source is the object as presented by reason, which serves as the form of the act. On the other hand, the source of the will's movement *quantum ad exercitium* is its own movement, or even, God's original movement.

Thomas needs to distinguish the source of an act's goodness from the source of its specification. For example, the goodness of the midwives' act, their fear of God and benevolence toward the Jews, differs from the source of the wrongness of their action, the formal object wherein they contradict in spoken word what they have in mind. The formal movement describes whether they in their own personal freedom move themselves and their reason toward right presentation, acceptance, and execution. The actual specification of the act describes the matter of its presentation, acceptance, and execution. Unfortunately, Thomas does not apply that distinction directly to moral theology.

He does, however, make a similar distinction between the virtues and charity. The virtues have their source in rightly ordered objects presented by reason, accepted by the will, and executed by the intending agent. That source is the form that specifies particular virtues. On the other hand, there is charity. Its source is union, and as form it only moves the person toward seeking greater union. Here, for Thomas, is the threshold between the formal movement of the agent, which has its source in union with God, and the actual specification of the intention of an agent, which has its source in the rightly ordered object. This is the insight and the distinction that Thomas made in 1270.

The distinction does not appear in the treatise on sin. Only one source of movement appears in these questions, namely the object. Thomas remains in the realm of specification, though he often tries to reach goodness. He introduces the excuse of ignorance, the excuse of the passions, the veniality of mortal sins, and finally even good motivation in the attempt to exceed specification. Yet, though Thomas introduces the cause of movement *quantum ad exercitium*, that is, the fear of God, in the treatises on sin, he does not distinguish it (as he had previously) as belonging to another order. Indeed, only in discussions about sin, do we find the last end used so arbitrarily in its relation to the object.

On the question of freedom, Thomas explicitly distinguishes the two orders of motivation and intention. Further, between the virtues and charity, Thomas implicitly distinguishes the two. In the treatise on sin, however, Thomas does not make this distinction. Why does Thomas not distinguish the self-movement of the agent from what the agent does?

I have stated that the issue is Thomas's starting point, the object. In the same way, the object is the starting point for discussing the morality of acts and virtues. But Thomas is careful to keep the last end out of that discourse. He reserves the last end for his discussion on charity, in which he establishes a separate order and a separate measure. In the discussion on sin, however, he mixes the end and objects together and refers to the last end materially, a departure from the way charity works formally. Is this an oversight? Is it simply that Thomas did not appreciate the two orders with their respective sources and measures? Or is there another reason? I do not know. For that reason, I argue only that the distinction was not thematized.

Perhaps the problem results from this: if Thomas sees charity as seeking greater union, then badness is seeking lesser union. But charity could not have such a contradictory. Since Thomas realizes that we cannot intend "evil" per se, perhaps, he realizes as well that the order of charity has no real contradictory: we cannot seek lesser union. This is speculation. But notwithstanding this difficulty, Thomas was also familiar with the dictum of Gregory and Bernard: "To stand still on the way to God is to go back." With that one phrase Thomas could have discussed badness, not as seeking to do "evil," but as the failing to strive. With it, Thomas could have avoided the difficulties of the diminishment and the destruction of charity. He could have spoken of sin in relation to people's daily motivations and still maintained that people do not intend "evil." Instead, Thomas turned to the object.

*   *   *

At this point, I ask what have we done? First, we have reread Thomas. Second, we have developed the distinction. Third, we have discovered in Thomas a relationship described between the will and reason that has never been worked out by advocates of the distinction. Fourth, we have seen that the discussion of the act can remain within the question of rightness and that the notions of "end" and "intention" as used by Thomas often do not mean goodness, but rightness. Fifth, we have seen that contrary to others' suggestions, virtue can quite easily be discussed in the context of rightness. Sixth, we have seen charity not simply as the complement of reason, but as a moral description distinct from that of reason. Seventh, we have critiqued Thomas's position on sin, realizing new questions concerning the concepts of mortal and venial sins and challenging his position on the diminishment of charity. Finally, we have seen that goodness and rightness describe two different realities.

As I conclude, I ask another question, one only obliquely referred to throughout this work, but one that arises in the case of the lying midwives. Thomas never explicitly, to my knowledge, presents a case of one who acts out of charity but does the wrong or disordered intended act. He does state, however, that venial sins or wrong acts are acts that are not referred to God. Yet is that true? Are we not growing in charity despite the traces of disorders or wrongnesses within ourselves? Are there not even some areas of our lives in which the disorders are more than simply traces? Can we, like the midwives, not offer these to God?

I do not propose that we offer our sinfulness to God, which is, our failure to strive for greater union. In our sinfulness we offer God nothing. But in our goodness, can we not offer the disordered as well as the rightly ordered dimensions of ourselves? Can we not offer what we have attained and what we are striving to attain? Are not all our strivings, be they right or wrong, capable of being presented to the One who made us, loves us, and delivers us? If we only offer the rightnesses, then perhaps we have not yet begun to encounter the fullness of that union which we seek, and more important, into which we have been invited. Broken as we are, we offer God our entire selves, willing that there be no limit in our striving.

Chronology of Thomas Aquinas's Works

The chronology and classification of the works are those given by James A. Weisheipl and the *New Catholic Encyclopedia*, and they are keyed as follows:

A: Theological Syntheses
B: Academic Disputations
C: Expositions of Holy Scripture
D: Expositions on Aristotle
E: Other Expositions

F: Polemical Writings
G: Treatises on Special Subjects
H: Expert Opinions
I: Letters
J: Liturgical Pieces and Sermons

*　　　　　*　　　　　*

1224/25	Born at Roccasecca in Caserta
1230/31 to 1239	Benedictine oblate at Monte Cassino
1239 to 1244	Studied at the University of Naples
1244, late April	Joined Dominicans at Naples
1244 to 1245	Detained at home by his family

G: *De fallaciis ad quosdam nobiles artistas* (1244–45)
I: *De propositionibus modalibus* (1244–1245)

1245 to 1248	In Paris for novitiate and study
1248 to 1252	In Cologne with Albert the Great

C: *Expositio super Isaiam ad litteram* (1249–52)
Postilla super Jeremiam (possibly at this time)
Postilla super Threnos (possibly at this time)

1252 to 1256	Sententiarius at Paris

A: *Scriptum super libros Sententiarum* (1252–56)
E: *Expositio super librum Boethii De trinitate* (any time between 1252–59)
G: *De ente et essentia ad fratres et socios suos* (1252–56)
De principiis naturae ad fratrem Sylvestrum (1252–56)

1256 to 1259	Regent master in theology at Paris

A: *Summa contra gentiles* (begun 1259)
B: *De veritate* (1256–59)
      Quaestiones de quodlibet 7–11 (1256–59)
C: *Lectura super Matthaeum. Reportatio* (probably 1256–59)
      Commendatio Sacrae Scripturae (1256)
E: *Expositio in librum Boethii De hebdomadibus* (1256–59)
F: *Contra impugnantes Dei cultum et religionem* (1256)
G: *Compendium theologiae ad fratrem Reginaldum socium suum: De fide* (probably begun 1259)

1260 to 1261   In Naples

A: *Summa contra gentiles* (in progress)
G: *Compendium theologiae ad fratrem Reginaldum socium suum: De fide* (in progress)

1261 to 1265   In Orvieto as Lector

A: *Summa contra gentiles* (finished 1264)
C: *Expositio in Job ad litteram* (1261–64)
      Catena aurea (begun 1263)
G: *Compendium theologiae ad fratrem Reginaldum socium suum: De fide* (probably completed 1265)
H: *Contra errores Graecorum* (1263)
 I: *De articulis fidei et Ecclesiae sacramentis* (1261–65)
      Expositio super primam et secundam Decretalem ad Archidiaconum Tudertinum (probably 1261–65)
      De rationibus fidei contra Saracenos, Graecos et Armenos (1264)
      De emptione et venditione ad tempus (1262)
 J: *Officium de festo Corporis Christi* (1264)

1265 to 1268   In Rome: opened studium, Regent Master

A: *Summa theologiae I* (1266–68)
      Summa theologiae II (begun, only a few questions, spring 1268)
B: *De potentia* (1265–66)
      De malo (1266–67, excluding q.6)
      De spiritualibus creaturis (1267–68)
C: *Catena aurea* (finished 1267)
D: *Sententia super De anima* (1267–68)
E: *Expositio super Dionysium De divinis nominibus* (1265–67)
G: *De regno* (authenticated up to II.4, 1265–67)
H: *Responsio ad fr. Joannem Vercellensem de articulis 108* (1265–66)

1269 to 1272   Second regency at Paris

A: *Summa theologiae II* (finished, spring 1272)

Summa theologiae III (begun, only a few questions, spring 1272)
B: *De anima (1269)*
De virtutibus in communi; De caritate; De corr. fraterna; De spe; De virt. cardinalibus (1269–72)
De malo q.6: De libero arbitrio (1270)
De unione verbi incarnati (1272)
Quaestiones de quodlibet 1–6, 12 (1269–72)
C: *Lectura super Johannem. Reportatio (1269–72)*
Expositio et lectura super Epistolas Pauli Apostoli (1270–72)
D: *Sententia super Peri hermenias (1270–71)*
Sententia super Posteriora Analytica (1269–72)
Sententia super Meteora (possibly 1269–73)
Sententia super Metaphysicam (1269–72)
Sententia libri Politicorum (probably 1269–72)
Sententia super Physicam (1270–71)
Sententia libri Ethicorum (1271)
E: *Expositio super librum De causis (1271–72)*
F: *De perfectione spiritualis vitae (1269–70)*
Contra doctrinam retrahentium a religione (1271)
De unitate intellectus contra Averroistas (1270)
De aeternitate mundi contra murmurantes (1271)
H: *De forma absolutionis sacramentalis (probably 1269)*
De secreto (1269)
Responsio ad fr. Johannem Vercellensem de articulis 42 (1271)
I: *De motu cordis (1270–71)*
De mixtione elementorum (probably 1270–71)
Responsio ad lectorem Venetum de 30 & de 36 (before April 1271)
Epistola ad comitissam Flandriae (1271)
De sortibus ad Dominum Jacobum (1271)

1272 to 1273   Regency at Naples

A: *Summa theologiae III (ends with q.90.4)*
C: *Postilla super Psalmos (1272–73)*
D: *Sententia de caelo et mundo (1272–73)*
Sententia super libros De generatione et corruptione (1272–73)
G: *Compendium theologiae ad fratrem Reginaldum socium suum: De spe (1272–73)*
De angelis (1272–73)
I: *Responsio ad Bernardum Abbatem Casinensem (perhaps on way to Lyons, 1274)*
J: *Collationes super Credo in Deum (1273)*
Collationes super Pater Noster (1273)
Collationes super Ave Maria (1273)
Collationes de decem praeceptis (1273)

1274, March 7   Died at Fossanova in the Campania

* * *

There is no agreement regarding dates for the following works:

D: *Sententia de sensu et sensato Sententia de memoria et treminiscentia*
I: *Epistola exhortatoria de modo studendi*
Responsio ad lectorem Bisuntinum de articulis 6
De occultis operationibus naturae
De iudiciis astrorum
J: *Orationes: Adoro te, Gratias tibi ago, etc.*

Note: The above chronology is adapted from Eschmann in James A. Weisheipl. *Friar Thomas D'Aquino*, 2nd ed. Washington, D.C.: The Catholic University of America Press, 1983.

Bibliography in Four Parts

I. THOMAS'S WORKS

All citations from the *Commentary on the Sentences* were taken from the Vivès Edition, Volumes VII–XI, Paris, 1953–1954.

All other citations from Thomas's writings were taken from the Marrietti Edition, Torino, 1950–.

Thomas Aquinas. *On Charity*. Translated by Lottie Kendzierski. Milwaukee: Marquette University Press, 1960.

_____. *Compendium of Theology*. Translated by Cyril Vollert. St. Louis: B. Herder Book Co., 1947.

_____. *The Summa Theologiae*. Translated by the English Dominicans. London: Oates and Washbourne, 1912–1936.

_____. *On Truth*. Translated by Robert Mulligan et al. Chicago: Henry Regnery Company, 1952.

_____. *On the Truth of the Catholic Faith*. Translated by Anton Pegis et al. Notre Dame: University of Notre Dame Press, 1975.

_____. *On the Virtues in General*. Translated by John Reid. Providence: Providence College Press, 1951.

Unless otherwise noted all translations cited in this work were taken from the above texts. Citations from other writings of Thomas which appear in this work were translated into English by the author.

II. COMMENTARIES ON SAINT THOMAS AQUINAS

Abbà, Guiseppe. *Lex et Vertus*. Las-Roma: Biblioteca di Scienze Religiose 56, 1983.

_____. "La Nuova concezione dell' habitus virtuoso nella *SummaTheologiae* di San Tommaso D'Aquino." *Salesianum* 43 (1981): 71–118.

Adler, Mortimer. "A Question about Law." In *Essays in Thomism*. Edited by Robert Brennan, 207–236. New York: Sheed and Ward, 1942.

Anscombe, G. E. M., and Peter Geach. *Three Philosophers*. Ithaca: Cornell University Press, 1961.

Armstrong, Ross. *Primary and Secondary Precepts in Thomistic Natural Law Teaching*. The Hague: Martinus Nijhoff, 1966.

Auer, Alfons. "L'autonomia della morale secondo Tommaso d'Aquino." In *Fede Cristiana e Agire Morale*. Edited by Klaus Demmer and Bruno Schüller, 32–61. Assisi: Cittadella Editrice, 1980.

Battaglia, Anthony. *Toward a Reformulation of Natural Law*. New York: Seabury Press, 1981.

Blanche, F. "Sur la langue technique de Saint Thomas d'Aquin." *Revue de Philosophie* 30 (1930): 7–30.

Bourke, Vernon. "Aquinas and Recent Theories of Right." *American Catholic Philosophical Association* 48 (1974): 187–197.

———. *Aquinas' Search for Wisdom*. Milwaukee: The Bruce Publishing Company, 1965.

———. "The Nicomachean Ethics and Thomas Aquinas." In *St. Thomas Aquinas, 1274–1974, Commemorative Studies*, 239–259. : Toronto: Pontifical Institute of Medieval Studies, 1974.

———. "Right Reason as the Basis for Moral Action." *Atti del Congresso Internazionale* 5:122–128. Naples: Edizioni Dominicane Italiane, 1974.

———. "The Role of Habitus in the Thomistic Metaphysics of Potency and Act." In *Essays in Thomism*. Edited by Robert Brennan, 103–109. New York: Sheed and Ward, 1942.

———. "Voluntariness and the Insanity Plea." In *Thomistic Papers*, 1. Edited by Victor Brezik, 45–64. Houston: Center for Thomistic Studies, 1984.

———. *Will in Western Thought*. New York: Sheed and Ward, 1964.

Boyle, Leonard. *The Setting of the Summa Theologiae of Saint Thomas*. Toronto: Pontifical Institute of Medieval Studies, 1982.

———. "The Quodlibets of St. Thomas and Pastoral Care." *The Thomist* 38 (1974): 232–256.

Brennan, Robert, ed. *Essays in Thomism*. New York: Sheed and Ward, 1942.

Brown, Oscar James. *Natural Rectitude and Divine Law in Aquinas*. Studies and Text, 55. Toronto: Pontifical Institute of Medieval Studies, 1981.

Bujo, Bénézet. *Moralautonomie und Normenfindung bei Thomas von Aquin*. Paderborn: Schöningh, 1979.

Capone, Dominico. "Antropologia, coscienza, e personalità." *Studia Moralia* 4 (1966): 73–113.

———. *Intorno alla Verità Morale*. Rome: Gregorian University Press, 1951.

———. "Ritorno a S. Tommaso per una visione personalistica in teologia morale." *Rivista di Teologia Morale* 1 (1969): 85–103.

Carlin, David. "Assimilating Kohlberg to Aquinas." *The Thomist* 45 (1981): 124–131.

Chesterton, G. K. *Saint Thomas Aquinas: The Dumb Ox*. Garden City: Doubleday & Co., 1956.

Chenu, Marie-Dominique. *Toward Understanding Saint Thomas*. Chicago: Henry Regnery Company, 1963.

Colavechio, Xavier. *Erroneous Conscience and Obligations*. STD dissertation, The Catholic University of America, 1967.

Copleston, Frederick. *Aquinas*. Baltimore: Penguin Books, 1955.

Crowe, Frederick. "Complacency and Concern in Saint Thomas Aquinas." *Theological Studies* 20 (1959): 1–39, 198–230, 343–395.

_____. "Universal Norms and the concrete 'Operabile' in Saint Thomas Aquinas." *Sciences Ecclésiastique* 7 (1955): 115–150, 257–292.

Crowe, Michael. "St. Thomas and Ulpian's Natural Law." *St. Thomas Aquinas, 1274–1974, Commemorative Studies*, 261–282. Toronto: Pontifical Institute of Medieval Studies, 1974.

D'Arcy, Eric. *Conscience and its Right to Freedom*. London: Sheed and Ward, 1961.

Dedek, John. "Freedom of the Catholic Conscience." *Chicago Studies* 7 (1968): 115–125.

_____. "Intrinsically Evil Acts: The Emergence of a Doctrine." *Recherches de théologie ancienne et médiévale* 50 (1983): 191–226.

_____. "Intrinsically Evil Acts: An Historical Study of the Mind of St. Thomas." *The Thomist* 43 (1979): 385–413.

_____. "Moral Absolutes in the Predecessors of St. Thomas." *Theological Studies* 38 (1977): 654–680.

Dewan, Lawrence. "The Real Distinction between Intellect and Will." *Angelicum* 57 (1980): 557–593.

Dianich, Severino. *L'Opzione Fondamentale nel Pensiero di S. Tommaso*. STD dissertation, Gregorian University, 1968.

Doherty, Reginald. *The Judgments of Conscience and Prudence*. River Forest, Illinois: The Aquinas Library, 1961.

Donagan, Alan. "The Scholastic Theory of Moral Law in the Modern World." *Aquinas: A Collection of Critical Essays*. Edited by Anthony Kenny, 325–339. London: Macmillan Press, 1969.

Eckert, Willehad, ed. *Thomas von Aquino*. Mainz: Matthias–Grünewald Verlag, 1974.

Egenter, Richard. "Über die Bedeutung der Epikie im sittlichen Leben." *Philosophisches Jahrbuch* 53 (1940): 115–127.

Endres, Josef. "Anteil der Klugheit am Erkennen des konkreten Wahren und an dem Wollen des wahrhaft Guten." *Studia Moralia* 1 (1963): 221–263.

_____. *Menschliche Grundhaltungen*. Salzburg: Otto Müller Verlag, 1958.

Engelhardt, Paulus, ed. *Sein und Ethos*. Mainz: Matthias-Grünewald Verlag, 1964.

Ernst, Wilhelm. "Klassiche und Moderne Begrundung der Sittlichkeit im Hoch und Spat-mittellalter." *Concilium* 17 (1981): 769–774.

Eschmann, Thomas. "Saint Thomas's Approach to Moral Philosophy." *American Catholic Philosophical Association* 31 (1957): 25–33.

_____. "Studies on the Notion of Society in St. Thomas Aquinas." *Medieval Studies* 8 (1946): 1–42; 9 (1947): 19–53.

Fabro, Cornelio. "Orizzontalità e verticalità della libertà." *Angelicum* 48 (1971): 302–354.

————. "Philosophy and Thomism Today." *American Catholic Philosophical Association* 48 (1974): 44–54.

Falanga, Anthony. *Charity the Form of the Virtues According to Saint Thomas.* Washington, D.C.: The Catholic University of America Press, 1948.

Farrell, Walter. *A Companion to the Summa.* 4 vols. London: Sheed and Ward, 1938.

————. *The Natural Moral Law According to St. Thomas and Suarez.* Ditchling: St. Dominic's Press, 1930.

Festugière, A. "La notion du péché présentée par S. Thomas." *New Scholasticism* 5 (1931): 332–341.

de Finance, Joseph. "Autonomie et théonomie." *Gregorianum* 56 (1975): 207–235.

————. *Essai sur l'agir humain.* Rome: Gregorian University Press, 1962.

————. *Ethique Generale.* Rome: Gregorian University Press, 1967.

————. *Être et agir dans la philosophie de Saint Thomas.* Paris: Beauchesne et Fils, 1945.

Finnis, John. *Natural Law and Natural Rights.* Oxford: Clarendon Press, 1980.

Fuchs, Josef. *Natural Law: A Theological Approach.* Dublin: Gill and Son, 1965.

————. *Theologia Moralis Generalis.* Rome: Gregorian University Press, 1971.

Garrigou-Lagrange, Reginald. *Reality: A Synthesis of Thomistic Thought.* St. Louis: B. Herder Book Co., 1950.

Gauthier, René. "Quelques questions à propos du commentaire de S. Thomas sur le *De Anima,*" *Angelicum* 51 (1974): 419–472.

Gigante, Mario. *Genesi e struttura dell'atto libero in S. Tommaso.* Naples: Giannini Editore, 1980.

Gilleman, Gerard. *The Primacy of Charity in Moral Theology.* Westminster, Maryland: The Newman Press, 1959.

Gilson, Étienne. *The Christian Philosophy of Saint Thomas Aquinas.* London: Gollancz Ltd., 1957.

————. *The Elements of Christian Philosophy.* Garden City, New York: Doubleday & Co., 1960.

————. *A Gilson Reader.* Edited by Anton Pegis. Garden City, New York: Doubleday & Co., 1957.

Golding, Martin. "Aquinas and Some Contemporary Natural Law Theories." *American Catholic Philosophical Association* 48 (1974): 238–247.

Golser, Karl. *Gewissen und objektive Sittenordnung.* Wien: Wiener Dom-Verlag, 1975.

Grabmann, Martin. *The Interior Life of St. Thomas Aquinas.* Milwaukee: The Bruce Publishing Company, 1951.

————. *Thomas Aquinas: His Personality and Thought.* New York: Longmans, Green and Co., 1928.

Grisez, Germain. "The First Principle of Practical Reason." In *Aquinas: A Collection of Critical Essays.* Edited by Anthony Kenny, 340–382. London: Macmillan Press, 1969.

Harvey, John. "The Nature of the Infused Moral Virtues." *Proceedings of Tenth Annual Convention of Catholic Theological Society of America* 1955: 172–221.

Hörmann, Karl. "Die Bedeutung der konkreten Wirklichkeit für das sittliche Tun nach Thomas von Aquin." *Theologisch-praktische Quartalschrift* 123 (1975): 118–129.

Horváth, Tibor. *Caritas est in ratione*. Münster: Aschendorff Verlag, 1966.

Janssens, Louis. "St. Thomas and the Question of Proportionality." *Louvain Studies* 9 (1982): 26–46.

Junges, José Roque. *Consciencia y discernimento*. STD dissertation, Gregorian University, 1986.

Keenan, James. "Distinguishing Charity as Goodness and Prudence as Rightness." *The Thomist* 56 (1992): 389–411.

Kenny, Anthony. *Aquinas*. Oxford: Oxford University Press, 1980.

———. *Aquinas: A Collection of Critical Essays*. London: Macmillan Press, 1969.

———. *Will, Freedom and Power*. Oxford: Basil Blackwell, 1975.

Klubertanz, George. "Causality and Evolution." *The Modern Schoolman* 18 (1941): 11–14.

———. "Causality in the Philosophy of Nature." *The Modern Schoolman* 19 (1942): 29–32.

———. "Ethics and Theology." *The Modern Schoolman* 27 (1949): 29–39.

———. *Habits and Virtues*. New York: Meredith Publishing Co., 1965.

———. "Presidential Address: The Empiricism of Thomistic Ethics." *American Catholic Philosophical Association* (1957): 1–24.

———. "The Root of Freedom in St. Thomas's Later Works." *Gregorianum* 42 (1961): 701–724.

———. *Saint Thomas Aquinas on Analogy*. Chicago: Loyola University Press, 1960.

———. "Une theorie sur les vertus morales 'naturelles' et 'surnaturelles.'" *Revue Thomiste* 59 (1959): 565–575.

———. "The Unity of Human Activity." *The Modern Schoolman* 27 (1950): 75–103.

Kluxen, Wolfgang. "Analogie." *Historisches Wörterbuch der Philosophie* 1. Edited by Joachim Ritter, 214–227. Basel: Schwabe and Co., 1971.

———. "Anima Separata und Personsein bei Thomas von Aquin." In *Thomas von Aquino*. Edited by Willehad Eckert, 96–116. Mainz: Matthias-Grünewald Verlag, 1974.

———. *Philosophische ethik bei Thomas von Aquin*. Hamburg: Felix Meiner Verlag, 1980.

———. *Thomas von Aquin im philosophischen Gespräch*. Munich: Karl Alber, 1975.

Knauer, Peter. "The Hermeneutic Function of the Principle of Double Effect." In *Moral Norms and Catholic Tradition, Readings in Moral Theology* 1. Edited by Charles Curran and Richard McCormick, 1–39. New York: Paulist Press, 1979.

Kramer, Herbert. *The Indirect Voluntary or Voluntarium in Causa*. Ph.D. dissertation, The Catholic University of America, 1935.

Kristeller, Paul Oskar. *Medieval Aspects of Renaissance Learning*. Durham: Duke University Press, 1974.

Laguna, Justo. "La doctrina de Santo Tomás sobre el pecado." *L'Agire Morale*, 499–509. Naples: Edizioni Dominicane Italiane, 1974.

Land, Philip and George Klubertanz. "Practical Reason, Social Fact, and the Vocational Order." *The Modern Schoolman* 28 (1951): 239–266.

Langan, John P. "Beatitude and Moral Law in Saint Thomas." *Journal of Religious Ethics* 5 (1977): 183–195.

———. *Desire, Beatitude, and the Basis of Morality in Thomas Aquinas.* Ph.D. dissertation, University of Michigan, 1979.

———. "Morality, Egoism and Punishment in Thomas Aquinas." *Heythrop Journal* 22 (1981): 378–393.

———. "Sins of Malice in the Moral Psychology of Thomas Aquinas." *The Annual of the Society of Christian Ethics* 12 (1987): 179–198.

———. "The Unity of the Virtues." *Harvard Theological Review* 72–73 (1979): 81–95.

Lauer, Rosemary. "St. Thomas' Theory of Intellectual Causality." *The New Scholasticism* 28 (1954): 299–319.

Lonergan, Bernard. "The Future of Thomism." In *A Second Collection.* Edited by William Ryan, 43–53. London: Darton, Longman, and Todd, 1974.

———. "St. Thomas's Thought on *Gratia Operans.*" *Theological Studies* 3 (1942): 533–578.

Lottin, Odon. "Les éléments de la Moralité des Actes chez Saint Thomas D'Aquin." *Revue néo-scolastique* 23–24 (1921–22): 281–313, 389–429; 25 (1923): 20–56.

———. *Morale Fondamentale.* Tournai: Desclée et Cie, 1954.

———. "La preuve de la liberté humaine chez Thomas d'Aquin." *Recherches de théologie ancienne et médiévale* 23 (1956): 323–330.

———. *Principes de morale.* Louvain: Éditions du Mont César, 1946.

———. "Les vertus morales acquises sont-elles de vraies vertus?" *Recherches de théologie ancienne et médiévale* 20 (1953): 13–39; 21 (1954): 101–129.

———. *Psychologie et Morale aux XIIe et XIIIe siècles.* 6 vols. Gembloux: Duculot, 1942–1954.

———. "La valeur normative de la conscience morale." *Ephemerides Theologicae Lovanienses* 9 (1932): 409–431.

McDonnell, Kevin. "Aquinas and Hare on Fanaticism." *American Catholic Philosophical Association* 48 (1974): 218–227.

McInerny, Ralph. *St. Thomas Aquinas.* Notre Dame: University of Notre Dame Press, 1977.

MacMahon, Kevin. *On the Deontology of the Magisterium to Teach Natural Law.* Ph.D. dissertation, Marquette University, 1984.

Mahoney, John. *Seeking the Spirit.* London: Sheed and Ward, 1981.

———. *The Spirit of God and the Sons of God.* STD dissertation, Gregorian University, 1967.

Maritain, Jacques. *The Angelic Doctor.* New York: Dial Press, 1931.

———. *Moral Philosophy.* Translated by M. Suther. New York: Charles Scribner's Sons, 1964.

———. *Neuf Leçons sur les notions premières de la philosophie morale.* Paris: Téqui, 1950.

Maurer, Armand. *Medieval Philosophy.* New York: Random House, 1962.

May, William. "Aquinas and Janssens on the Moral Meaning of Human Acts." *The Thomist* 48 (1984): 566–606.

Merken, Paul. "Transformations of the Ethics of Aristotle in the Moral Philosophy of Thomas Aquinas." In *Atti del Congresso Internazionale* 5:151–164. Naples: Edizioni Dominicane Italiane, 1974.

Merks, Karl-Wilhelm. *Theologische Grundlegung der sittlichen Autonomie.* Düsseldorf: Patmos, 1978.

Mieth, Dietmar. "Norma morale e autonomia dell'uomo. Problema della legge naturale e sua relazione con legge nuova." In *Problemi e Prospettive di Teologia Morale.* Edited by Tullo Goffi, 173–198. Brescia: Editrice Queriniana, 1976.

Milhaven, John Giles. "Moral Absolutes and Thomas Aquinas." In *Absolutes in Moral Theology.* Edited by Charles Curran, 154–185. Washington, D.C.: Corpus Books, 1968.

Molinaro, Aniceto. "Coscienza e Norma Etica." In *Vita Nuova in Cristo.* Edited by Tullo Goffi and Giannino Piana, 449–490. Brescia: Editrice Queriniana, 1983.

Mongillo, Dalmazio. "Le Componenti della bontà morale." *Studia Moralia* 15 (1977): 483–502.

———. "L'elemento primario della legge naturale in S. Tommaso." In *La Legge Naturale.* Edited by L. Rossi, 101–123. Bologna: Edizioni Dehoniane, 1970.

———. "L'esistenza cristiana: Peccato e conversione." In *Vita Nuova in Cristo.* Edited by Tullo Goffi and Giannino Piana, 491–552. Brescia: Editrice Queriniana, 1983.

———. "La teonomia come autonomia dell'uomo in Dio." In *Fede Cristiana e Agire Morale.* Edited by Klaus Demmer and Bruno Schüller, 62–85. Assisi: Cittadella Editrice, 1980.

Mullady, Brian. *The Meaning of the Term "Moral" in St. Thomas Aquinas.* Vatican City: Libreria Editrice Vaticana, 1986.

Naus, John. *The Nature of the Practical Intellect According to St. Thomas Aquinas.* Rome: Gregorian University Press, 1969.

Noonan, John. "An Almost Absolute Value in History." In *The Morality of Abortion: Legal and Historical Perspectives.* Edited by John Noonan, 1–59. Cambridge: Harvard University Press, 1970.

———. "Masked Men: Person and Persona in the Giving of Justice." *American Catholic Philosophical Association* 48 (1974): 228–237.

Nygren, Anders. *Agape and Eros.* Chicago: University of Chicago Press, 1953.

O'Connell, Timothy. *Principles for a Catholic Morality.* New York: Seabury Press, 1978.

O'Connor, Daniel. *Aquinas and Natural Law.* London: Macmillan Press, 1967.

Oeing-Hanhoff, Ludger. "Mensch und Recht nach Thomas von Aquin." *Philosophisches Jahrbuch* 82 (1975): 10–30.

———. "Theologie des Wortes bei Thomas von Aquin." *Zeitschrift für Theologie und Kirche* 66 (1969): 437–465.

———. "Thomas von Aquin und die gegenwärtige katholische Theologie." In *Thomas von Aquino*. Edited by Willehad Eckert, 245–306. Mainz: Matthias-Grünewald, 1974.

———. "Zur thomistischen Freiheitslehre." *Scholastik* 31 (1956): 161–181.

O'Neil, Charles. *Imprudence in St. Thomas*. Milwaukee: Marquette University Press, 1955.

———. "Prudence, the Incommunicable Wisdom." In *Essays in Thomism*. Edited by Robert Brennan, 187–204. New York: Sheed and Ward, 1942.

Owens, Joseph. "Aquinas as Aristotelian Commentator." In *St. Thomas Aquinas, 1274–1974, Commemorative Studies*, 213–238. Toronto: Pontifical Institute of Medieval Studies, 1974.

———. "Ideology and Aquinas." *Thomistic Papers* 1. Edited by Victor Brezik, 135–152. Houston: Center for Thomistic Studies, 1984.

Pangle, Thomas. "A Note on the Theological Foundation on the Just War Doctrine." *The Thomist* 43 (1979): 464–473.

Pesch, Otto. "Freiheit." In *Historisches Wörterbuch der Philosophie* 2. Edited by Joachim Ritter, 1083–1088. Basel: Schwabe and Co., 1972.

———. "Philosophie und Theologie der Freihet bei Thomas von Aquin in quaest. disp 6 *De malo*." *Münchener Theologische Zeitschrift* 13 (1962): 1–25.

———. "Sittengebote, Kultvorschriften, Rechtssatzungen." In *Thomas von Aquino*. Edited by Willehad Eckert, 488–518. Mainz: Matthias-Grünewald, 1974.

———. "Thomas von Aquin über Schlafen und Baden." *Theologische Quartalschrift* 151 (1971): 155–159.

Petrin, Jean. *Connaissance speculative et Connaissance pratique*. Ottawa: Éditions de l'Université, 1948.

Phelan, Gerald. *Some Illustrations of St. Thomas' Development of the Wisdom of Saint Augustine*. Chicago: Argus Press, 1946.

Pieper, Josef. *The Four Cardinal Virtues*. Notre Dame: University of Notre Dame Press, 1980.

———. *Guide to Thomas Aquinas*. New York: Random House, 1962.

———. *The Silence of Saint Thomas*. Chicago: Henry Regnery Co., 1957.

Pinckaers, Servais. "Autonomie et heteronomie en morale selon S. Thomas d'Aquin." In *Autonomie: Dimensions éthiques de la liberté*. Edited by Carolos Josaphat Pinto de Oliviera and Dietmar Mieth, 104–123. Fribourg: University of Fribourg, 1978.

———. "Eudämonismus und sittliche Verbindlichkeit in der Ethik des heiligen Thomas." In *Sein und Ethos*. Edited by Paulus Engelhardt, 267–305. Mainz: Matthias-Grünewald, 1964.

———. "La Loi de l'evangile ou Loi nouvelle selon Saint Thomas." In *Loi et Evangile*, 57–79. Geneva: Labor et Fides, 1981.

———. "Le rôle de la fin dans l'action morale selon Saint Thomas." In *Le Renouveau de la Morale*. Tournai: Casterman, 1964.

———. "Der Sinn für die Freundschaftsliebe als Urtatsache der thomistischen Ethik." In *Sein und Ethos*. Edited by Paulus Engelhardt, 228–235. Mainz: Matthias-Grünewald, 1964.

_____. "Virtue is not a Habit." *Cross Currents* 12 (1962): 65–82.

Pizzuti, Giuseppe. "Natura, implicazioni e limiti del concetto di 'circumstantia' in Tommaso d'Aquino." In *L'Etica della Situazione.* Edited by Pietro Piovani, 55–72. Naples: Guida, 1974.

Pope, Stephen. "Aquinas on Almsgiving, Justice and Charity." *Heythrop Journal* 32 (1991): 167–191.

_____. "Expressive Individualism and True Self-Love: A Thomistic Perspective." *Journal of Religion* 71 (1991): 384–399.

_____. "The Order of Love and Recent Catholic Ethics." *Theological Studies* 52 (1991): 255–288.

Porter, Jean. "Desire for God: Ground of the Moral Life in Aquinas." *Theological Studies* 47 (1986): 48–68.

_____. "Perennial and Timely Virtues." In *Changing Values and Virtues.* Edited by Dietmar Mieth and Jacques Pohier, 60–68. Edinburgh: T. & T. Clark, Ltd., 1987.

_____. *The Recovery of Virtue: The Relevance of Aquinas for Christian Ethics.* Louisville: Westminster, 1990.

Regan, Richard. "Aquinas on political obedience and disobedience." *Thought* 56 (1981): 77–88.

Reilly, Richard. "Weakness of Will: The Thomistic Advance." *American Catholic Philosophical Association* 48 (1974): 198–207.

Reiner, Hans. "Beatitudo und Obligatio bei Thomas von Aquin." In *Sein und Ethos.* Edited by Paulus Engelhardt, 306–328. Mainz: Matthias-Grünewald, 1964.

_____. "Wesen und Grund der sittlichen Verbindlichkeit (Obligatio) bei Thomas von Aquin." In *Sein und Ethos.* Edited by Paulus Engelhardt, 236–266. Mainz: Matthias-Grünewald, 1964.

Rescher, Nicholas. "Morality in Government and Politics." *American Catholic Philosophical Association* 48 (1974): 259–265.

Riesenhuber, Klaus. "The Bases and Meaning of Freedom in Thomas Aquinas." *American Catholic Philosophical Association* 48 (1974): 99–111.

_____. *Die Transzendenz der Freiheit zum Guten: Der Wille in der Anthropologie und Metaphysik des Thomas von Aquin.* Munich: Berchmanskolleg Verlag, 1971.

Rousselot, Pierre. *The Intellectualism of Saint Thomas.* London: Sheed and Ward, 1935.

Ryan, John. "The Problem of Truth." In *Essays in Thomism.* Edited by Robert Brennan, 65–79. New York: Sheed and Ward, 1942.

Schlüter, Dietrich. "Der Wille und das Gute bei Thomas von Aquin." *Freiburger Zeitschrift für Theologie und Philosophie* 8 (1971): 88–136.

Scholz, Franz. "Possibilità e impossibilità dell'agire indiretto." In *Fede Cristiana e Agire Morale.* Edited by Klaus Demmer and Bruno Schüller, 289–311. Assisi: Cittadella Editrice, 1980.

_____. "Problems of Norms Raised by Ethical Borderline Situations: Beginnings of a Solution in Thomas Aquinas and Bonaventure." In *Moral Norms and Catholic Tradition, Readings in Moral Theology* 1. Edited by

Charles Curran and Richard McCormick, 158–183. New York: Paulist Press, 1979.

Schmitz, Kenneth. "Another Look at Objectivity. *American Catholic Philosophical Association* 48 (1974): 86–98.

Scott, David. *Egocentrism and the Christian Life: A Study of Thomas Aquinas and Martin Luther and an Attempted Reformulation.* Ph.D. dissertation, Princeton University, 1968.

Siedl, von Horst. "Das Sittliche Gute (als Glückseligkeit) nach Aristoteles." *Philosophisches Jahrbuch* 82 (1975): 31–53.

Sertillanges, Antonin. *Foundations of Thomistic Philosophy.* Springfield: Templegate Publishers, 1931.

———. *La Philosophie Morale de Saint Thomas D'Aquin.* Paris: Libraire Felix Alcan, 1922.

———. *Rectitude.* New York: McMullen Books, 1953.

Sheehan, Peter. "Aquinas on Intentionality." In *Aquinas: A Collection of Critical Essays.* Edited by Anthony Kenny, 307–321. London: Macmillan Press, 1969.

Simon, Yves. *Critique de la Connaissance Morale.* Paris: Desclée de Brouwer et Cie, 1934.

———. *A General Theory of Authority.* Notre Dame: University of Notre Dame Press, n.d.

Simonin, H. D. "La Notion d'intention dans l'oeuvre de S. Thomas d'Aquin." *Revue des Sciences Philosophiques et Théologiques* 19 (1930): 445–463.

Stanke, Gerhard. *Die Lehre von den 'Quellen der Moralität.'* Regensburg: Friedrich Pustet, 1984.

Steinbüchel, Theodor. *Der Zweckgedanke in der Philosophie des Thomas von Aquino.* Münster: Aschendorff Verlag, 1912.

Tracy, David. "St. Thomas and the Religious Dimension of Experience: The Doctrine of Sin." *American Catholic Philosophical Association* 48 (1974): 166–176.

van Ouwerkerk, Conrad. *Caritas et Ratio: Étude sur le double principe de la vie morale chrétienne d'après S. Thomas d'Aquin.* Nijmegen: Drukkerij Gebr. Janssen, 1956.

Van Roo, William. *Grace and Original Justice According to Saint Thomas.* Rome: Analecta Gregoriana, 1955.

———. "Law of the Spirit and Written Law." *Gregorianum* 37 (1956): 417–443.

Verbeke, Gerard. "Fatalism and Freedom According to Nemesius and Thomas Aquinas." In *St. Thomas Aquinas, 1274–1974, Commemorative Studies,* 283–313. Toronto: Pontifical Institute of Medieval Studies, 1974.

Virt, Günter. *Epikie—Verantwortlicher Umgang mit Normen.* Mainz: Matthias-Grünewald, 1983.

von Rintelen, Fritz-Joachim. "The Good and the Highest Good in the Thought of Aquinas." *American Catholic Philosophical Association* 48 (1974): 177–186.

Wadell, Paul. *Friends of God: Virtues and Gifts in Aquinas.* New York: Peter Lang, 1991.

Wallace, William. *The Role of Demonstration in Moral Theology: A Study of Methdology in St. Thomas Aquinas.* Washington, D.C.: Thomist Press, 962.
Weisheipl, James. *Friar Thomas d'Aquino.* 2nd ed. Washington, D.C.: The Catholic University of America Press, 1983.
Welp, Dorothée. *Willensfreiheit bei Thomas von Aquin.* Fribourg: Universitätsverlag, 1979.

III. THE DISTINCTION: MORAL GOODNESS AND MORAL RIGHTNESS

Anscombe, G. E. M. *Ethics, Religion and Politics.* Oxford: Basil Blackwell, 1981.
————. *Intention.* Oxford: Basil Blackwell, 1957.
Baier, Kurt. "Reasoning in Practical Deliberation." In *The Moral Judgment.* Edited by Paul Taylor, 277–296. Englewood Cliffs, New Jersey: Prentice-Hall, 1963.
Barker, S. "Thought and Action." *The Philosophical Review* 71 (1962): 392–394.
Brandt, Richard. "Hare: Freedom and Reason." *Journal of Philosophy* 61 (1964): 139–150.
Cahill, Lisa. "Teleology, Utilitarianism, and Christian Ethics." *Theological Studies* 42 (1981): 601–629.
Carlon, Keith. "R. M. Hare and Moral Theology." *Louvain Studies* 8 (1980): 30–46.
Carney, Frederick. "The Virtue-Obligation Controversy." *Journal of Religious Ethics* 1 (1973): 5–19.
————. "On Frankena and Religious Ethics." *Journal of Religious Ethics* 3 (1975): 7–26.
Connery, John. "Catholic Ethics: Has the Norm for Rule-Making Changed?" *Theological Studies* 42 (1981): 232–250.
————. "The Teleology of Proportionate Reason." *Theological Studies* 44 (1983): 489–496.
Coventry, John. "Christian Conscience." *The Heythrop Journal* 7 (1966): 145–160.
Demmer, Klaus. "La competenza normativa del magistero ecclesiastico in morale." In *Fede Cristiana e Agire Morale.* Edited by Klaus Demmer and Bruno Schüller, 144–169. Assisi: Cittadella Editrice, 1980.
————. *Deuten und Handeln.* Freiburg, Switzerland: Universitätsverlag, 1985.
————. "Erwägungen zum intrinsece malum." *Gregorianum* 68 (1987): 613–637.
————. "Hermeneutische Probleme der Fundamentalmoral." In *Ethik im Kontext des Glaubens.* Edited by Dietmar Mieth and Francesco Compagnoni, 101–119. Freiburg, Switzerland: Universitätsverlag, 1978.
————. *Leben in Menschenhand.* Freiburg, Switzerland: Universitätsverlag, 1987.
————. "Sittlicher Anspruch und Geschichtlichkeit des Verstehens." In *Heilsgeschichte und Ethische Normen.* Edited by Hans Rotter, 64–98. Freiburg: Herder, 1984.

_____. "Sittlich handeln als Zeugnis geben." *Gregorianum* 64 (1983): 453–485.
_____. "Sittlich handeln aus Erfahrung." *Gregorianum* 59 (1978): 661–690.
Di Ianni, Albert. "The Direct/Indirect Distinction in Morals." In *Moral Norms and Catholic Tradition, Readings in Moral Theology* 1. Edited by Charles Curran and Richard McCormick, 215–243. New York: Paulist Press, 1979.
Edel, Abraham. "The Logical Structure of Moore's Ethical Theory." In *The Philosophy of G. E. Moore*. Edited by Paul Schilpp, 135–177. New York: Tudor Publishing Co., 1952.
Ewing, A. "Hare and the Universalisation Principle." *Philosophy* 39 (1964): 71–74.
Farley, Margaret. *Personal Commitments*. San Francisco: Harper & Row, 1989.
Foot, Philippa. *Virtues and Vices*. Oxford: Basil Blackwell, 1981.
Frankel, Charles. "An Examination of the Place of Reason in Ethics." *Journal of Philosophy* 48 (1951): 734–736.
Frankena, William. "Conversations with Carney and Hauerwas." *Journal of Religious Ethics* 3 (1975) 45–62.
_____. *Ethics*. 2nd Ed. Englewood Cliffs, New Jersey: Prentice-Hall, 1973.
_____. "The Ethics of Love Conceived as an Ethics of Virtue." *Journal of Religious Ethics* 1 (1973): 21–31.
_____. "Is Morality Logically Dependent on Religion? In *Divine Commands and Morality*. Edited by P. Helm, 14–34. Oxford: Oxford University Press, 1981.
_____. "McCormick and the Traditional Distinction." In *Doing Evil to Achieve Good*. Edited by Richard McCormick and Paul Ramsey, 145–164. Chicago: Loyola University Press, 1978.
_____. *Perspectives on Morality: Essays of William Frankena*. Edited by Kenneth Goodpaster. Notre Dame: University of Notre Dame Press, 1976.
_____. "The Philosopher's Attack on Morality." *Philosophy* 49 (1974): 345–356.
_____. "Public Education and the Good Life." *Harvard Educational Review* 30 (1961): 413–426.
_____. "Recent Conceptions of Morality." In *Morality and Language of Conduct*. Edited by Hector Castañada and George Nakhnikian, 1–24. Detroit: Wayne University Press, 1963.
_____. *Thinking about Morality*. Ann Arbor: University of Michigan Press, 1980.
_____. "Under What Net?" *Philosophy* 48 (1973): 319–326.
Fuchs, Josef. *Christian Ethics in a Secular Arena*. Washington, D.C.: Georgetown University Press, 1984.
_____. *Christian Morality: The Word Becomes Flesh*. Washington, D.C.: Georgetown University Press, 1987.
_____. "Control over Human Life." *Theology Digest* 32 (1985): 247–252.
_____. *Essere del Signore*. Rome: Gregorian University Press, 1981.
_____. *Human Values and Christian Morality*. Dublin: Gill and Macmillan, 1970.
_____. "Moral Aspects of Human Progress." In *Theology Meets Progress*. Edited by Philip Land, 145–170. Rome: Gregorian University Press, 1971.

_____. *Personal Responsibility and Christian Morality.* Washington, D.C.: Georgetown University Press, 1983.

_____. "Sin and Conversion." *Theology Digest* 14 (1966): 292–301.

_____. *Sussidi 1980 per lo Studio della Teologia Morale Fondamentale.* Rome: Gregorian University Press, 1980.

Gaffney, James. "On Paranesis and Fundamental Moral Theology." *Journal of Religious Ethics* 11 (1983): 23–34.

Gallagher, John. *Time Past, Time Future: An Historical Study of Catholic Moral Theology.* New York: Paulist Press, 1990.

Garnett, A. "Moore's Theory of Moral Freedom." In *The Philosophy of G. E. Moore.* Edited by Paul Schilpp, 177–200. New York: Tudor Publishing Co., 1952.

Geach, Peter. "Good and Evil." In *Theories of Ethics,* 64–73. Oxford: Oxford University Press, 1967.

_____. *The Virtues.* Cambridge: Cambridge University Press, 1977.

Hampshire, Stuart. "Reply to Walsh on Thought and Action." *Journal of Philosophy* 60 (1963): 410–424.

_____. *Thought and Action.* London: Chatto and Windus, Ltd., 1959.

Hare, R. H. "Broad's Approach to Moral Philosophy." In *Essays on Philosophical Method,* 1–19. London: Macmillan Press, 1971.

_____. "Conventional Morality," "Decision," Deliberation," "Descriptivism," "Emotivism," "Ethics," "Goodness," "Intention," "Prescriptivism," "Relativism," "Right and Wrong," "Subjectivism, Ethical." *A Dictionary of Christian Ethics.* Edited by John Macquarrie. London: SCM Press, 1967.

_____. *Freedom and Reason.* Oxford: Clarendon Press, 1962.

_____. *The Language of Morals.* Oxford: Oxford University Press, 1964.

_____. *Moral Thinking.* Oxford: Clarendon Press, 1981.

_____. "Wrongness and Harm." in *Essays on Moral Concepts,* 92–109. Berkeley: University of California Press, 1972.

Hauerwas, Stanley. "Obligation and Virtue Once More." *Journal of Religious Ethics* 3 (1975): 27–44.

Hoose, Bernard. *Proportionalism: The American Debate and Its European Roots.* Washington, D.C.: Georgetown University Press, 1987.

Janssens, Louis. "Norms and Priorities in a Love Ethics." *Louvain Studies* 6 (1977): 207–238.

_____. "Ontic Good and Evil." *Louvain Studies* 12 (1987): 62–82.

_____. "Ontic Evil and Moral Evil." In *Moral Norms and Catholic Tradition, Readings in Moral Theology* 1. Edited by Charles Curran and Richard McCormick, 40–93. New York: Paulist Press, 1979.

Jonsen, Albert, and Stephen Toulmin. *The Abuse of Casuistry.* Berkeley: University of California Press, 1988.

Kaufmann, Hilde. " 'Schuld' und 'Sünde.' " *Theologische Quartalschrift* 160 (1980): 175–182.

Keenan, James. "Prophylactics, Toleration and Cooperation: Contemporary Problems and Traditional Principles." *International Philosophical Quarterly* 29 (1989): 205–225.

———. "Taking Aim at the Principle of Double Effect." *International Philosophical Quarterly* 28 (1988): 201–205.

———. "Töten oder Sterbenlassen?" *Stimmen der Zeit* 201 (1983): 825–837.

———. "Virtue Ethics: Making a Case as It Comes of Age." *Thought* 67 (1992): 115–127.

———. "What is Good and What is Right? A New Distinction in Moral Theology." *Church* 5 (1989): 22–30.

Langan, John P. "Augustine on the Unity and the Interconnection of the Virtues." *Harvard Theological Review* 72 (1979): 81–95.

McCormick, Richard. "Bishops as Teachers and Jesuits as Listeners." *Studies in the Spirituality of the Jesuits* 28 (1986).

McDermott, John. "Moral Systems: Maritain and Schüller Compared." *Divus Thomas* (1985): 3–23.

Mackie, John. *Ethics: Inventing Right and Wrong.* New York: Penguin Books, 1977.

May, William E. *Moral Absolutes.* Marquette: Marquette University Press, 1989.

Mieth, Dietmar. "Autonome Moral im Christlichen Kontext." *Orientierung* 40 (1976): 31–34.

———. "Autonomy of Ethics—Neutrality of the Gospel." *Concilium* 155 (1982): 32–39.

———. *Die neuen Tugenden.* Düsseldorf: Patmos, 1984.

———. "Wieweit kann man 'Schuld' und 'Sünde' trennen?" *Theologische Quartalschrift* 160 (1980): 184–191.

Mieth, Dietmar, and Jacques Pohier. *Changing Values and Virtues.* Edinburgh: T. & T. Clark, Ltd., 1987.

Moore, G. E. *Ethics.* London: Thornton Butterworth Ltd., 1912.

———. *Principia Ethica.* Cambridge: Cambridge University Press, 1903.

———. "A Reply to My Critics." In *The Philosophy of G. E. Moore.* Edited by Paul Schilpp, 533–688. New York: Tudor Publishing Co., 1952.

Moser, Antonio, and Bernardino Leers. *Moral Theology: Dead Ends and Alternatives.* Maryknoll, New York: Orbis Books, 1990.

Nampiaparambil, Alberto. *Ethics of R. M. Hare.* STD dissertation, Gregorian University, 1964.

O'Connor, Daniel. "Thought and Action." *Philosophy* 36 (1961): 231–233.

Paton, H. J. "The Alleged Independence of Goodness." In *The Philosophy of G. E. Moore.* Edited by Paul Schilpp, 113–134. New York: Tudor Publishing Co., 1952.

———. "An Examination of the Place of Reason in Ethics." *Philosophy* 27 (1952): 81–84.

Patrick, Anne. "Narrative and the Social Dynamics of Virtue." In *Changing Values and Virtues.* Edited by Dietmar Mieth and Jacques Pohier, 69–80. Edinburgh: T. & T. Clark, Ltd., 1987.

Phillips, Dewi. "God and Ought." In *Divine Commands and Morality*, 175–180. Oxford: Oxford University Press, 1981.

———. *Through a Darkening Glass.* Notre Dame: Notre Dame University Press, 1982.

Rahner, Karl. "The Commandment of Love in Relation to the Other Commandments." In *Theological Investigations* 5:439–459. Baltimore: Helicon Press, 1966.

———. "Reflections on the Unity of the Love of Neighbor and the Love of God." In *Theological Investigations* 6:231–252. Baltimore: Helicon Press, 1969.

———. "The Theology of Freedom." In *Theological Investigations* 6:178–196. Baltimore: Helicon Press, 1969.

Rawls, John. "An Examination of the Place of Reason in Ethics." *The Philosophical Review* 60 (1951): 572–580.

Richman, Richard. "Geach: The Virtues." *The Philosophical Review* 87 (1978): 626–632.

Ross, W. D. "Right Acts." In *The Moral Judgment*. Edited by Paul Taylor, 21–32. Englewood Cliffs, New Jersey: Prentice-Hall, 1963.

———. *The Right and the Good*. Oxford: Clarendon Press, 1930.

Schüller, Bruno. *Die Begründung sittlicher Urteile*. Düsseldorf: Patmos, 1980.

———. "Can Moral Theology Ignore Natural Law?" *Theology Digest* 15 (1967): 94–99.

———. "The Debate on the Specific Character of Christian Ethics." In *The Distinctiveness of Christian Ethics, Readings in Moral Theology* 2. Edited by Charles Curran and Richard McCormick, 207–233. New York: Paulist Press, 1980.

———. "Direct Killing/Indirect Killing." In *Moral Norms and Catholic Tradition, Readings in Moral Theology* 1. Edited by Charles Curran and Richard McCormick, 138–157. New York: Paulist Press, 1979.

———. "The Double Effect in Catholic Thought: A Reevaluation." In *Doing Evil to Achieve Good*. Edited by Richard McCormick and Paul Ramsey, 165–192. Chicago: Loyola University Press, 1978.

———. "Gewissen und Schuld." In *Das Gewissen*. Edited by Josef Fuchs, 34–55. Düsseldorf: Patmos, 1979.

———. "L'Importanza dell'Esperienza per la Giustificazione delle Norme di Comportamento Morale." In *Fede Cristiana e Agire Morale*. Edited by Klaus Demmer and Bruno Schüller, 312–343. Assisi: Cittadella Editrice, 1980.

———. "Mortal Sin—Sin unto Death?" *Theology Digest* 16 (1968): 232–235.

———. "Neuere Beiträge zum Thema 'Begründung sittlicher Normen.'" *Theologische Berichte* 4. Edited by Franz Furger, 109–181. Zurich: Benziger Verlag, 1974.

———. "Die Quelle der Moralität." *Theologie und Philosophie* 59 (1984): 535–559.

———. "Remarks on the Authentic Teaching of the Magisterium of the Church." In *The Magisterium and Morality, Readings in Moral Theology* 3. Edited by Charles Curran and Richard McCormick, 14–33. New York: Paulist Press, 1982.

———. "Various Types of Grounding for Ethical Norms." In *Moral Norms and Catholic Tradition, Readings in Moral Theology* 1. Edited by Charles Curran and Richard McCormick, 184–198. New York: Paulist Press, 1979.

———. "What Ethical Principles are Universally Valid?" *Theology Digest* 19 (1971): 23–28.

———. *Wholly Human.* Washington, D.C.: Georgetown University Press, 1985.

Scriven, Michael. "Thought and Action." *Mind* 71 (1962): 100–107.

Smith, Janet. "Can Virtue Be in the Service of Bad Acts?" *The New Scholasticism* 58 (1984): 357–373.

Strawson, Peter. "Social Morality and Individual Ideal." *Philosophy* 36 (1961): 1–17.

Swinburne, R. "Duty and the Will of God." In *Divine Commands and Morality*, 120–134. Oxford: Oxford University Press, 1981.

Toulmin, Stephen. *An Examination of the Place of Reason in Ethics.* Cambridge: Cambridge University Press, 1950.

Urmson, James. " 'Good' as a Grading Word." In *The Moral Judgment.* Edited by Paul Taylor, 211–237. Englewood Cliffs, New Jersey: Prentice-Hall, 1963.

———. "Saints and Heroes." In *Moral Concepts.* Edited by Joel Feinberg, 60–73. Oxford: Oxford University Press, 1967.

Wadell, Paul. *Friendship and the Moral Life.* Notre Dame: University of Notre Dame Press, 1989.

Wallace, James. *Virtues and Vices.* Ithaca: Cornell University Press, 1978.

Walsh, James. "Remarks on Thought and Action." *Journal of Philosophy* 60 (1963): 57–65.

IV. OTHER RELATED WORKS

Aristotle. *The Nicomachean Ethics.* Translated by J. Thomson. London: Penguin Books, 1984.

Arntz, Joseph. "Natural Law and its History." *Concilium* 5 (1965): 23–32.

Attard, Mark. *Compromise in Morality.* STD dissertation, Gregorian University, 1976.

Bastianel, Sergio. *Autonomia Morale del Credente.* Naples: Morcelliana, 1980.

Böckle, Franz. *Fundamental Moral Theology.* Dublin: Gill and Macmillan Ltd., 1980.

Boelaars, H. "Riflessioni sul Voto." *Studia Moralia* 16 (1978): 129–165.

Cahill, Lisa S. "Sex, Marriage and Community in Christian Ethics." *Thought* 58 (1983): 72–81.

Carpentier, René. "Conscience." In *Dictionnaire de Spiritualité Ascetique et Mystique* 2: col. 1548–1575. Paris: Beauschesne, 1953.

Chiavacci, Enrico. "La Legge Naturale ieri e oggi." *Nuove Prospettive di Morale Conjugale.* Edited by Franco Festorazzi, 61–91. Brescia: Editrice Queriniana, 1969.

Chirico, Peter. "Tension, Morality and Birth Control." *Theology Digest* 16 (1968): 104–110.

Connery, John. "Morality of Consquences." In *Moral Norms and Catholic Tradition, Readings in Moral Theology* 1. Edited by Charles Curran and Richard McCormick, 244–266. New York: Paulist Press, 1979.

Cooper, Eugene. "Fundamental Option." *Irish Theological Quarterly* 39 (1972): 383–393.

———. "The Notion of Sin in Light of the Fundamental Option." *Louvain Studies* 9 (1983): 363–382.

Crowe, Frederick. "The Conscience of the Theologian." In *Conscience: Its Freedom and Limitations*. Edited by William Bier, 312–332. New York: Fordham University Press, 1971.

———. "Dialectic and the Ignatian Spiritual Exercises." *Science et Esprit* 30 (1978): 111–127.

———. "Doctrines and Historicity in the Context of Lonergan's 'Method.'" *Theological Studies* 38 (1977): 115–124.

———. "Dogma Versus the Self-Correcting Process of Learning." *Theological Studies* 31 (1970): 605–624.

———. "Early Jottings on Bernard Lonergan's Method in Theology." *Science et Esprit* 25 (1973): 121–138.

———. "The Exploration of Lonergan's New Notion of Value." *Science et Esprit* 29 (1977): 123–143.

Curran, Charles. "Method in Moral Theology." *Studia Moralia* 18 (1980): 107–128.

———. *A New Look at Christian Morality*. Notre Dame: Fides Publishers, Inc., 1968.

D'Arcy, Martin. *Christian Morals*. New York: Longmans, Green and Company, 1937.

Deman, Th. "Péché." in *Dictionnaire de Théologie*, 12:col. 140–275. Paris: Libraire Letouzey et Ané, 1933.

Demmer, Klaus. "Cristologia e morale: Orientamenti per una proposta sistematica." In *Cristologia e Morale: IX Congresso dei Teologi Moralisti*, 83–108. Bologna: Edizioni Dehoniane, 1982.

———. "The Evangelical Counsels." *Communio* (1984): 3–18.

———. "Elementi base de un'anthropologia cristiana." In *Problemi e Prospettive di Teologia Morale*. Edited by Tullo Goffi, 31–74. Brescia: Editrice Queriniana, 1976.

———. "The Irrevocable Decision." *Communio* (1974): 293–308.

Dolan, Joseph. "Conscience in the Catholic Theological Tradition." In *Conscience, Its Freedom and Limitations*. Edited by William Bier, 9–19. New York: Fordham University Press, 1971.

Donagan, Alan. *The Theory of Morality*. Chicago: University of Chicago Press, 1977.

Fagothey, Austin. *Right and Reason*. St. Louis: C. V. Mosby Company, 1959.

Ford, John, and Gerald Kelly. *Contemporary Moral Theology*. Westminster, Maryland: The Newman Press, 1958.

Gervais, Pierre. "Péché." In *Dictionnaire de Spiritualité Ascetique et Mystique* 12:col. 790–853. Paris: Beauschesne, 1984.

Ginters, Rudolf. *Valori, Norme et Fede Cristiana.* Casale Monferato: Marietti, 1982.

Hallett, Garth. *Christian Moral Reasoning: An Analytic Guide.* Notre Dame: University of Notre Dame Press, 1983.

Haring, Bernard. "Magistero." In *Dizionario Enciclopedico di Teologia Morale,* 583–594. Rome: Paoline, 1981.

Hamel, Edouard. "Alleanza e Legge." *Rassegna di Teologia* 16 (1975): 513–533.

———. "La Legge Nuova per una comunita nuova." *Civiltà Cattolica* 124 (1973): 351–360.

———. "La scelta morale tra coscienza e legge." *Rassegna di Teologia* 17 (1976): 121–136.

———. "La theologie morale entre l'Ecriture et la raison." *Gregorianum* 56 (1975): 273–319.

Hauerwas, Stanley. *A Community of Character.* Notre Dame: University of Notre Dame Press, 1981.

———. *Suffering Presence.* Notre Dame: University of Notre Dame Press, 1986.

———. *Truthfulness and Tragedy.* Notre Dame: University of Notre Dame Press, 1977.

Holderegger, Adrian. "Per una fondazione storica dell'etica." In *Vita nuova in Cristo.* Edited by Tullo Goffi and Giannino Piana, 175–220. Brescia: Editrice Queriniana, 1983.

Hughes, Gerard. *Authority in Morals.* London: Sheed and Ward, 1978.

———. *Moral Decisions.* London: Darton, Longman and Todd, 1980.

———. "Killing or Letting Die." *The Month* 236 (1975): 42–45.

Hürth, Franz. "Metaphysica, psychologica, theologica hodierna conscientiae christianae problemata." *Analecta Gregoriana* 68 (1954): 393–414.

Jung, Patricia, and Thomas Shannon, editors. *Abortion and Catholicism.* New York: Crossroads, 1988.

Kant, Immanuel. *Critique of Practical Reason.* Translated by Lewis White Beck. Indianapolis: Bobbs-Merrill, 1956.

———. *Foundations of the Metaphysics of Morals.* Translated by Lewis White Beck. Indianapolis: Bobbs-Merrill, 1969.

Kass, Leon. "Practicing Ethics." *The Hastings Center Report* 20 (1990): 5–12.

Keane, Philip. *Christian Ethics and Imagination.* New York: Paulist Press, 1984.

———. "The Objective Moral Order: Reflections on Recent Research." *Theological Studies* 43 (1982): 260–278.

———. *Sexual Morality.* New York: Paulist Press, 1977.

Keenan, James. "What is Morally New in Genetic Manipulation?" *Human Gene Therapy* 1 (1990): 289–298.

Kelly, Gerard. "Pope Pius XII and the Principle of Totality." *Theological Studies* 16 (1955): 373–396.

Kiely, Bartholomew. "The Impracticality of Proportionalism." *Gregorianum* 66 (1985): 655–686.

———. *Psychology and Moral Theology.* Rome: Gregorian University Press, 1980.

Klingl, Alfons. "Sequela di Cristo: Un Concetto di Teologia Morale." In *Fede Cristiana e Agire Morale.* Edited by Klaus Demmer and Bruno Schüller, 86–108. Assisi: Cittadella Editrice, 1980.

Knauer, Peter. "The Hermeneutic Function of the Principle of Double Effect." In *Moral Norms and Catholic Tradition, Readings in Moral Theology* 1. Edited by Charles Curran and Richard McCormick, 1–39. New York: Paulist Press, 1979.

Komonchak, Joseph. "Moral Pluralism and the Unity of the Church." *Concilium* 150 (1981): 89–94.

Korff, Wilhelm. "Nature or Reason as the Criterion for the Universality of Moral Judgments." *Concilium* 150 (1981): 82–88.

Kramer, Hans. "Scelte Irrevocabili." In *Problemi e Prospettive di Teologia Morale.* Edited by Tullo Goffi, 117–138. Brescia: Editrice Queriniana, 1976.

Lonergan, Bernard. "Christ as Subject: A Reply." In *Collection*. Edited by Frederick Crowe, 164–197. New York: Herder, 1967.

———. "The Dehellenization of Dogma." In *A Second Collection*. Edited by William Ryan and Bernard Tyrrell, 11–32. London: Darton, Longman, and Todd, 1974.

———. "An Interview with Fr. Bernard Lonergan, S.J." In *A Second Collection*. Edited by William Ryan and Bernard Tyrrell, 209–230. London: Darton, Longman, and Todd, 1974.

———. "Cognitional Structure." In *Collection*. Edited by Frederick Crowe, 221–239. New York: Herder, 1967.

———. *Insight*. London: Darton, Longman, and Todd, 1983.

———. *Method in Theology*. New York: Seabury Press, 1972.

———. "Openness and Religious Experience." In *Collection*. Edited by Frederick Crowe, 190–201. New York: Herder, 1967.

———. *The Subject*. Milwaukee: Marquette University Press, 1968.

———. "The Transition from a Classicist World-View to Historical Mindedness." In *A Second Collection*. Edited by William Ryan and Bernard Tyrrell, 1–9. London: Darton, Longman, and Todd, 1974.

Lotz, Johannes B. "La Metafisica come fondamento dei valori etici e sociali." *Sapienza* 34 (1981): 5–18.

McCloskey, H. J. *Meta-Ethics and Normative Ethics.* The Hague: Martinus Nijhoff, 1969.

McCormick, Richard. *Ambiguity in Moral Choice*. Marquette: Marquette University Press, 1973.

———. *Notes in Moral Theology 1965 through 1980*. Lanham, Maryland: University Press of America, 1981.

———. *Notes in Moral Theology 1981 through 1984*. Lanham, Maryland: University Press of America, 1984.

MacIntyre, Alasdair. *After Virtue*. Notre Dame: University of Notre Dame Press, 1981.

———. *Whose Justice? Which Rationality?* Notre Dame: University of Notre Dame Press, 1988.

McMahon, John. "What Does Christianity Add to Atheistic Humanism?" *Cross Currents* 18 (1968): 129–150.

Macquarrie, John, ed. *A Dictionary of Christian Ethics*. London: SCM Press Limited, 1984.

———. "Rethinking Natural Law." In *The Distinctiveness of Christian Ethics, Readings in Moral Theology* 2. Edited by Charles Curran and Richard McCormick, 121–145. New York: Paulist Press, 1980.

Maguire, Daniel. *The Moral Choice*. Minneapolis: Winston Press, 1978.

Mahoney, John. *The Making of Moral Theology*. Oxford: Clarendon Press, 1987.

Meilaender, Gilbert. *Friendship*. Notre Dame: University of Notre Dame Press, 1981.

———. *The Limits of Love*. University Park: The Pennsylvania State University Press, 1987.

Milhaven, John Giles. "Toward an Epistemology of Ethics." *Theological Studies* 27 (1966): 228–241.

Mortimer, R. C. *Christian Ethics*. London: Hutchinson House, 1950.

Niebuhr, H. Richard. *Christ and Culture*. New York: Harper & Row, 1956.

Pinckaers, Servais. "La question des actes intrinsèquement mauvais." *Revue Thomiste* 82 (1982): 181–212.

———. "Ockham and the Decline of Moral Theology." *Theology Digest* 26 (1978): 239–241.

———. "La théologie morale a la period de la grande Scolastique." *Nova et Vetera* 52 (1977); 118–131.

Post, Werner. "Tolerance." *Sacramentum Mundi* 6:262–267. London: Burns and Oates, 1968.

Rahner, Karl. *The Dynamic Element in the Church*. London: Burns and Oates, 1964.

———. "Reflections on Obedience." *Cross Currents* 10 (1960): 363–374.

Rawls, John. *A Theory of Justice*. Cambridge: Harvard University Press, 1971.

Regan, Augustine. *Thou Shalt Not Kill*. Dublin: Mercier, 1979.

Rigali, Norbert. "Christ and Morality." In *The Distinctiveness of Christian Ethics, Readings in Moral Theology* 2. Edited by Charles Curran and Richard McCormick, 111–120. New York: Paulist Press, 1980.

———. "The Moral Act." *Horizons* 10 (1983): 252–266.

———. "New Epistemology and the Moralist." *Chicago Studies* 11 (1972): 237–244.

———. "The Unity of the Moral Order." *Chicago Studies* 8 (1969): 125–144.

Rossi, Leandro, and Ambrogio Valsecchi, eds. *Dizionario Enciclopedico dei Teologia Morale*. Rome: Paoline, 1981.

Schillebeeckx, Edward. "La 'loi naturelle' et l'ordre du salut." In *Dieu et L'Homme*, 228–246. Bruxelles: CEP, 1965.

Schmitz, Philipp. *Menschsein und sittliches Handeln*. Würzburg: Echter, 1980.

Schoonenberg, Piet. "Original Sin and Man's Situation." *Theology Digest* 15 (1967): 203–208.

Simon, Yves. *The Definition of Moral Virtue*. New York: Fordham University Press, 1986.

Stöckle, Bernhard. *Dizionario di Etica Cristiana*. Assisi: Cittadella Editrice, 1978.

Ugorji, Lucius. *The Principle of Double Effect*. Frankfurt am Main: Peter Lang, 1985.

Vacek, Edward. "Proportionalism: One View of the Debate." *Theological Studies* 46 (1985): 286–314.

van Ouwerkerk, Conrad. "Gospel Morality and Human Compromise." *Concilium* 5 (1965): 5–12.

_____. "Secularism and Christian Ethics." *Concilium* 25 (1967): 133–136.

Veatch, Henry. *Rational Man: A Modern Interpretation of Aristotelian Ethics.* Bloomington: Indiana University Press, 1962.

Vereecke, Louis. "La Conscience selon Saint Alphonse de Liguori." *Studia Moralia* 21 (1983): 259–273.

_____. "L'éthique sexuelle des moralistes post-tridentins." *Studia Moralia* 13 (1975): 175–196.

_____. "Mariage et plaisir sexuel chez les théologiens de l'époque moderne (1300–1789)." *Studia Moralia* 18 (1980): 245–268.

Wittgenstein, Ludwig. *The Blue and Brown Books.* New York: Harper & Row, 1965.

_____. *Philosophical Investigations.* New York: Macmillan, 1958.

Index

Abelard, Peter, 3
Aristotle, 12, 83; on natural aptitude for virtue, 51; *exercitium*, 56
Attainment: rightness, 8–11. *See also* Charity
Augustine, 12–13, 170; definition of virtue, 94, 142–143
Averroists, Latin, 40, 44
Avicenna: on *exercitium*, 51, 56, 105

Benevolence: charity, 124; moral goodness, 11, 14, 54–56
Bernard: 3, 166, 181
Boyle, Leonard, 39

Charity: attains last end, 95, 100, 138–139; command of, 124, 128–130, 136, 163–164; destroyed by mortal sin, 138, 158; efficient form, 128; form of the virtues, 102, 109, 124, 128, 163, 164, 181; grace, 137–141; heart, 140–141, 143; love, 122–124; measure of, 124, 130–132, 137, 140, 172, 173, 174; moral goodness, 3, 11, 13, 95, 168; "mother," 129; motivation, 125, 134–135, 136, 138, 141, 163; neighbor love, 134–137; primary *exercitium*, 129, 141, 148; related to faith and hope, 125; right making, 124; theological virtue, 49, 54; union with God, 95–96; 124–127, 133, 135, 165, 181; venial sin, 158–161. *See also* Benevolence; Command; *Exercitium*; Merit
Choice: external act, 66; distinguishing *quid* from *circa quid*, 78–79; rightness, 14. *See also* Intention
Circumstances: *circa quid*, 77–79; *cur*, 79; defined, 77–79; excuse, 4, 7, 155; of the act, 173; *quid*, 77–79
Command, 50; distinct from elicit, 129, 133, 163, 164; sin, 152. *See also* Charity
Commentary on the Sentences: culpable ignorance, 25; distinguishes two modes of acting, 41–42; identifies goodness with perfection, 96; lying midwives, 169–171; *materia circa quam* identified with end, 42, 75; reason moving the will, 26; sin, 29; venial sin, 160; will's autonomy, 24
Compendium of Theology: identifies goodness with perfection, 96
Conveniens, 47, 49–50, 53

De caritate: command, 129; form, 128; motivation, 134; Peter's denial, 167
De malo: *I*, identifies goodness with perfection, 96–97; *III*, culpable ignorance, 25; *VI*, 40–49